IMAGES
of America

TAMPA'S WESTSHORE

On the Cover: Super-Test Amusement Park, located at 2924 North Dale Mabry Highway, offered many fun things for families in the Westshore community. Among the attractions were carnival rides, a miniature zoo, and this carousel that children of all ages loved. (Courtesy of the Tampa–Hillsborough County Public Library System.)

IMAGES
of America

TAMPA'S WESTSHORE

Joshua McMorrow-Hernandez

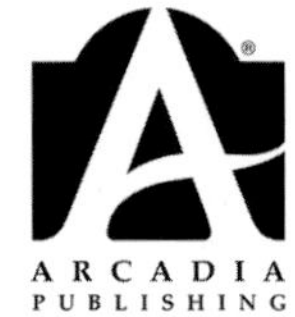

ISBN 978-1-4671-0696-2

Published by Arcadia Publishing
Charleston, South Carolina

Printed in the United States of America

Library of Congress Control Number: 2021936785

For all general information, please contact Arcadia Publishing:
Telephone 843-853-2070
Fax 843-853-0044
E-mail sales@arcadiapublishing.com
For customer service and orders:
Toll-Free 1-888-313-2665

Visit us on the Internet at www.arcadiapublishing.com

For my family, my loved ones, and Tampa

Contents

Acknowledgments		6
Introduction		7
1.	Fun and Games	9
2.	Retail Therapy	25
3.	Gas, Food, and Lodging	41
4.	Scenes and Views	59
5.	Office Space	73
6.	Let's Fly Away	87
7.	In the Community	105
Bibliography		127

Acknowledgments

I would like to begin by recognizing St. Lawrence Catholic Church, my family's parish going back to the 1960s, not long after my maternal grandparents relocated from Braintree, Massachusetts, and built a home on the northern fringes of the Westshore community near Tampa International Airport. St. Lawrence Catholic Church founding pastor Msgr. Laurence Higgins was a dear family friend, and I feel grateful to have known him and to have had the opportunity to interview him years back for a history project that eventually led to the creation of this book. I also want to thank Fr. Daniel Kayajan, Audrey Boston, and Danah Lee for their assistance, as well as the Diocese of St. Petersburg for its.

The team at the Tampa–Hillsborough County Public Library System helped me on numerous occasions in sourcing historic images, many of which fill the pages of this book. Also of great assistance was Andrew Huse at the University of South Florida Library Special Collections Department, with Jennifer Dietz and Alison Smith tirelessly scanning images from the City of Tampa Archives. Another important source for this book was the Florida State Archive.

There were also many individuals working independently or in coordination within larger organizations to provide me with images and information that are found in this book. They include Glenn Bomke, John Christen, Leslie Cunningham of the Harlem in Havana Project, Katie Dishman of Marriott, Mason Dixon of Q-105 FM, Rita Hattab of MacDonald Training Center, Julie Heath of Warner Bros. Clip and Still Licensing, Todd Keil, Katrina Kochneva at ZUMA Press, Ann Kulig of the Westshore Alliance, Kimi Lau-Costanzo, Ann Menchen of Hillsborough Community College, Mario Nunez of *The Tampa Natives Show*, Christine Osborn at Tampa International Airport, Dan Perez of TampaPix.com, Kevin Pytlak of Happy Hobo Trains, James Robiconti, Maria Williams Trippe, James Walker of Village Inn, Barry M. White, Michael Wigh and the Bell family, George Youdal, and Tony Zappone.

Several photographs appearing in this publication were selected from the Cinchett Collection, which is a valuable archive of historical Tampa photographs taken by the Cinchett family between 1949 and 1969 for their neon sign company (Cinchett Neon Signs Inc.), which operated in Tampa from 1947 to 1997. That collection was featured in another Arcadia Publishing book titled *Vintage Tampa Signs and Scenes* by author John Cinchett.

Any images appearing uncredited in this book are from the author's personal archive of photographs.

Introduction

Note: Those reading this book will notice various spellings of "Westshore" throughout. These are not typos but rather reflections of various historic and branding representations of the geographical name, generally spelled as "Westshore." However, original platting maps from the early 20th century show the name of West Shore Boulevard with "West" and "Shore" as two separate words. Meanwhile, retail landmark WestShore Plaza compounds the community's name and uses a capital "W" and "S" to distinguish "West" and "Shore." Other spelling variants exist and may be encountered throughout the community, which some may say is just as eclectic as its name's many spellings.

Westshore is one of Tampa's most energetic communities, covering more than 11 square miles in an area encompassing Tampa International Airport, Raymond James Stadium, Rocky Point, and countless other notable landmarks. The geographical boundaries of the Westshore community for the purposes of this book roughly align with Hillsborough Avenue to the north, Himes Avenue to the east, Kennedy Boulevard to the south, and Rocky Point to the west. The peninsular region of Tampa south of Westshore is reached by several major transportation arteries, including West Shore Boulevard, and is known as South Tampa—one of several Tampa neighborhoods whose residents shop and work in the Westshore area.

Those who have lived in Tampa for many years have seen Westshore grow into a dense urban community, one now anchored by Tampa International Airport, two regional shopping malls known as WestShore Plaza and International Plaza, Raymond James Stadium (home of the Tampa Bay Buccaneers National Football League franchise), George M. Steinbrenner Field (the spring training facility for Major League Baseball's New York Yankees), Al Lopez Park, Rocky Point Golf Course, and a vibrant mixed-use district known as Midtown Tampa. Then there are the seemingly countless office buildings that dot the Westshore community, which cumulatively offer millions of square feet of office space.

The Westshore area has long been known for its dense development of office space. In fact, by the 1990s, Westshore's claim to fame was being one of Florida's largest commercial real estate submarkets, then boasting nearly 10 million square feet of office space. Today, Westshore has transitioned into a vibrant live-work-play community, with increasing numbers of residents enjoying short commutes to prime office space, luxurious shopping and dining venues, and a growing number of parks and other recreational opportunities. But Westshore's story does not begin in the 1960s with the development of high-rise office towers or even in the 1920s with the establishment of an airfield that later became Tampa International Airport. Westshore's history goes back much further.

In the mid-19th century, Tampa was a small municipality that had grown from the US military outpost known as Fort Brooke, which was established in 1824 near where the southern reaches of downtown Tampa stand today. Settlers and enterprising individuals looking for vast stretches of inexpensive land near Tampa turned to the outlying areas east, north, and west of town. By the mid-1860s, agricultural interests and industrial entrepreneurs were platting the marshy scrub and pineland that became the Westshore region. One of the earliest known developments in this part of Tampa was a salt factory that once operated near where the city of Tampa's beachy Cypress Point Park is located today.

The sandy subtropical shores of Rocky Point lured many recreational visitors throughout the latter years of the 19th century and beyond, later inspiring the development of the nearby Rocky Point Golf Course, which was founded in 1911 by the Tampa Automobile Club and was then known as the Tampa Automobile and Golf Club. Becoming one of the first golf courses in Florida, the landmark was renamed Rocky Point Golf Club in 1917. It operated for many years until the outbreak of World War II, when the US government closed the golf course and incorporated the property into Drew Field, which originally opened in 1928 as a municipal airport but saw use as a US Army training center for combat aircrews during World War II.

After World War II, Florida saw a massive population boom. Countless northern tourists seeking sand, sun, and surf ended up staying in the state, and Tampa served as a destination for many of these new arrivals. Between 1940 and 1950, Tampa's population grew 15 percent, from 108,391 to 124,681. Further growth plus annexations of new neighborhoods incorporated into the city helped Tampa's population surge even further from 1950 to 1960, during which the headcount increased 120 percent to 274,970. During the 1950s and 1960s, many of Tampa's newest residents settled in the leafy northern suburban communities of Carrollwood and Forest Hills, as well as the decidedly more metropolitan neighborhoods being built near MacDill Air Force Base in South Tampa. In between sprang Westshore, which witnessed significant residential growth in the 1920s and 1930s but saw its identity morph into a commercial crossroads after World War II with the evolution of Tampa International Airport in the 1950s, construction of Interstate 4 in the early 1960s, and establishment of major hotels, sports complexes, and malls in the Westshore region during the next 20 years.

WestShore Plaza opened in 1967 as Tampa's first indoor shopping mall and continues operating today as one of the region's premier retail hubs. While Tampa International Airport had been operating in a facility that grew out of Drew Field, in 1971, it opened its modern-day terminal complex that, upon its unveiling, was hailed as one of the most revolutionary airports in the world.

On April 24, 1974, Tampa was awarded the National Football League's 27th franchise, which was purchased by Jacksonville attorney Hugh Culverhouse and became known as the Tampa Bay Buccaneers. The football team made its home in Tampa Stadium, which was built in 1967 and expanded with end zone seating and luxury skyboxes in time for the first Tampa Bay Buccaneers regular-season games in 1976. Less than a decade later, Tampa Stadium was the site of Super Bowl XVIII, which saw the Los Angeles Raiders defeat the Washington Redskins on January 22, 1984. It was Tampa's first Super Bowl, followed by several others in the years that came. These internationally televised football events helped put Tampa on the map, but they were not the Westshore community's only claims to fame.

During the last half of the 20th century, Westshore hosted a motorcade procession and speaking engagements by US president John F. Kennedy, saw a multiday revival by Christian evangelist Billy Graham, and served as center stage for English rock band Led Zeppelin—who in 1973 played a concert before some 57,000 people at Tampa Stadium that stood for many years as having the largest audience for a single musical artist performance ever. Additionally, Westshore fields many nationally acclaimed resorts and retail centers that continue drawing ever-larger numbers of businesses and tourist enterprises into the area.

Complementing downtown Tampa as a principal business district, the Westshore area today boasts more than 12 million square feet of commercial office space, over 100,000 employees, some 4,000 businesses, and an estimated 15,000 residents—all statistics that continue growing year by year. What Westshore will look like in the future occupies the dreams of many ambitious developers and community leaders. However, knowing the colorful story of this Tampa neighborhood can help everybody better understand why and how Westshore has become one of the most dynamic communities on the west coast of Florida.

One

Fun and Games

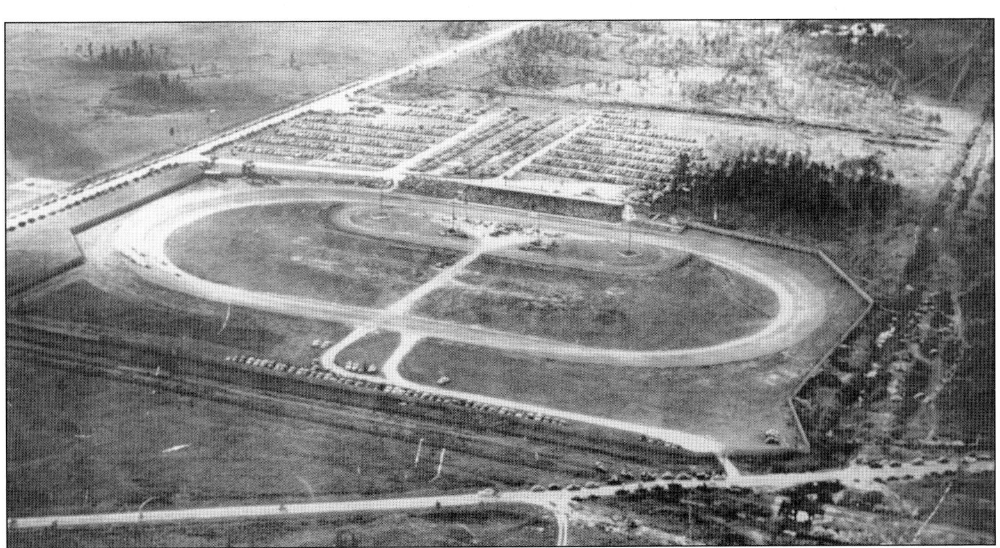

Speedway Park opened in August 1948 near the northwest corner of West Hillsborough Avenue and Anderson Road, north of modern-day Tampa International Airport. Billed as the "World's Fastest Half-Mile Dirt Track," the state-of-the-art auto-racing complex also boasted a quarter-mile track and hosted major racing events, including National AAA Big Car and 100-mile stock car events. Races saw colorful action involving late-model stock cars, modified stock cars, midget cars, and motorcycles.

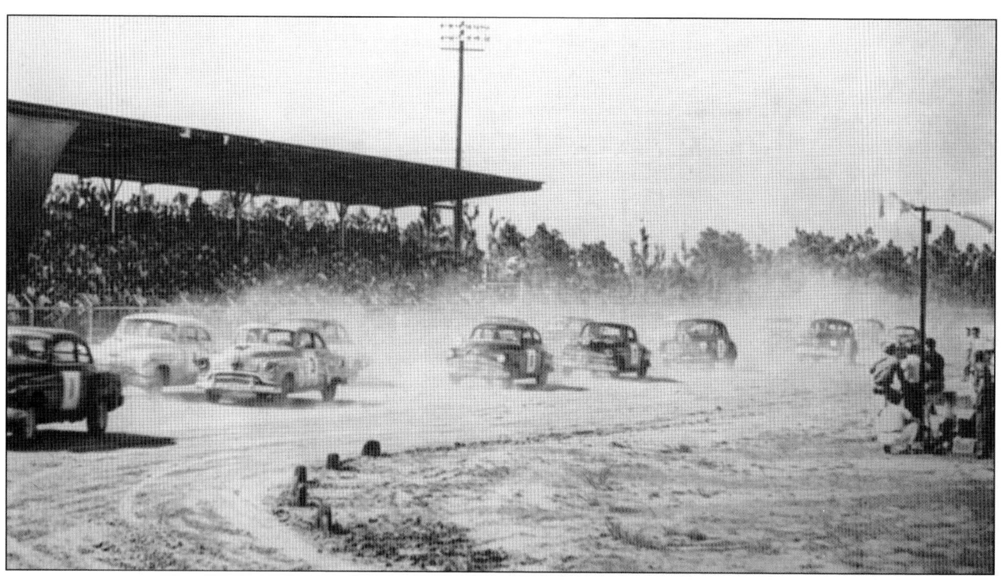

Above, drivers set the action on the pace lap right before the start of a 200-mile late-model stock car race around 1952. Below, driver Jimmy Thompson (left) claims the checkered flag as the winner of the Winter Championship 100-mile race and stands here beside Frank Dery Jr., owner of the Hudson Hornet that raced to victory in 1952.

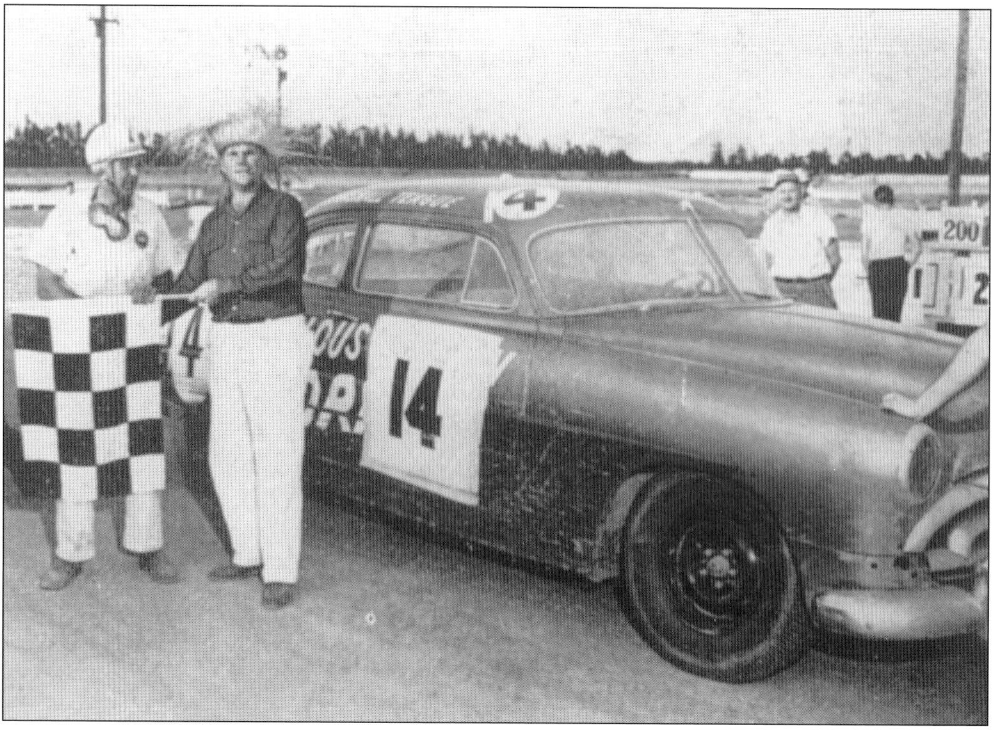

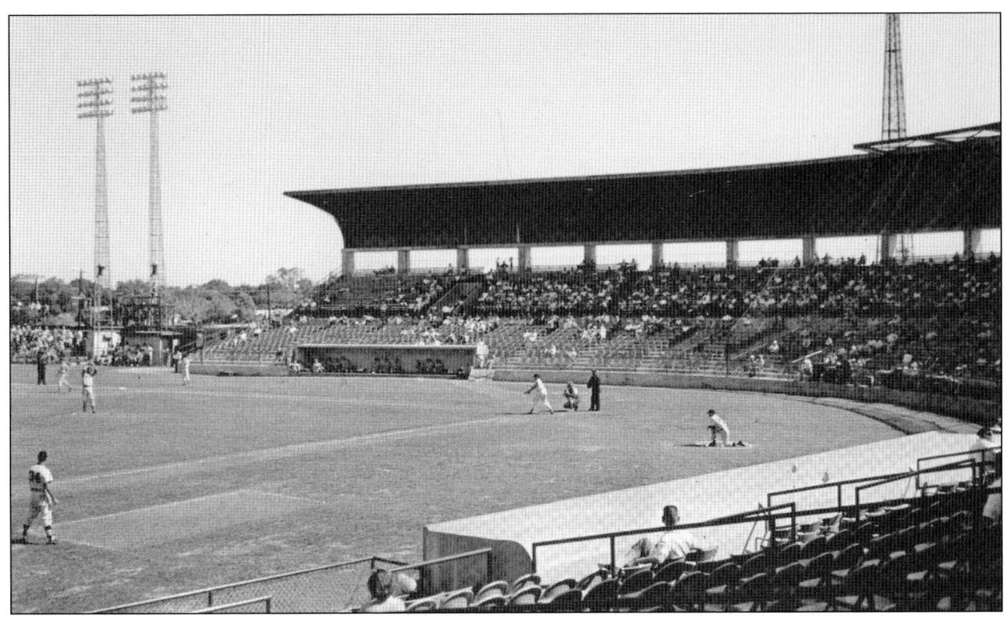

Al Lopez Field was a baseball stadium built near the northwest corner of Himes Avenue and Tampa Bay Boulevard. Named for Tampa-born baseball legend Al Lopez, the ballpark was the spring training home of the Chicago White Sox from 1955 through 1959 and Cincinnati Reds from 1960 through 1987. It also hosted the Tampa Tarpons minor-league team from 1957 through 1988. Left without a tenant after the departure of the Cincinnati Reds and Tampa Tarpons, Al Lopez Field was razed in 1989, and the land it sat upon was eventually used for Raymond James Stadium, which opened in 1998.

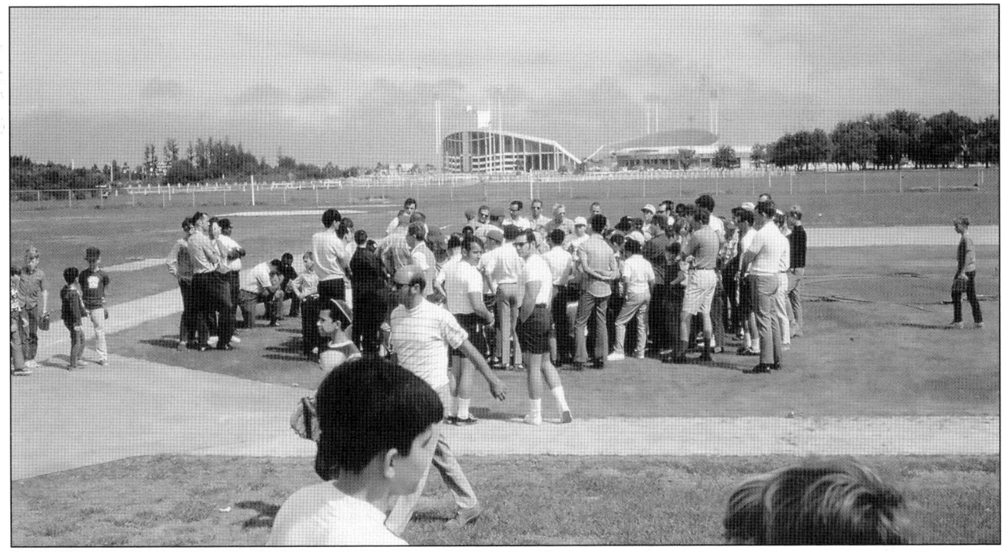

Tampa has long played host to the spring training affairs of various Major League Baseball teams, including the Cincinnati Reds, who began training at Plant Field near downtown Tampa in 1931. In 1960, they moved to Al Lopez Field, where they remained through 1987. Some of the team is seen in this 1970 image at a community event held at their training facility, dubbed Redsland, just south of Al Lopez Field and Tampa Stadium, both visible in the background. (Courtesy of the City of Tampa Archives.)

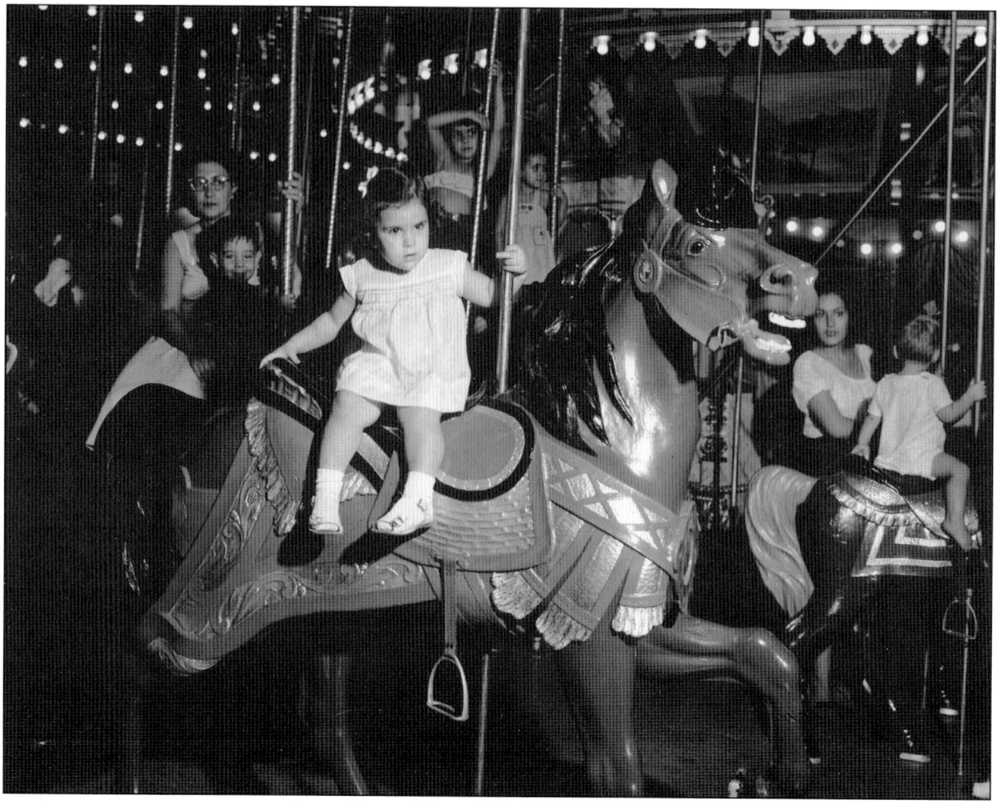

Super-Test Amusement Park was a family-friendly entertainment center located at the southwest corner of North Dale Mabry Highway and West Columbus Drive. It offered free admission via tickets that were distributed with purchases of gasoline at local Super-Test service stations and included many fun attractions, including a carousel (seen here), a roller coaster, a Ferris wheel, race cars, a miniature train, a menagerie, an ice cream parlor, and more. It was located at 2924 North Dale Mabry Highway from 1953 through 1964 and was owned and operated by Stanley Hughey and his son Mike Hughey. (Courtesy of the Tampa–Hillsborough County Public Library System.)

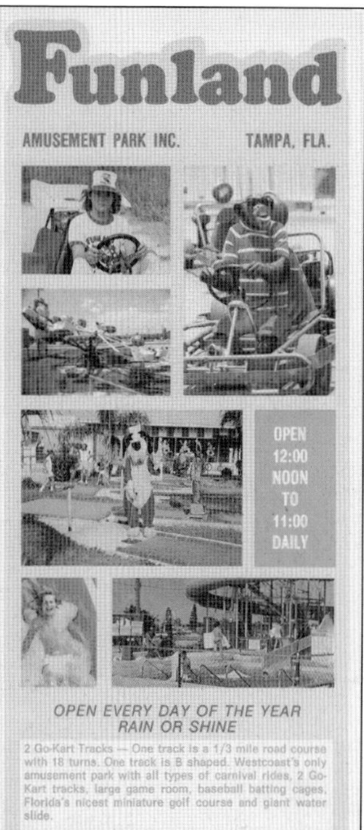

Funland Amusement Park was a family destination offering a one-third-mile-long road racing course, carnival-style rides, water slides, miniature golf, an arcade, and many other fun attractions. The entertainment complex was opened by Jim Frederiksen in 1974 at 4406 West Hillsborough Avenue, and it continued operations until 1983.

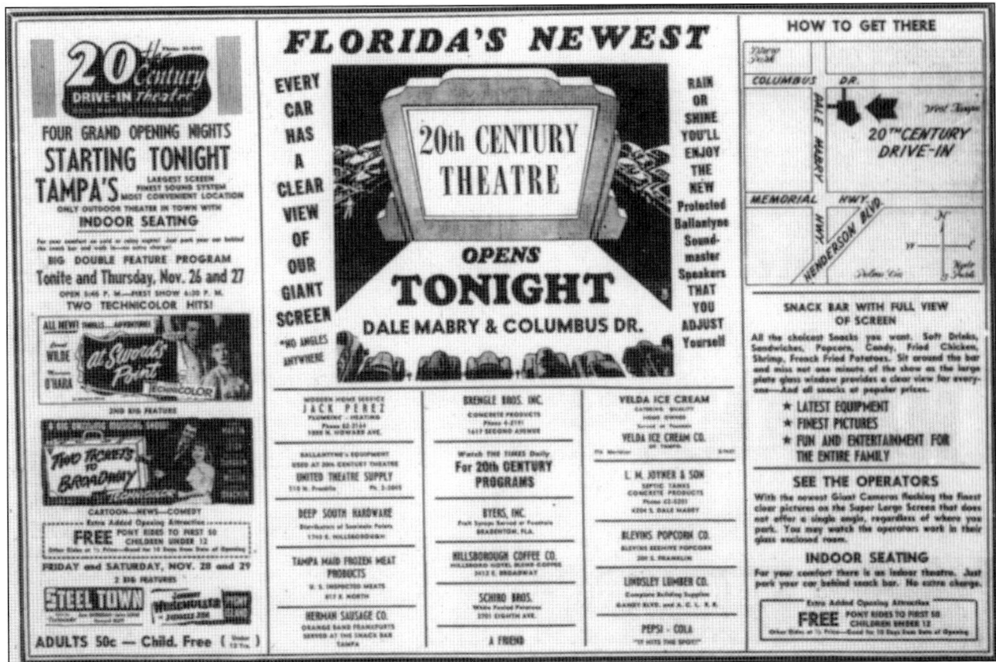

The 20th Century Drive-In Theatre opened southeast of North Dale Mabry Highway and West Columbus Drive on November 26, 1952. It closed in December 1980, by which time several other movie theaters had opened in Westshore, including Sundown Drive-In Theater in 1953, Loew's Tampa Theater (later renamed Austin Cinema) in 1968, Horizon Park 4 in 1971, and Tampa Bay Mall Cinema in 1976; all closed many years ago. AMC West Shore 14 at WestShore Plaza opened in 2000 and is the only mainstream movie theater still operating in the Westshore area. (© *Tampa Bay Times* via ZUMA Press.)

The Westshore area has seen a few bowling alleys over the years, including the long-defunct Tampa Bowling Center at 3611 West Grace Street, Crown Lanes at 5555 West Hillsborough Avenue (later renamed Pin Chasers), and Dale Mabry Lanes, pictured at right in 1967 at 1600 North Dale Mabry Highway. Opening in September 1959 as one of Florida's premier "bowling palaces," Dale Mabry Lanes hosted many tournaments and was popular with both league bowlers and those who played the sport on a more recreational level. The facility was purchased by the adjacent Jim Walter Corporation and closed in August 1979.

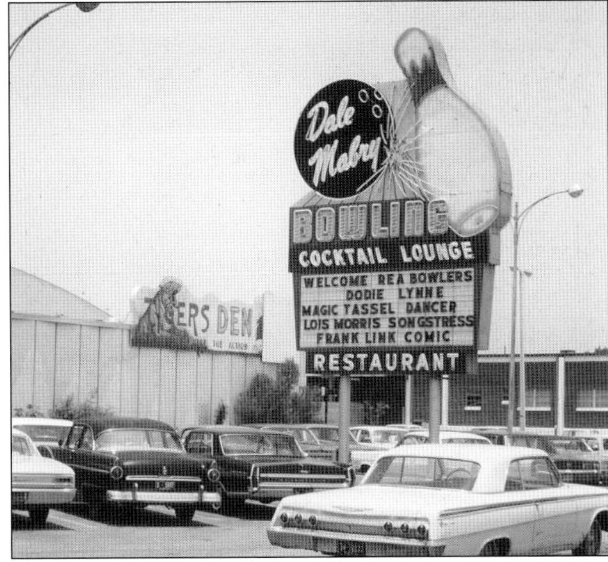

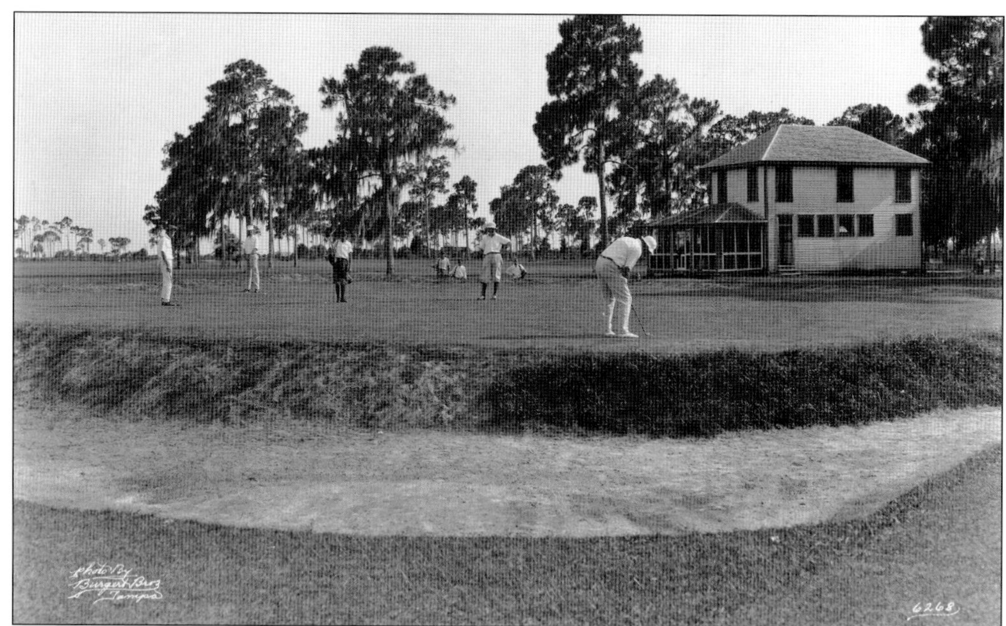

Opening in 1911 as Tampa Automobile and Golf Club, the course touted as among Florida's earliest was renamed Rocky Point Golf Club in 1917. World War II shut the course down by 1942, and the property was incorporated into adjacent Drew Army Air Field. Years after the war, in 1953, the US government conveyed the property to the City of Tampa. It was leased to J.S. "Curly" Hartman, who operated Rocky Point Golf Course from 1954 through 1978, after which the course was assumed by the Tampa Sports Authority. Afterward, Rocky Point Golf Course underwent a major redesign and opened on March 5, 1983, operating today as an 18-hole public course. (Both, courtesy of the Tampa–Hillsborough County Public Library System.)

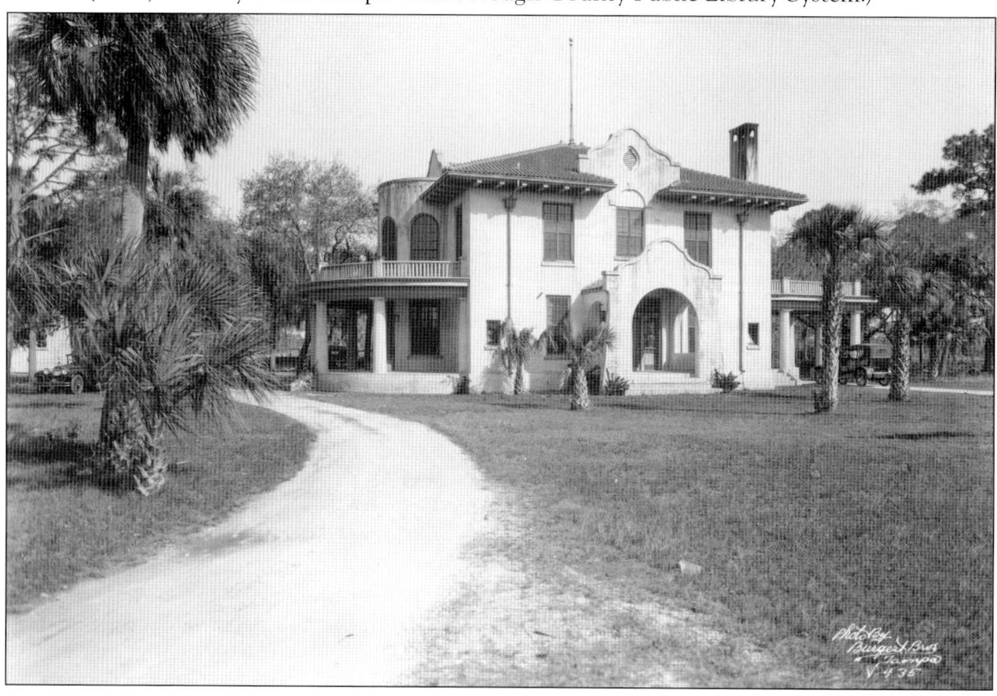

Loch Raven Golf Course was a par-three, 18-hole championship golf course located just south of Jesuit High School. Opened in 1960, the course was designed by George Cobb, who created more than 100 golf courses primarily around the Southeastern United States. The golf course eventually gave way to Tampa Bay Park, an office complex developed by the Landmarks Group of Atlanta that stripped the course of nine holes in 1978. The rest of the golf facility soon thereafter closed with the completion of Tampa Bay Park in 1981. (© *Tampa Bay Times* via ZUMA Press.)

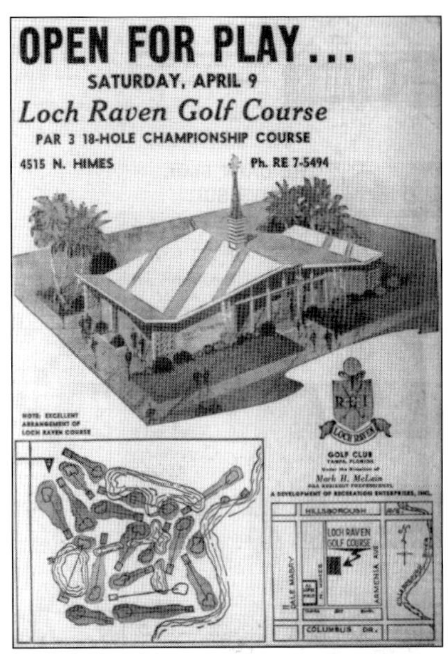

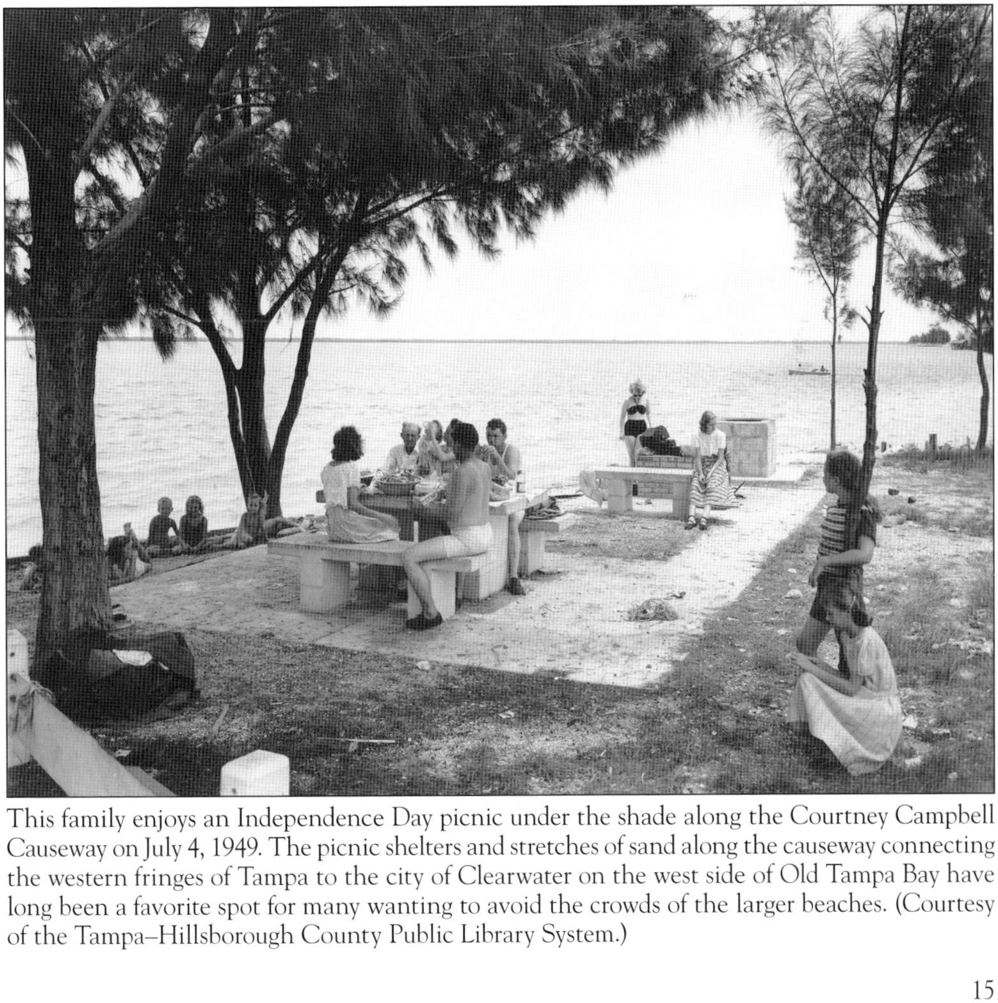

This family enjoys an Independence Day picnic under the shade along the Courtney Campbell Causeway on July 4, 1949. The picnic shelters and stretches of sand along the causeway connecting the western fringes of Tampa to the city of Clearwater on the west side of Old Tampa Bay have long been a favorite spot for many wanting to avoid the crowds of the larger beaches. (Courtesy of the Tampa–Hillsborough County Public Library System.)

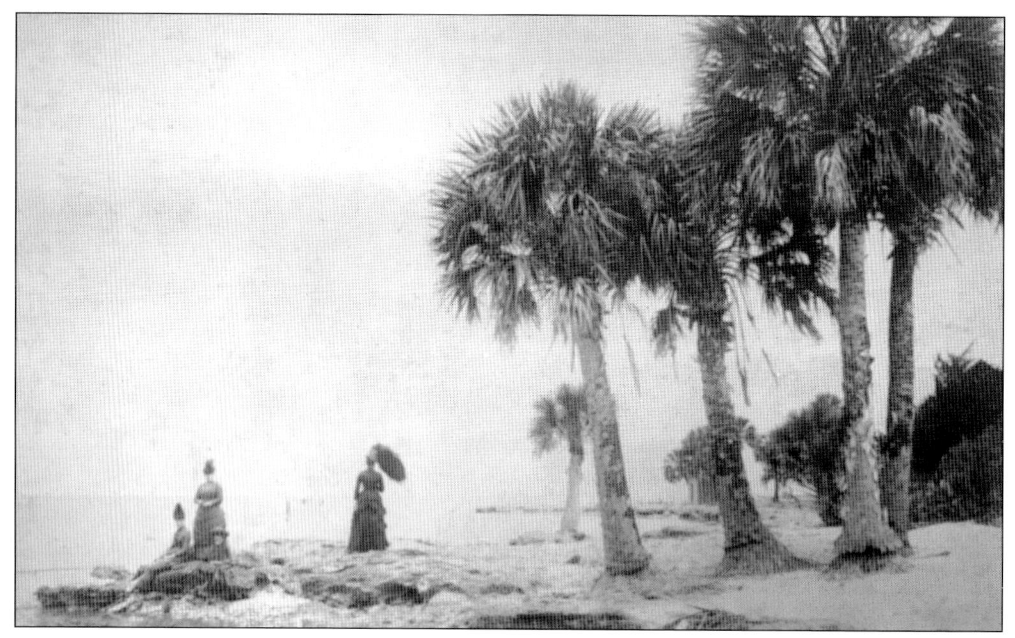

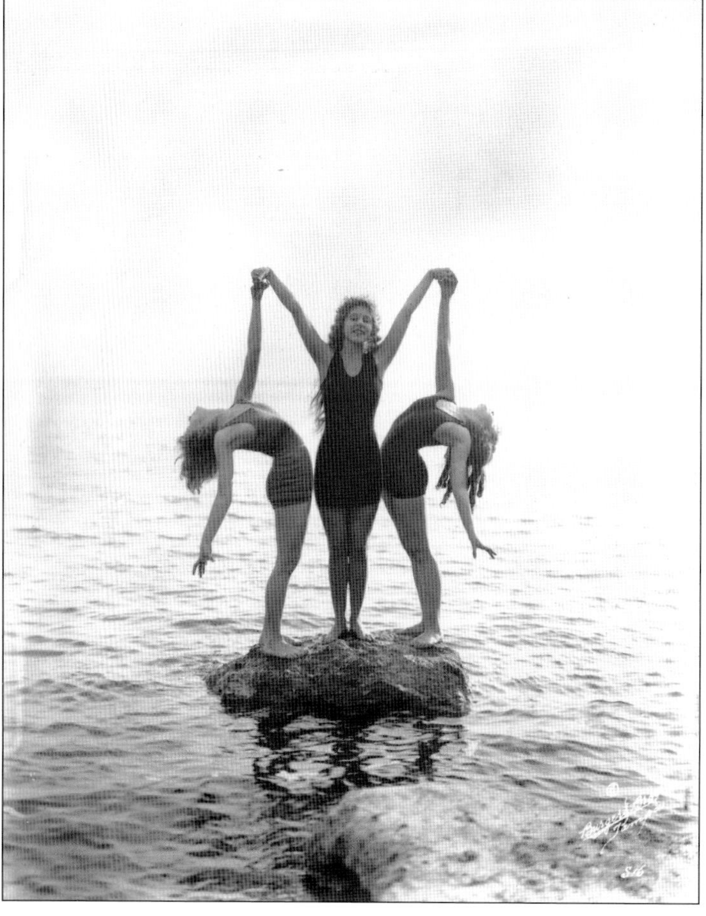

Rocky Point has been a beloved recreational spot since at least the late 19th century. Above, a family enjoys the sandy shores of Rocky Point in the 1880s. At left, three women from Madame Scovell's dancing school strike a skillful pose for the camera on March 28, 1922. (Above, courtesy of the University of South Florida Special Collections Department; left, courtesy of the Tampa–Hillsborough County Public Library System.)

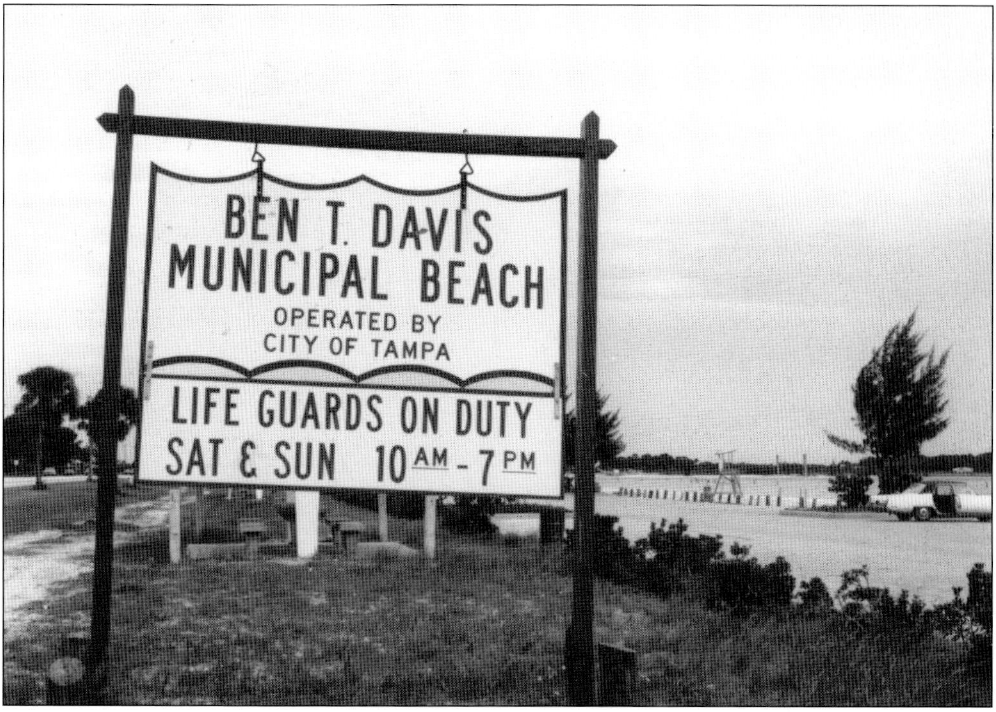

Ben T. Davis Beach, named for the owner of a dredging company that helped build the arterial link between Tampa and Clearwater in the late 1920s, has been a popular destination for revelers of the sand and sun for decades. Ben T. Davis Beach is located on the east side of the Courtney Campbell Causeway and is connected to Rocky Point. (Above, courtesy of the University of South Florida Special Collections Department; below, courtesy of the Florida State Archive.)

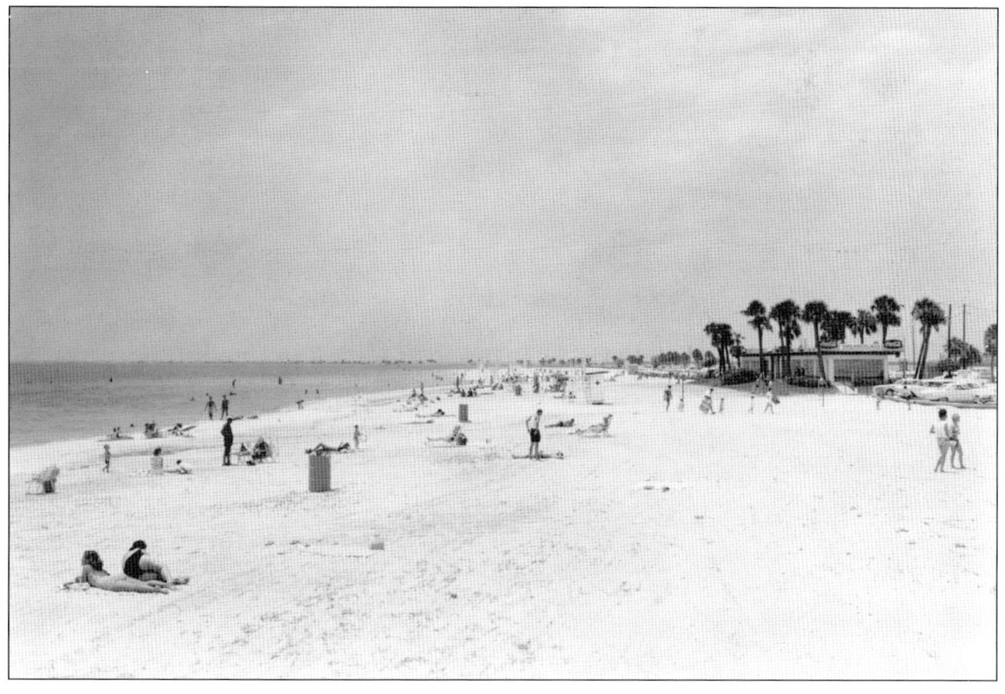

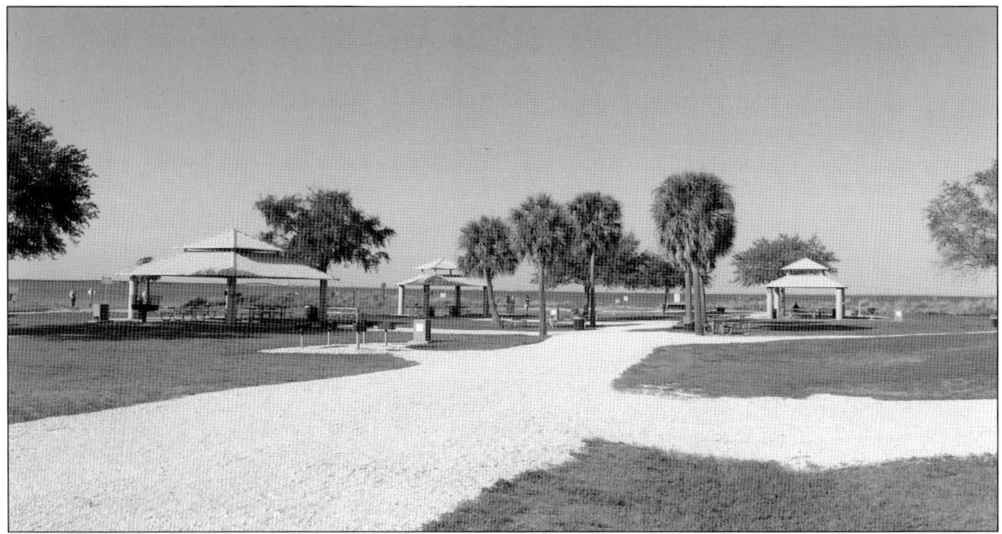

Long considered a hidden gem by locals, Cypress Point Park is a 35-acre beach and recreational green space operated by the City of Tampa. Along with its white, sandy shoreline, Cypress Point Park offers a .90-mile asphalt trail, 18-hole disc golf course, picnic pavilions, playground, and ample space for taking in sunset views over the waters of Old Tampa Bay.

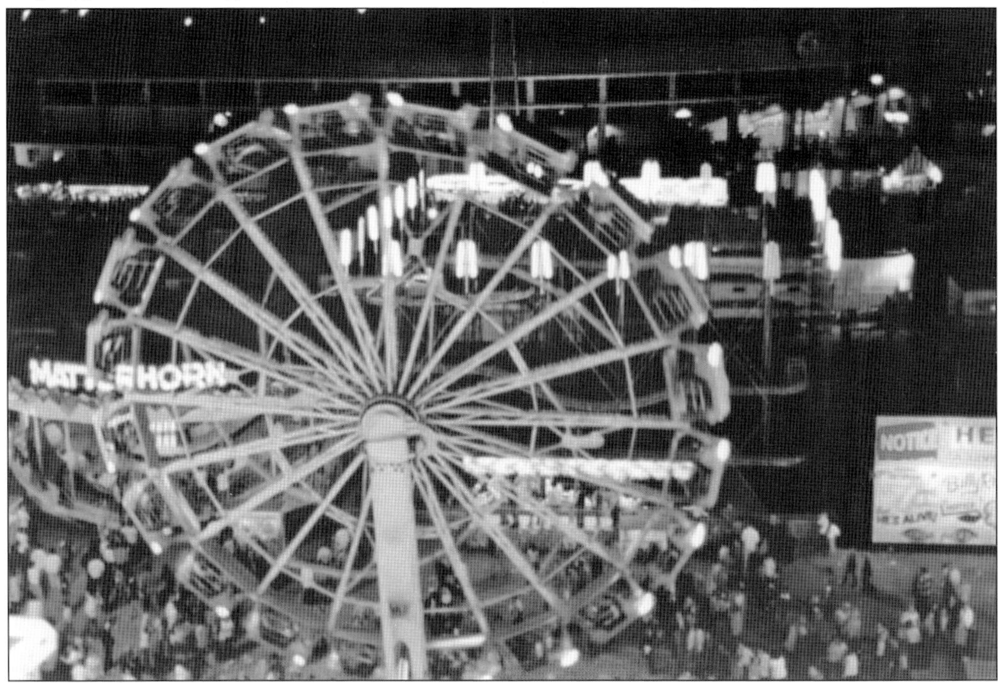

The Florida State Fair was first held in 1904 in downtown Tampa, where it remained until 1975. The following year marked a major transition for the Florida State Fair, when the annual event usually held in February began its shift away from downtown Tampa. For one year only, in 1976, the Florida State Fair was held adjacent to Tampa Stadium and Al Lopez Field, as seen here. In 1977, the Florida State Fair moved to the current site near the southwest corner of the Interstate 4 and US Route 301 interchange and now boasts more than 300 acres and several entertainment and exhibition venues. (Courtesy of Dan Perez.)

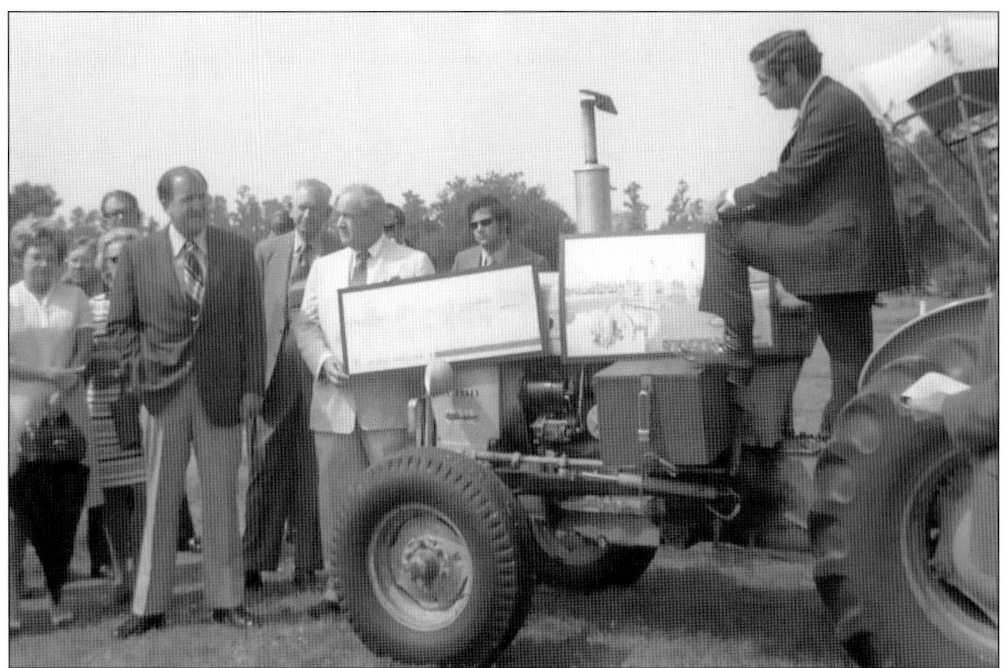

One of Tampa's most popular public recreational landmarks is Al Lopez Park, which was established as Horizon Park in the 1960s. Consisting of approximately 150 acres bound by Hillsborough Avenue to the north, Dr. Martin Luther King Jr. Boulevard to the south, Dale Mabry Highway to the west, and Himes Avenue to the east, the land under Al Lopez Park was once part of Drew Field before being purchased by the City of Tampa after World War II. In the above 1972 image, Tampa mayor Dick Greco operates earth-moving equipment during a ground-breaking ceremony, while the author plays with his sister and father near a picnic shelter in 1986 in the photograph below. (Above, courtesy of the City of Tampa Archives.)

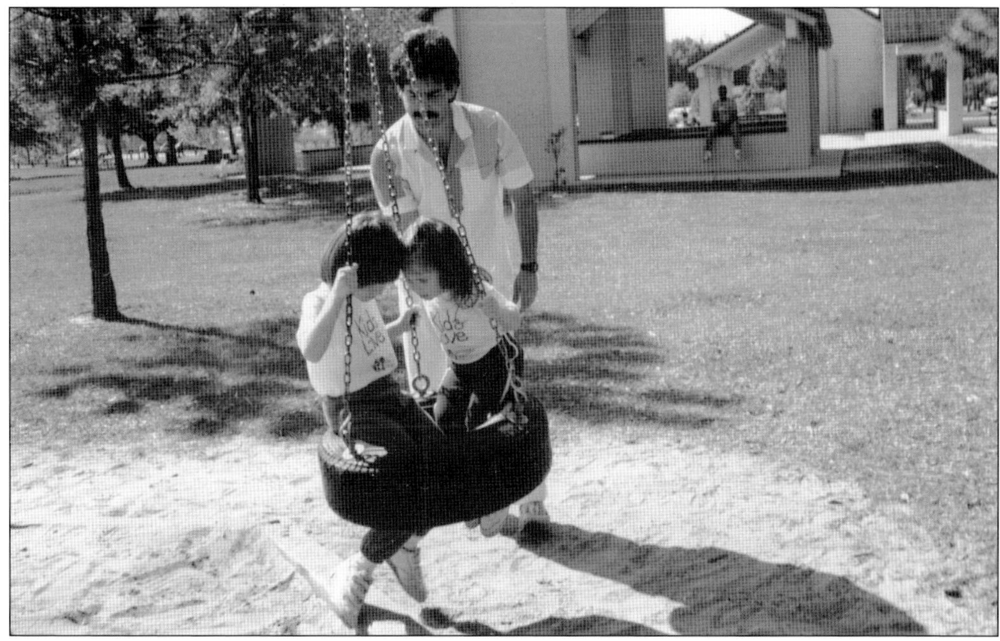

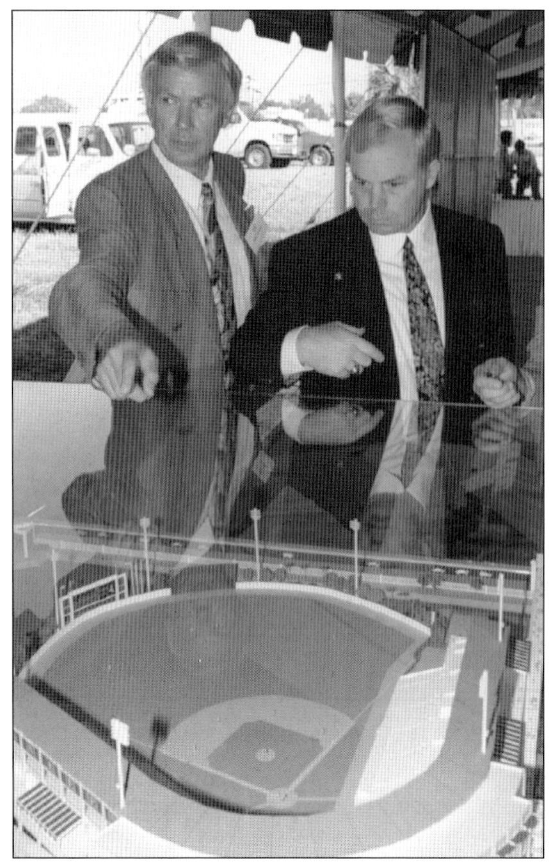

Ground-breaking ceremonies for Legends Field were held in October 1994, when the image at left was taken of New York Yankees general manager Gene Michael (left) and manager Buck Showalter (right) examining a detailed model of the team's new spring training facility. The 31-acre baseball complex, seen below, opened on March 1, 1996, across North Dale Mabry Highway from Tampa Stadium and was renamed George M. Steinbrenner Field in 2008 in honor of the principal owner of the New York Yankees; he became a major philanthropist in the Tampa area and gave to many local charitable organizations until his passing at the age of 80 in 2010. (Left, © Fraser Hale/*Saint Petersburg Times* via ZUMA Press; below, © Thomas Anderson/AFLO via ZUMA Press.)

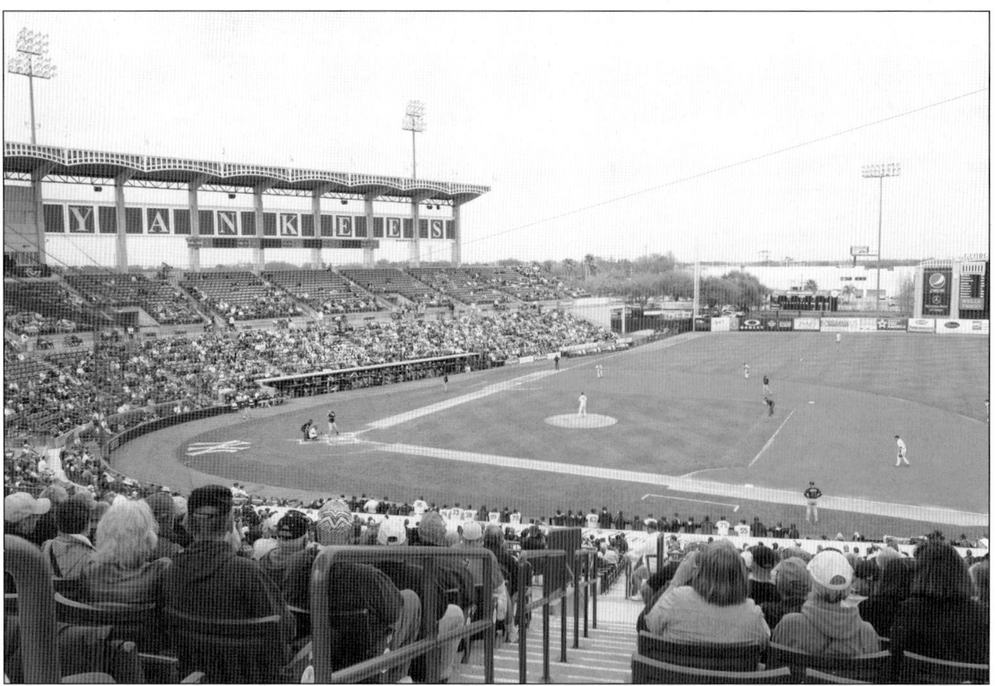

Tampa Stadium was built in 1967 on land formerly incorporated into Drew Army Air Field with the hopes of luring a National Football League franchise to the city. Construction on the original stadium, seen at right in the summer of 1967, cost $4.4 million. The football complex, seen below in 1971, opened on November 4, 1967, and seated 46,481 spectators in a pair of concrete grandstands with backless aluminum bleachers. During its earliest years, Tampa Stadium hosted various university football matchups and headlining concerts, including a 1973 Led Zeppelin show with 57,000 watching in what was then the largest crowd to ever watch a single artist perform. (Right, © Ricardo Ferro/*Tampa Bay Times* via ZUMA Wire; below, courtesy of Glenn Bomke.)

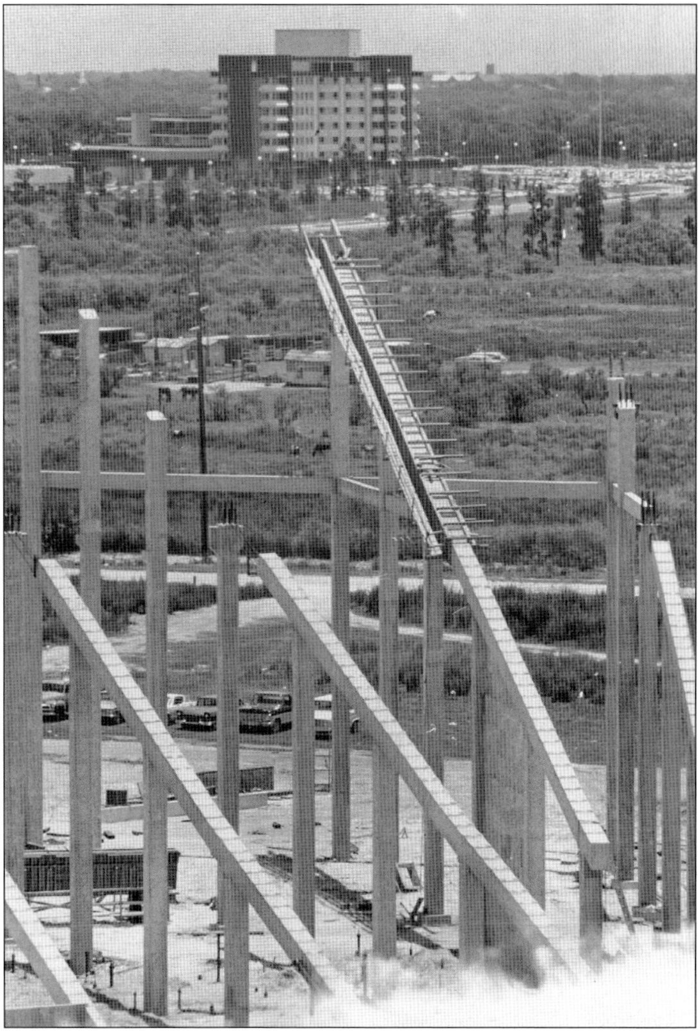

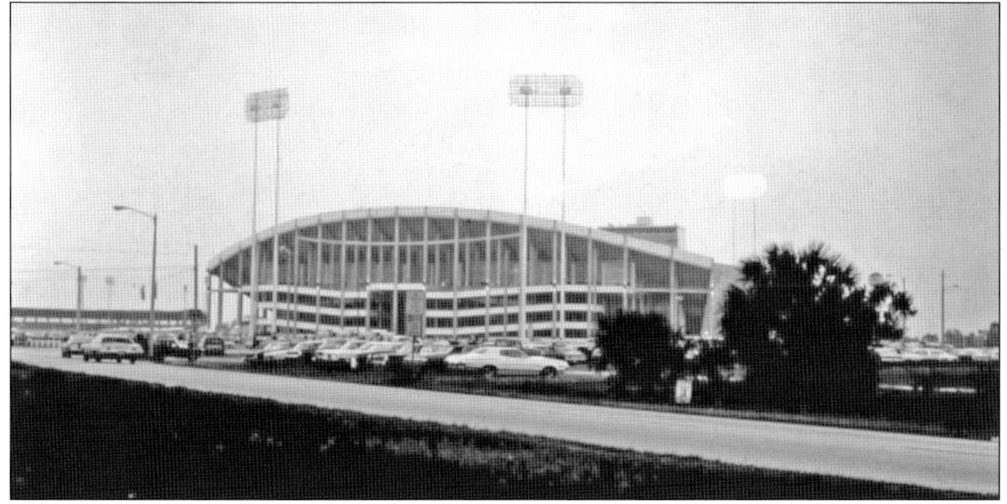

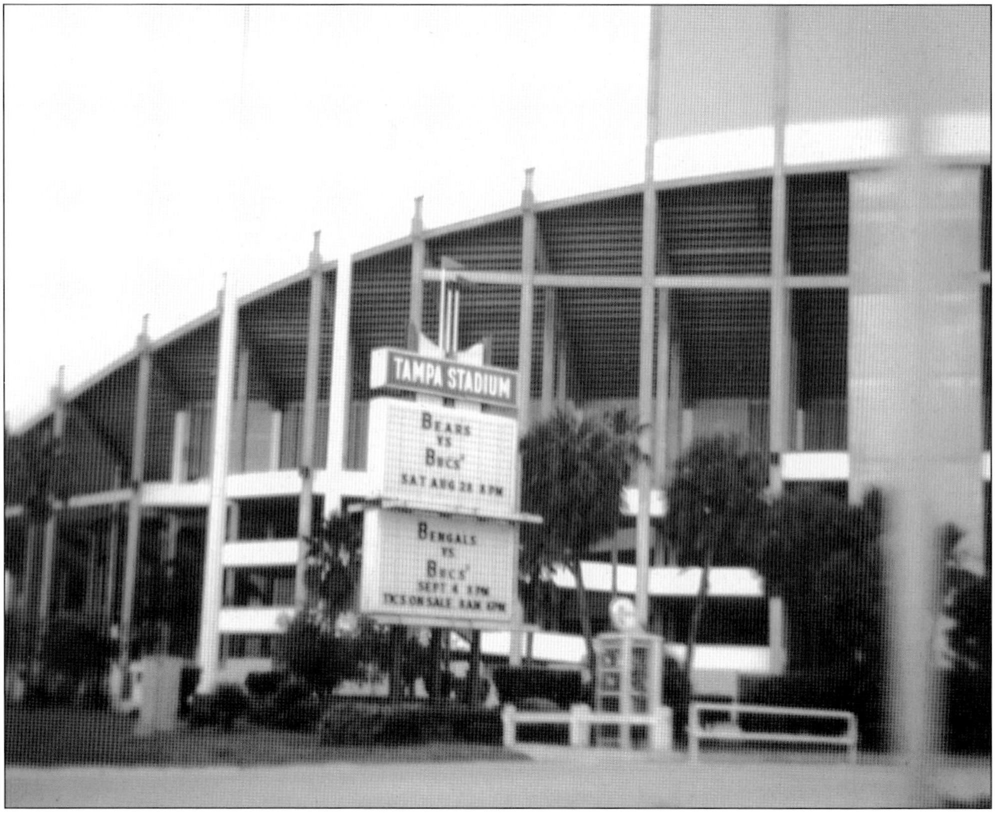

Tampa eventually scored its National Football League franchise in 1974 with an expansion team known as the Tampa Bay Buccaneers, originally owned by Hugh Culverhouse and later by the Glazer family. Above is a 1976 marquee showing upcoming matchups with the Chicago Bears and Cincinnati Bengals. Below, Chicago Bears offensive legend Walter Payton dives into the Tampa Bay Buccaneers defensive squadron at Tampa Stadium on November 1, 1981. The Buccaneers won that game 20 points to 10. (Above, courtesy of the Florida State Archive; below, © *Tampa Bay Times* via ZUMA Press.)

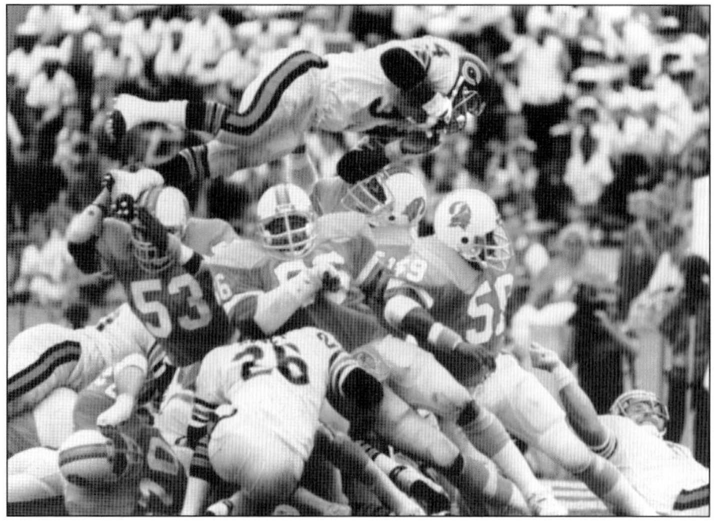

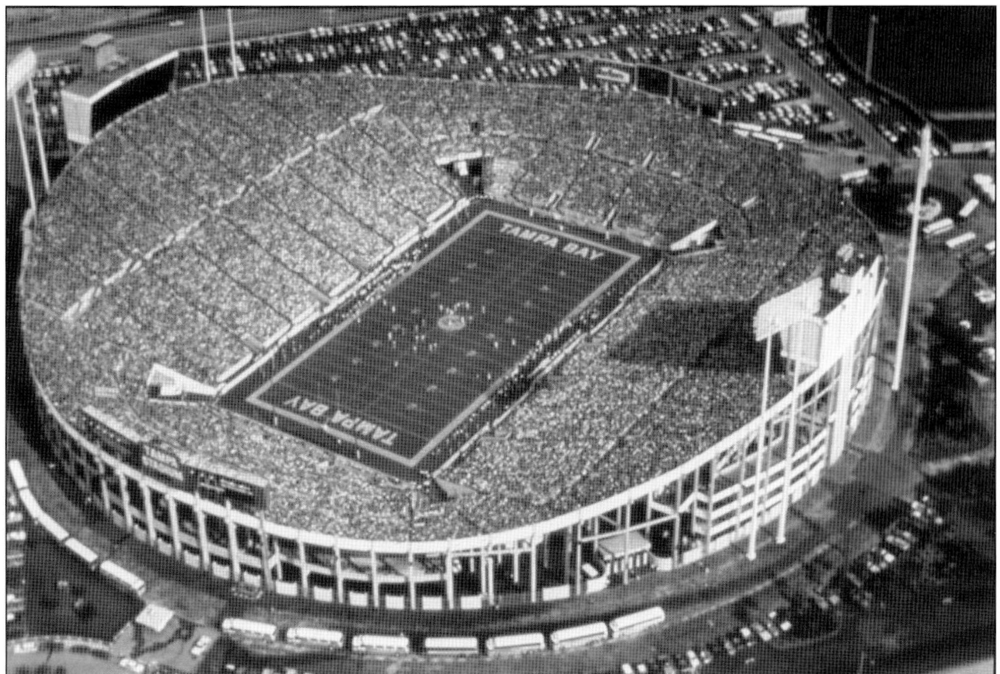

The arrival of the Tampa Bay Buccaneers in 1976 called for the construction of luxury boxes over the east grandstands and the enclosure of Tampa Stadium to form a bowl capable of holding more than 74,000 fans. Renovations were complete in time for the Tampa Bay Buccaneers' inaugural 1976 season and are seen above in the c. 1982 image. In 1983, further enhancements were made to the size of the eastern grandstand luxury boxes, as seen below, in time for Tampa's first Super Bowl in 1984. Tampa Stadium was lovingly nicknamed "the Big Sombrero" and was officially renamed Houlihan's Stadium from 1996 until its demolition in 1999 after being replaced by Raymond James Stadium the previous year. (Both, courtesy of the Florida State Archive.)

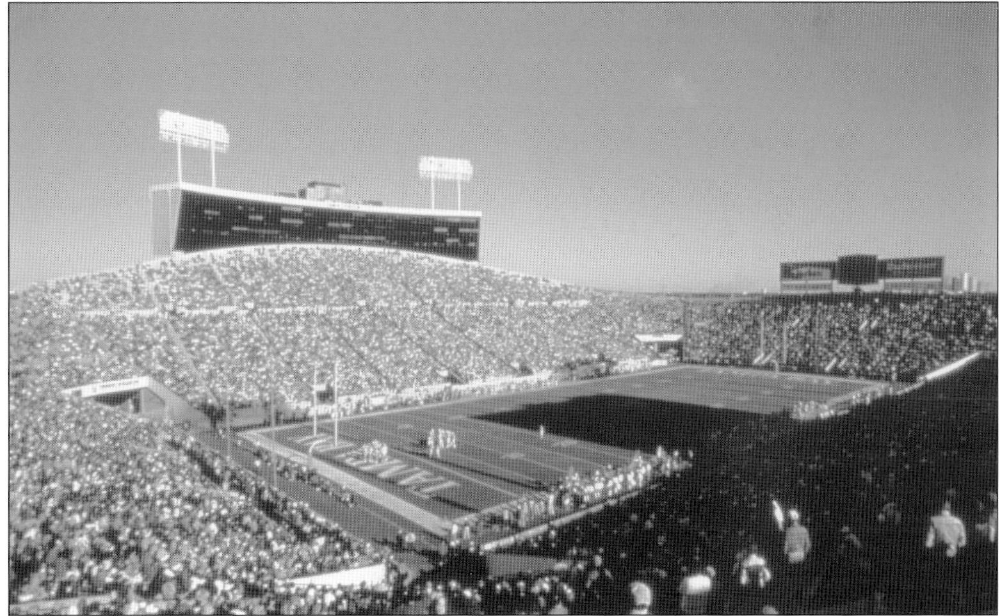

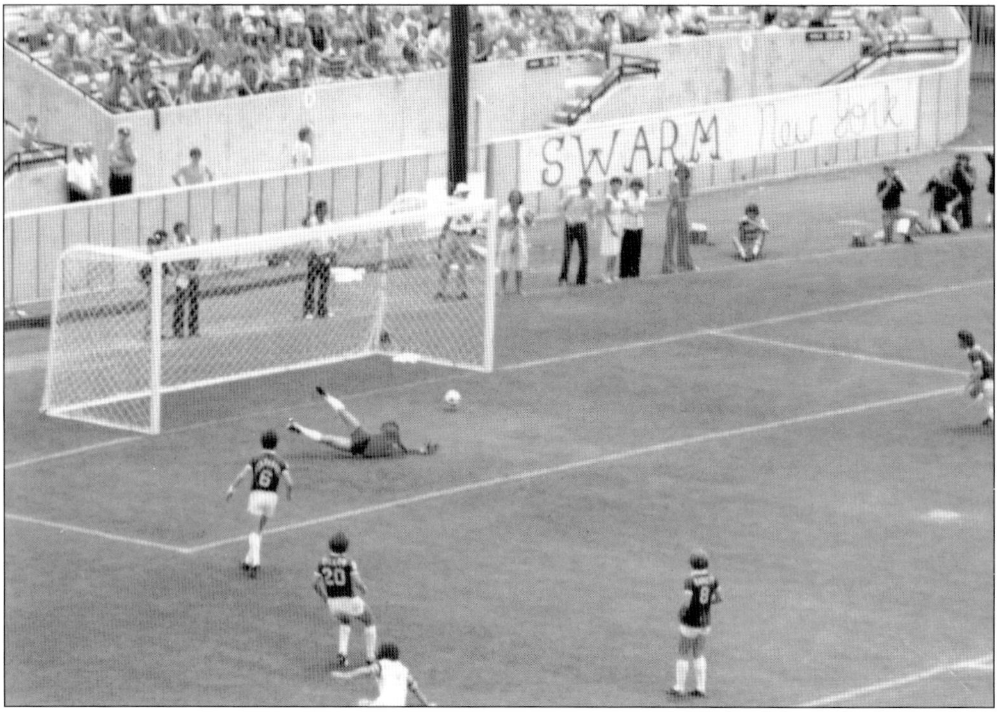

Tampa Stadium hosted much more than just Tampa Bay Buccaneers football games. It was the home of the Tampa Bay Rowdies professional soccer club (seen on the field above around 1980) from their inaugural season in 1975 through 1994. Annual events hosted at the Big Sombrero included monster truck rallies, college bowl games, and Budweiser American invitational equestrian showjumping events, one of which is seen below in the mid-1990s. (Above, courtesy of Dan Perez.)

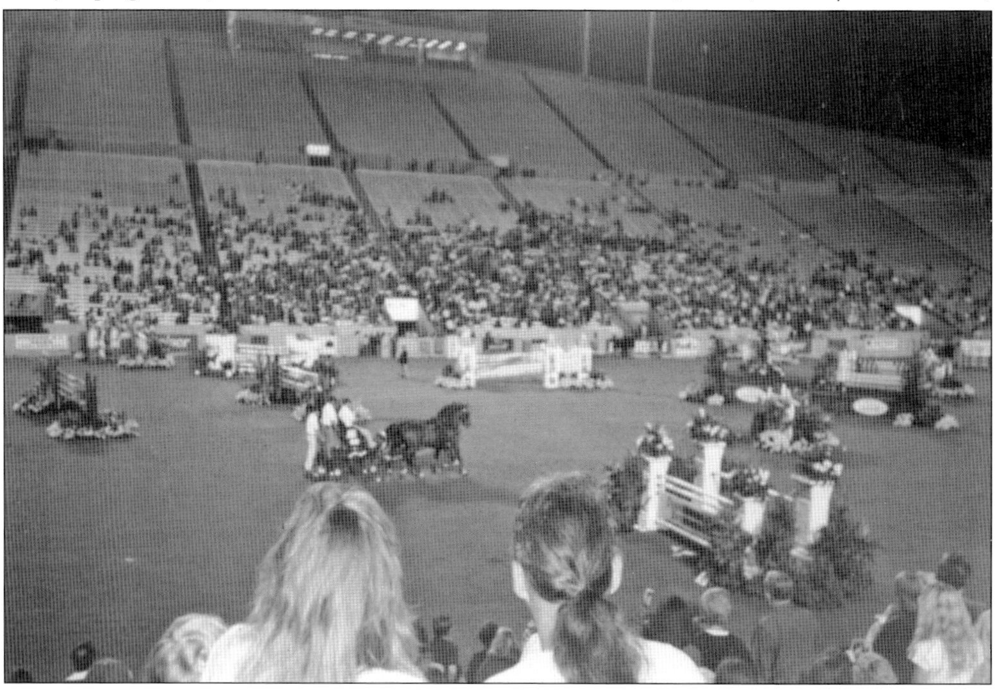

Two

Retail Therapy

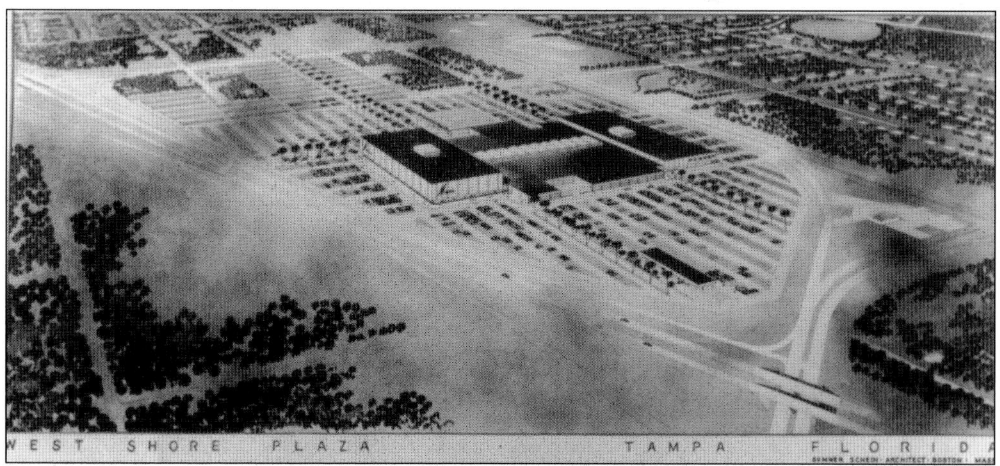

The announcement of WestShore Plaza in 1965 excited shoppers in Tampa, a city that had seen many new strip malls developed during the previous decade but none with indoor, climate-controlled corridors. WestShore Plaza, developed by Boston's Albert A. Manley, was planned as a $10-million project promising 40 stores and a convenient location central to shoppers in surrounding Tampa as well as those living just across the bay bridges in St. Petersburg and Clearwater. (Courtesy of the City of Tampa Archives.)

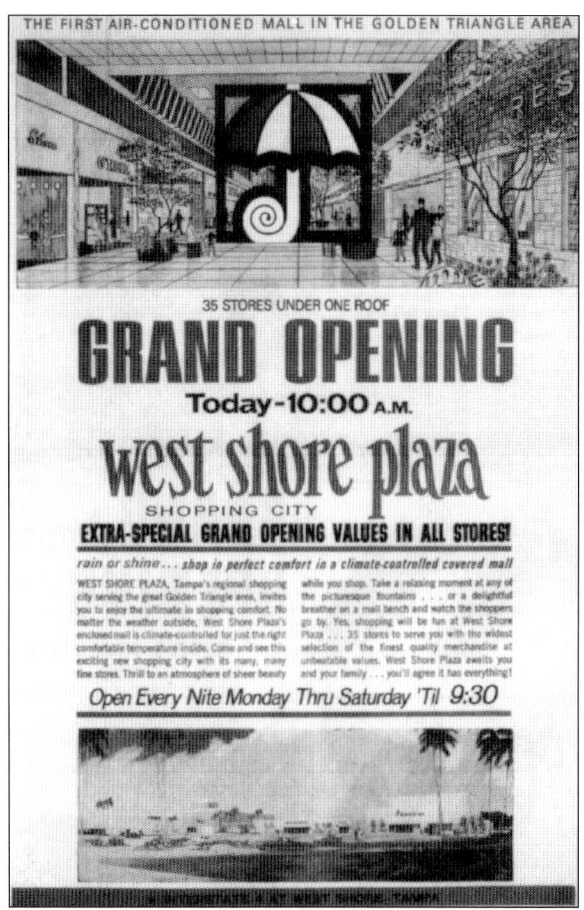

This full-page newspaper advertisement hails the arrival of WestShore Plaza on September 28, 1967, as Tampa's first enclosed shopping mall. Opening day saw the mall debut with 625,000 square feet of air-conditioned retail space, including a three-story Maas Brothers department store with 238,000 square feet of floor space on one end of the mall and a 209,000-square-foot, two-story J.C. Penney on the other. Additional retailers were to include a sprawling Woolworth's five-and-dime store, a Wolf Brothers clothing retailer, and a supermarket. (© *Tampa Bay Times* via ZUMA Press.)

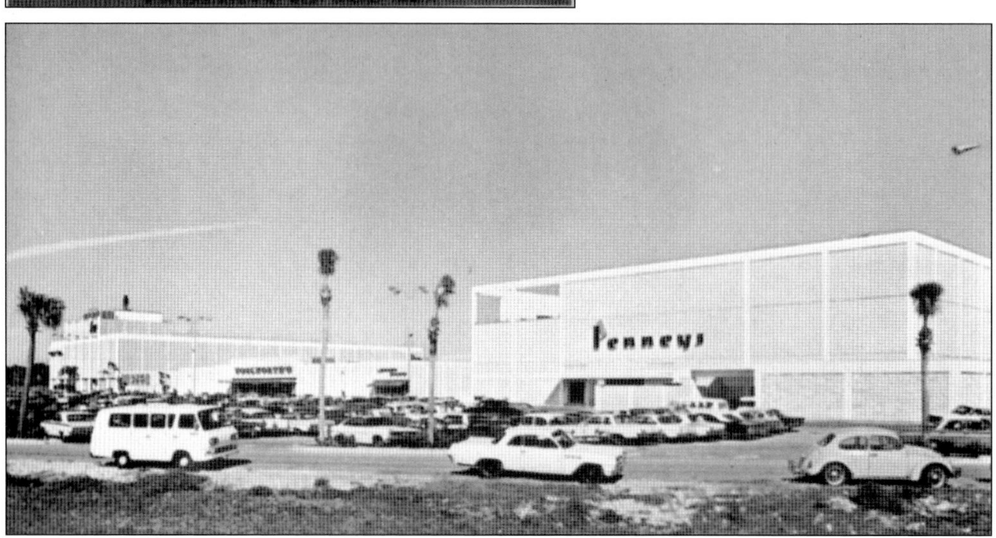

This late-1960s postcard shows anchors J.C. Penney in the foreground and Maas Brothers in the background. Also seen are major retailers Wolf Brothers adjacent to Maas Brothers and Woolworth's nearer to J.C. Penney. On the other side of the mall, unseen here, was a Pantry Pride supermarket, located approximately where the WestShore Plaza food court is today.

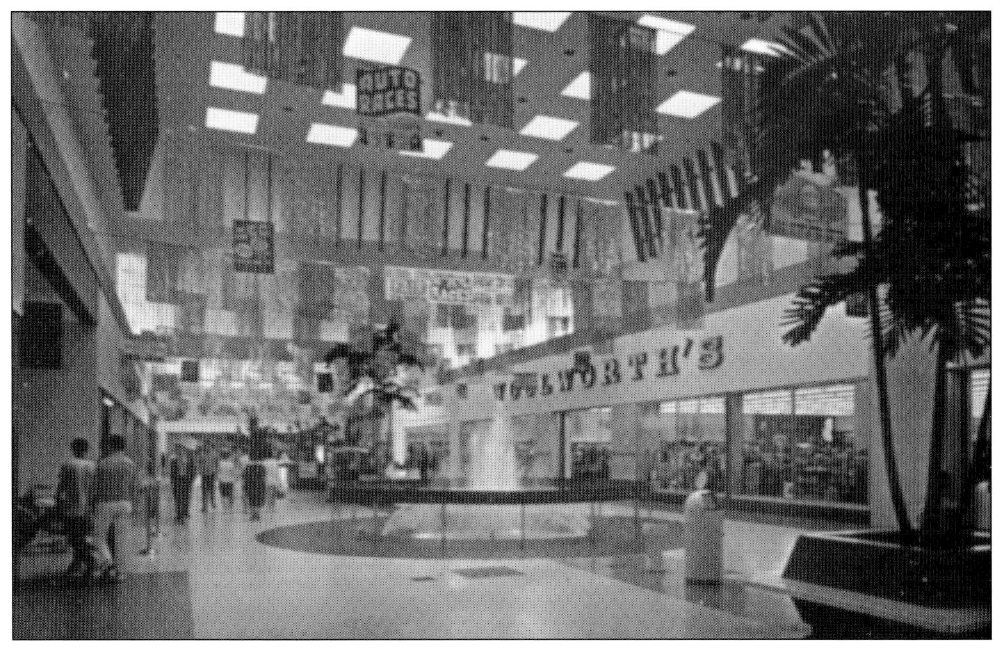

These views of WestShore Plaza date from around 1970 and show the main interior of the mall as seen near its central court. Prominently seen above is Woolworth's, with the entrance to J.C. Penney in the background. In the lower image, Hallmark Cards unfolds near the center of the mall, with a variety of other retailers to the left approaching the interior entrance of Maas Brothers.

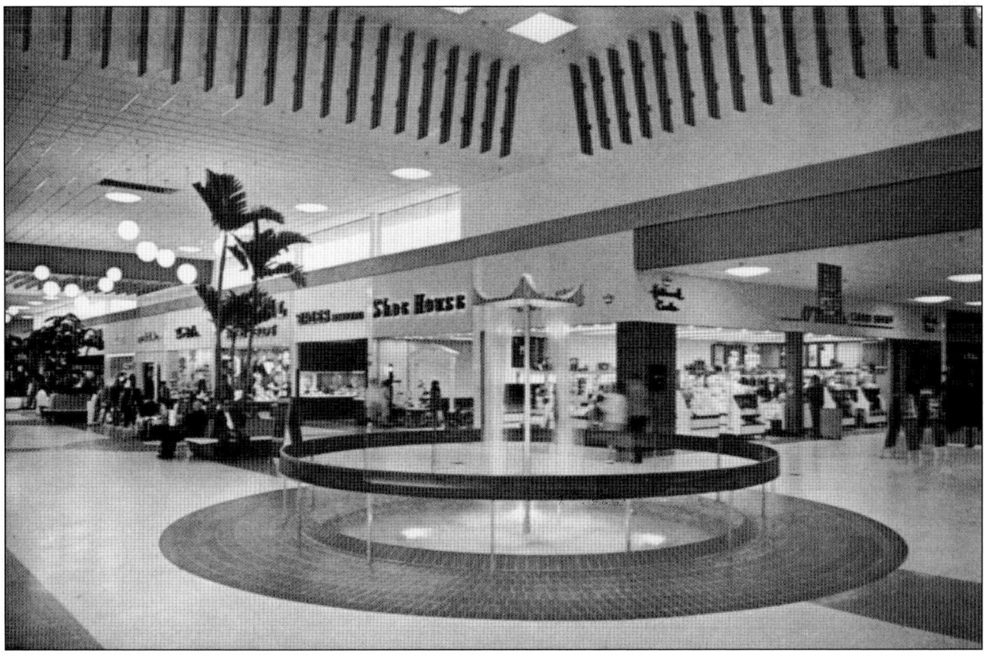

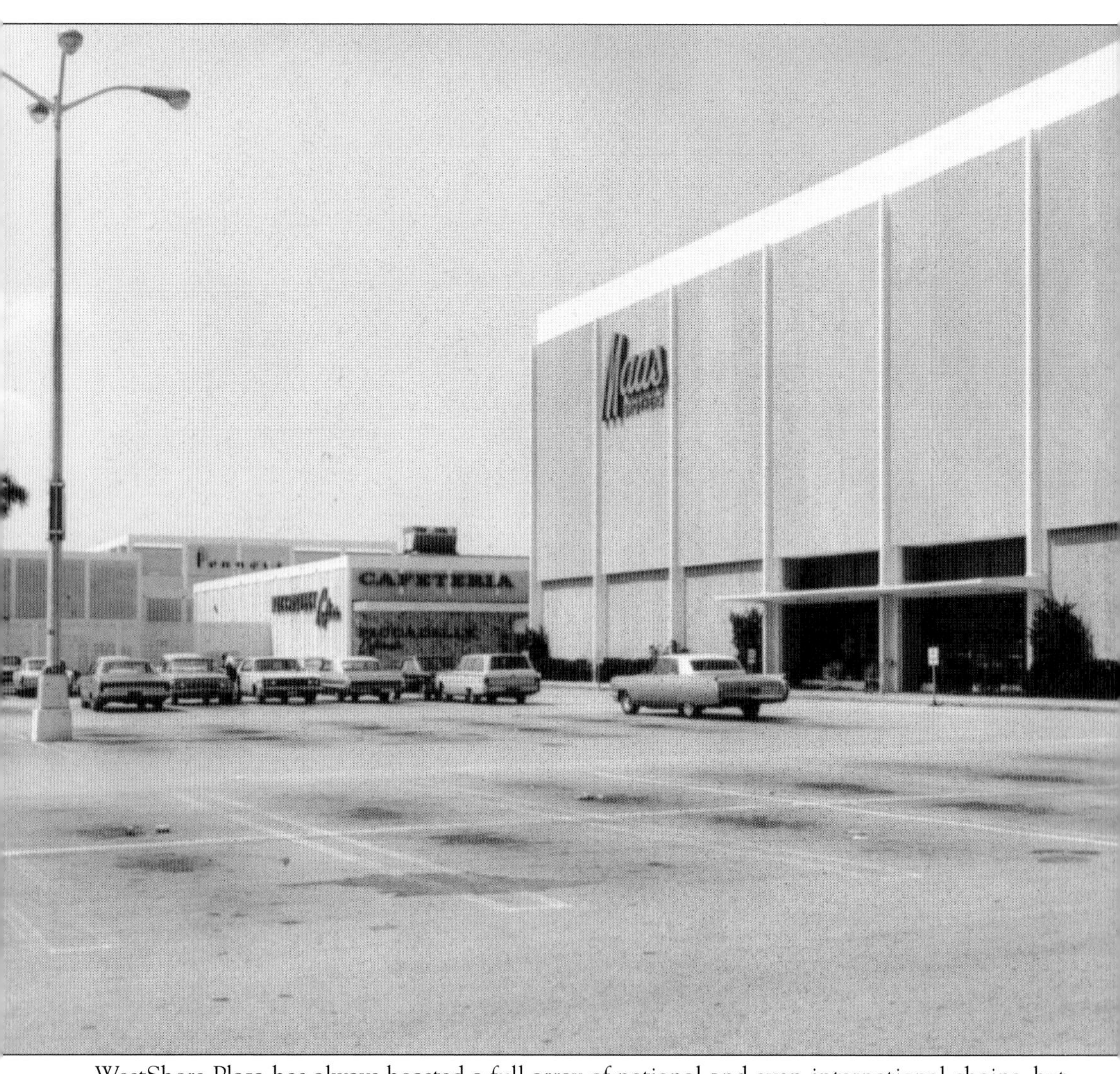

WestShore Plaza has always boasted a full array of national and even international chains, but three-story anchor Maas Brothers was truly a local department store. Maas Brothers was to Tampa's shoppers what Wanamaker's is to Philadelphians, Filene's to Bostoners, and Macy's to New Yorkers. Founded by brothers Abe and Isaac Maas in 1886, Maas Brothers became a department store of multigenerational popularity to the shoppers who frequented the main store in downtown Tampa, which closed with the rest of the 39-store chain in 1991 upon consolidating with Miami-based Burdines, itself defunct by 2005, when the latter was renamed in favor of its Macy's subsidiary. In this image, the WestShore Plaza Maas Brothers, which opened on October 28, 1966, eleven months before the rest of the mall, is seen from its east side with its neighbor Piccadilly Cafeteria in the mid-ground. Interestingly, this vantage point of the mall is visually obscured today by a two-story parking garage, built in 1974 when a third department-store anchor known as Robinson's of Florida joined the mall on its east side. (Courtesy of the City of Tampa Archives.)

Every great department store of the 20th century established time-honored holiday traditions, and this was certainly true for Maas Brothers. Christmas was a particularly cheerful time at Maas Brothers WestShore Plaza, where one might find the fanciful Talking Christmas Tree (right, with Maria Williams Trippe in 1970) or jolly old Saint Nick himself, as seen below with the author in 1981. (Right, courtesy of Maria Williams Trippe.)

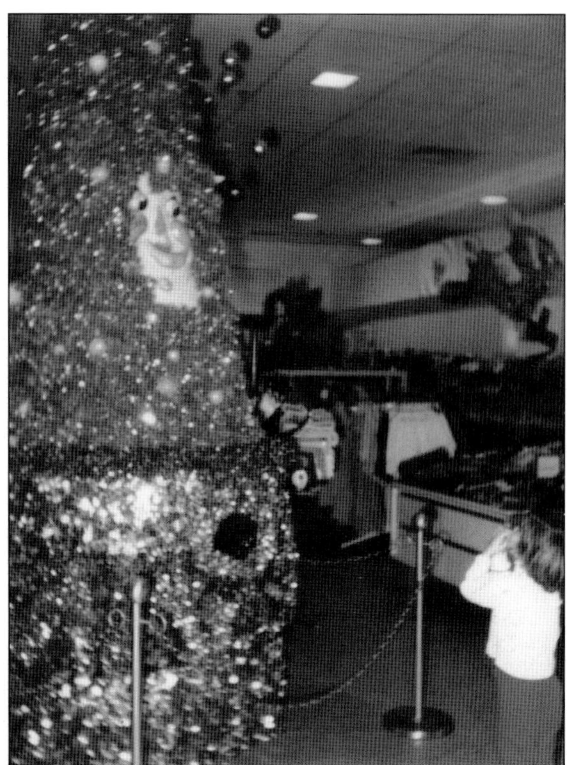

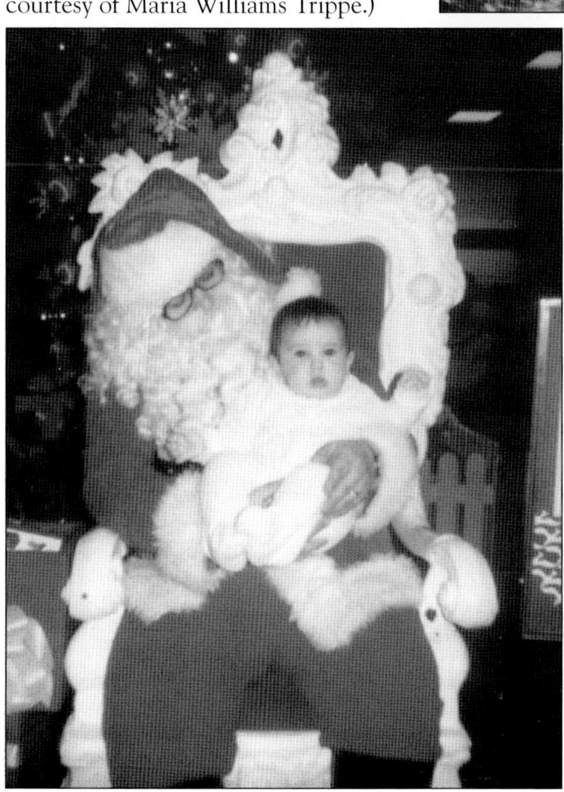

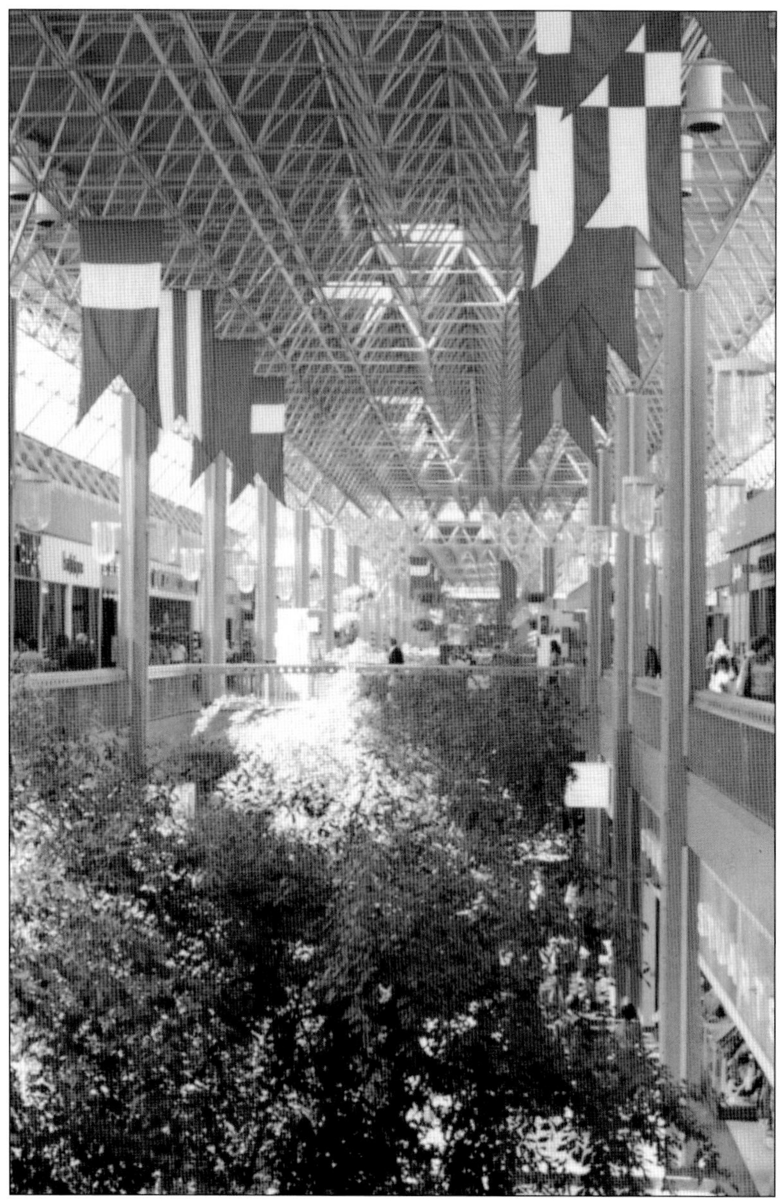

Tampa saw many new malls open in the decade following the debut of WestShore Plaza in 1967. Among these was Tampa Bay Center, which opened on August 5, 1976, on former pasture lands at the southeast corner of Himes Avenue and then–Buffalo Avenue. Tampa Bay Center was distinctive for its greenhouse-like main corridor, which allowed plenty of Florida sunshine to splash down upon shoppers inside. The interior of Tampa Bay Center also featured water fountains, live trees, and a glass elevator taking shoppers between the mall's lower and upper floors. Tampa Bay Center opened with Sears and Burdines and was joined in 1980 by Montgomery Ward as the mall's third anchor. Also opening with Tampa Bay Center was a two-screen cinema that operated until 1990; a food court on the upper floor came aboard in 1985. Eventually, new shopping malls opened within a few miles, helping bring an end to Tampa Bay Center, which closed in 2001 and was demolished to make room for a new training facility for the Tampa Bay Buccaneers professional football franchise. (Courtesy of Dan Perez.)

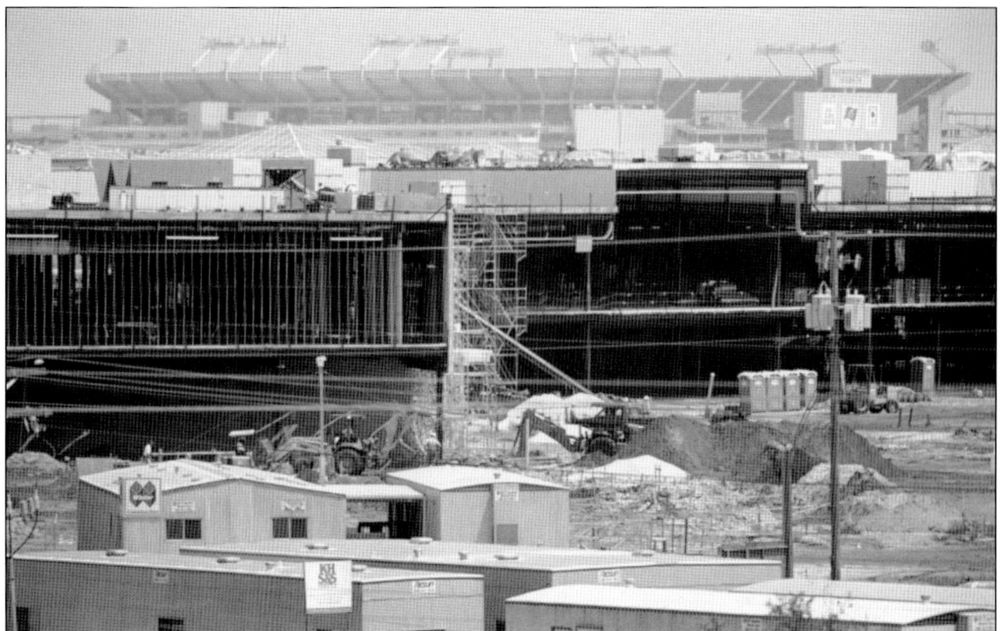

One of the newer malls that swayed shoppers from Tampa Bay Center was International Plaza, seen here under construction in 2000 with Raymond James Stadium in the background. The ritzy mall was built on land just southeast of Tampa International Airport formerly occupied by Tampa Airport Resort Golf and Racquet Club, which was situated at the northeast corner of West Shore Boulevard and Boy Scout Boulevard since the 1970s. Planning for International Plaza dates to 1986, but it would take over a dozen years to finalize the proposal and bring it to fruition. Construction began on the long-awaited mall in 1999. (© *Tampa Bay Times* via ZUMA Press.)

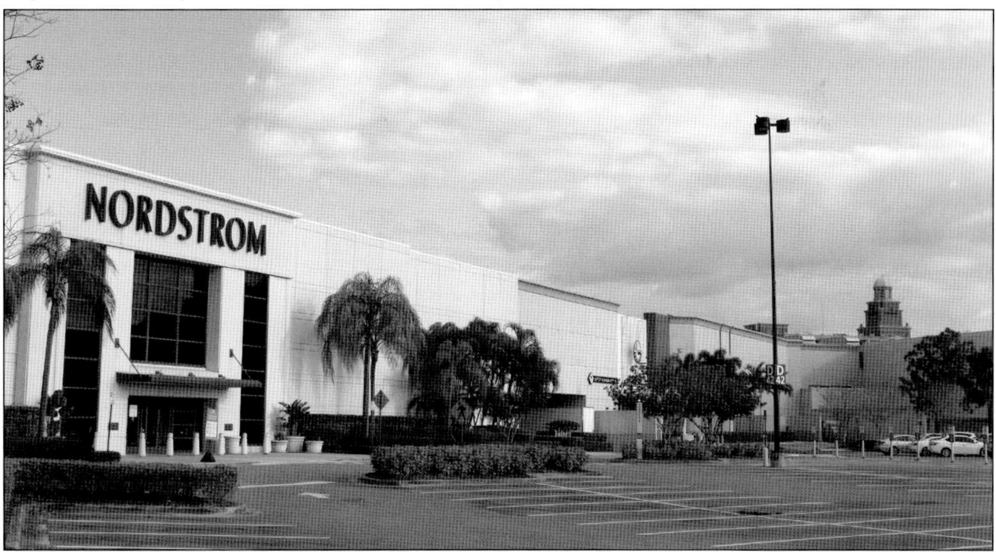

Seen above is Nordstrom, one of several high-end retailers at International Plaza. The mall opened on September 14, 2001, along with Neiman Marcus, Lord & Taylor, and Dillard's to round out the shopping hub's four department store anchors. Despite being located just one mile north of WestShore Plaza, both the earlier-built mall and the 1.2-million-square-foot International Plaza coexist well, drawing major crowds.

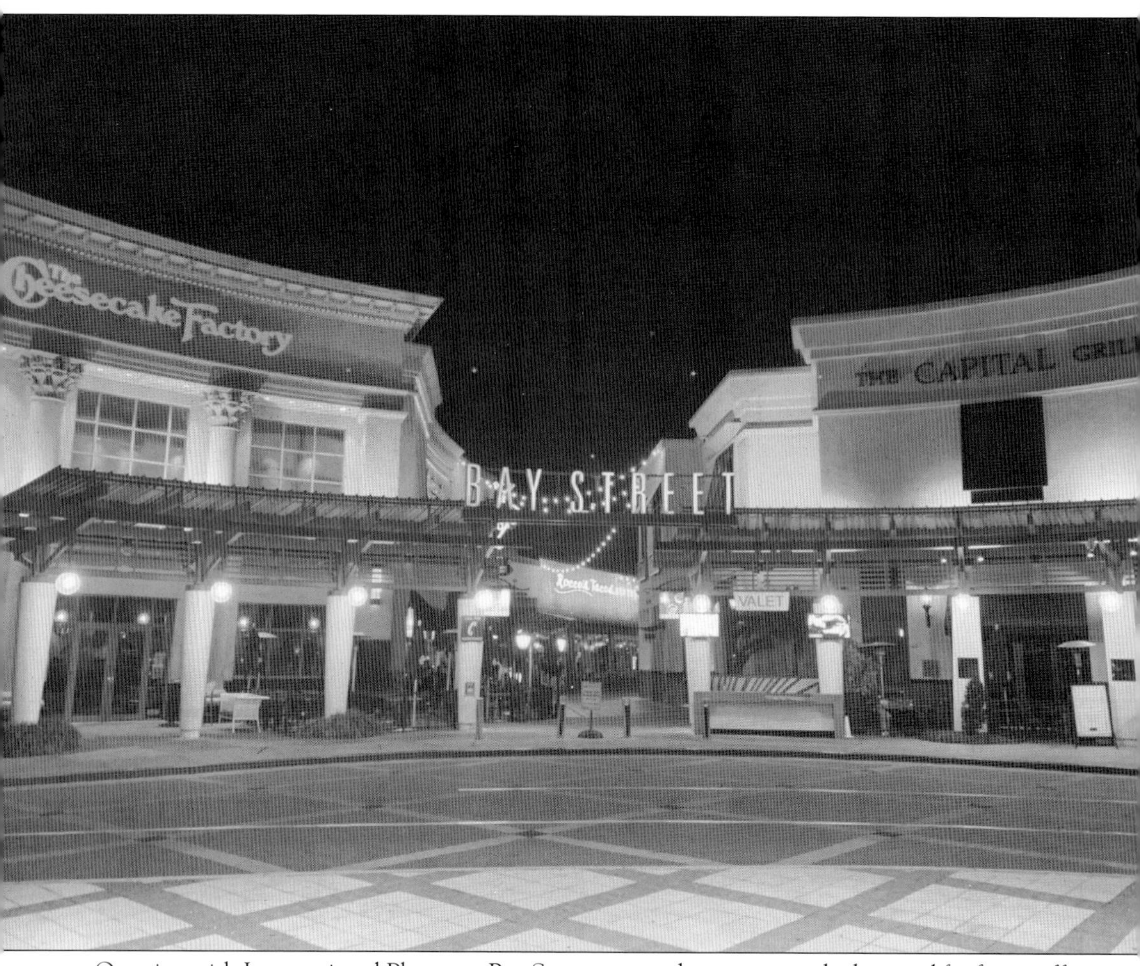

Opening with International Plaza was Bay Street, an outdoor promenade designed for foot traffic and mainly aimed at hungry foodies. This restaurant row opened with several major restaurants, including an 11,000-square-foot Cheesecake Factory. Among other earlier restaurants at Bay Street were Blue Martini, Bamboo Club, Gallery Bistro Tampa, Hollywood Java, Kahunaville, Prezzo, Profusion, TooJay's Original Gourmet Deli, and a French bakery called Ville du Pain. Many other restaurants have since come aboard to appease the ever-changing tastes of Tampa shoppers at International Plaza. Meanwhile, the upscale Renaissance Hotel opened adjacent to Bay Street in August 2004, making Bay Street a popular destination for the Westshore community, tying a large-scale resort with major restaurant and retail complexes.

Shoppers need money, and one place where they held their funds in safekeeping between shopping trips was the National Bank of Tampa, seen here on April 10, 1961, at 3439 West Hillsborough Avenue. The building changed hands many times over the years but still stands as a financial institution. (Courtesy of the Tampa–Hillsborough County Public Library System.)

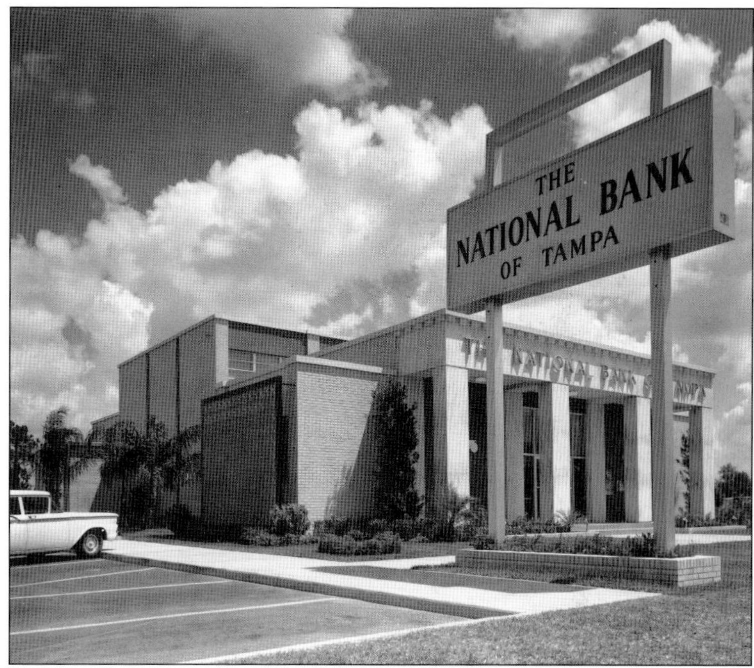

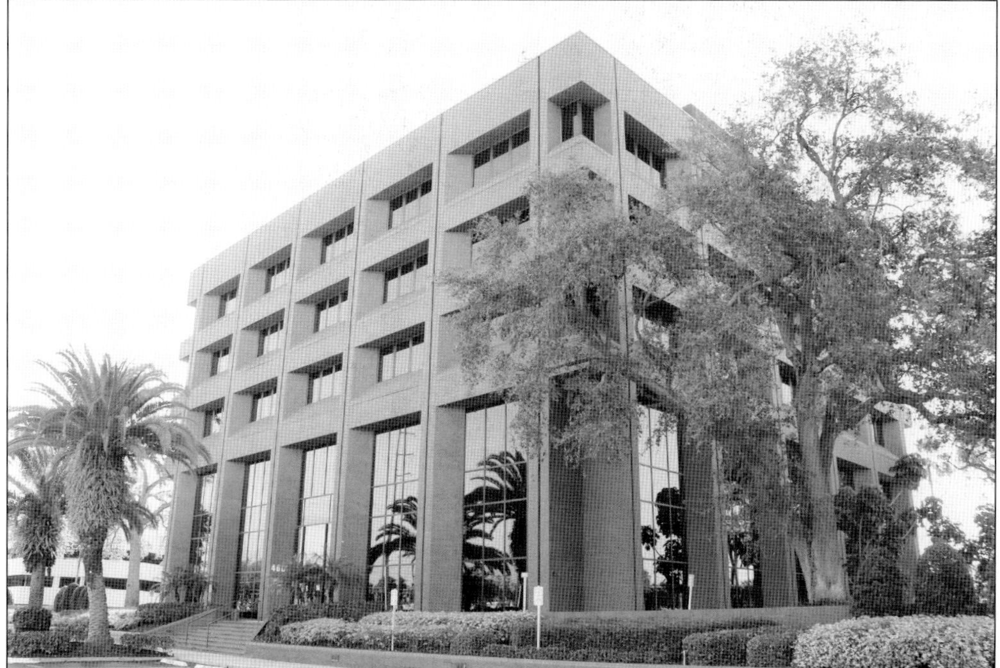

There was even more space for Tampa shoppers to secure their money (or apply for credit cards and loans) at this building, which opened at 4600 West Cypress Street in 1977 as the headquarters for Tampa-based Metropolitan Bank and Trust Company. That institution folded in 1982, and the office building has seen many other premier tenants since.

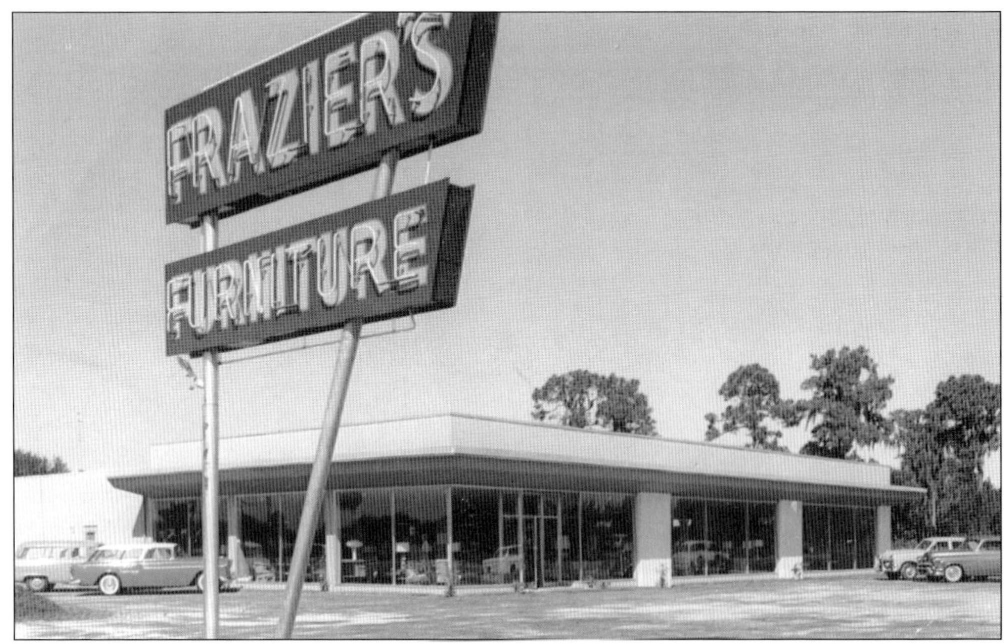

Frazier's Furniture was a 10,000-square-foot emporium of "the unusual at reasonable prices." The store, opened by furniture expert John T. Frazier at the northwest corner of North West Shore Boulevard and West Cypress Street in 1955, sold a wide variety of modern, early American, contemporary, Victorian, and traditional furnishings, as well as lamps, draperies, and rugs. The store also offered professional decorating services. The store closed by the late 1960s, and the building was later converted into a lounge, with the site subdivided to include a Shell gas station in 1970.

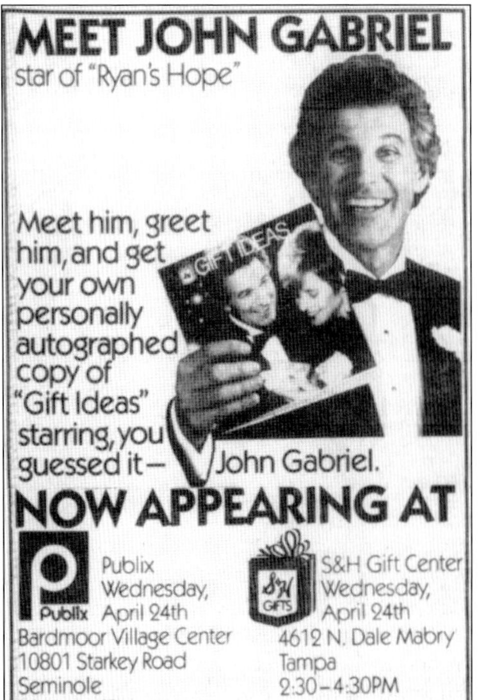

S&H Green Stamps was a nationwide rewards program by Sperry & Hutchinson company. These trading stamps were distributed in the Tampa Bay area by mainstream consumer outlets such as Publix supermarkets. Once enough were accumulated, the stamps could be redeemed for a variety of goods, including toys, housewares, and furnishings, such as could be found at the S&H Green Stamps Gift Center at 4612 North Dale Mabry Highway. As this newspaper advertisement announces, actor John Gabriel of soap opera *Ryan's Hope* made a promotional stop at the Westshore store on April 24, 1985. (© *Tampa Bay Times* via ZUMA Press.)

Horizon Park Shopping Center opened in 1971 near the southwest corner of North Dale Mabry Highway and West Hillsborough Avenue. It was originally anchored by Horizon Park 4 movie theater, Winn-Dixie grocery store, Madison Rexall Drug, and Bonanza Sirloin Pit steakhouse. Many other retailers have occupied spaces at the shopping center over the years, including Woolco department store, Luria's catalog showroom, The Home Depot, Mars Music, Pearl Artist & Craft Supply, and various restaurants, boutiques, and retailers. In the background of this 1972 photograph looking east along Hillsborough Avenue is Jim Harrell Pontiac. (Courtesy of Leto High School.)

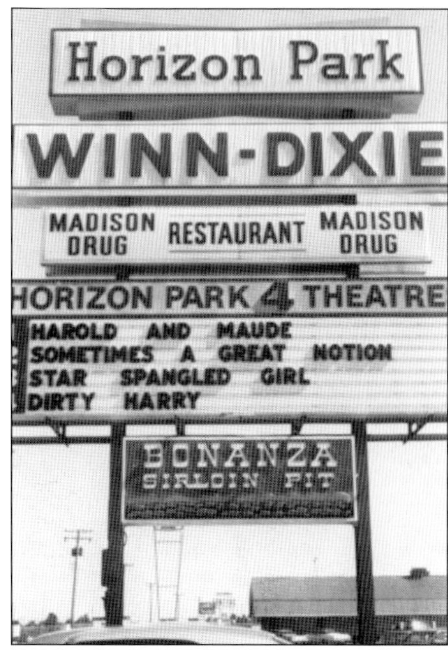

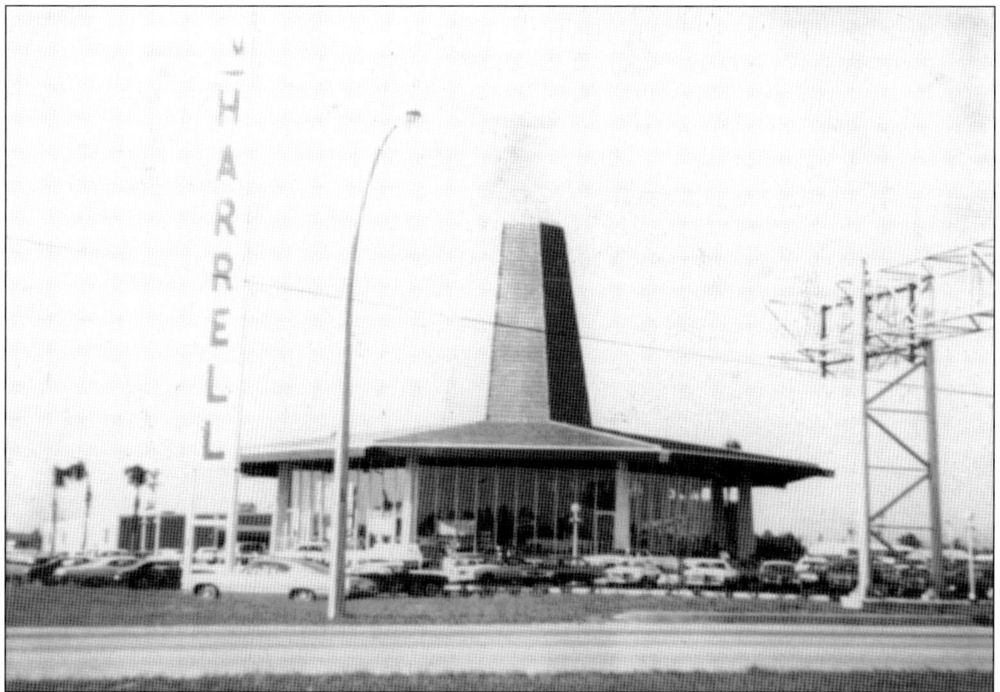

The Westshore district has seen many car dealerships, but perhaps none whose buildings were as architecturally distinctive as that of Jim Harrell Pontiac at 3800 West Hillsborough Avenue. Opening its doors at this location on December 8, 1967, Jim Harrell Pontiac spent many years in this unique building designed by Frank W. White, AIA/J. Priede Rodriguez, AIA, who incorporated a highly visible cone-shaped roof atop the large showroom reaching 82 feet over the interchange at West Hillsborough Avenue and North Dale Mabry Highway. While the building was demolished in 2005, a major car dealership still anchors the property. (Courtesy of Barry M. White.)

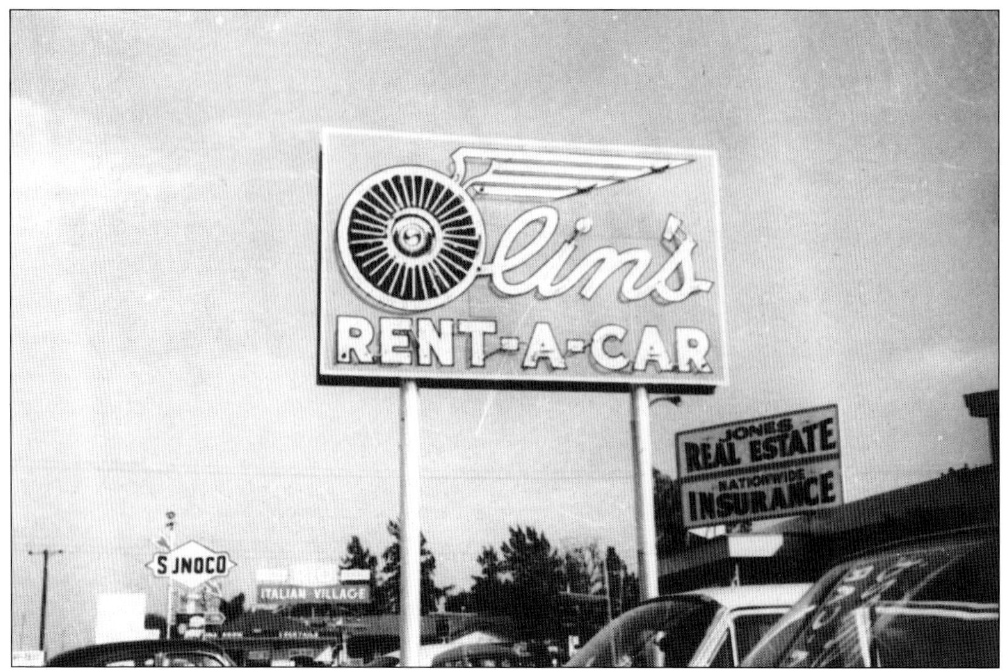

One could see Tampa Bay in a Chevrolet, or just about any other American-made car, by leasing a vehicle through Olin's Rent-A-Car, located near the intersection of North Dale Mabry Highway and West Spruce Street. Upon the opening of the newly expanded Tampa International Airport in 1971, the rental car company moved its Tampa location closer to the entrance of the jetport. (Courtesy of John Cinchett.)

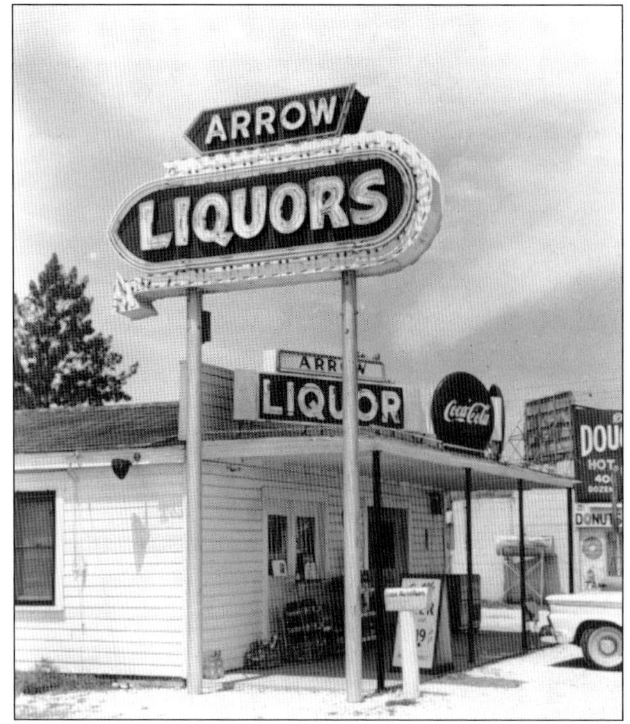

Arrow Liquors, seen here at 3716 West Columbus Drive, was one of many "packies" that have dotted the Westshore community. This site would later be ensconced into a shopping plaza that opened in 1972 and once included Kmart, Scan Design furniture store, and many other popular retailers. (Courtesy of John Cinchett.)

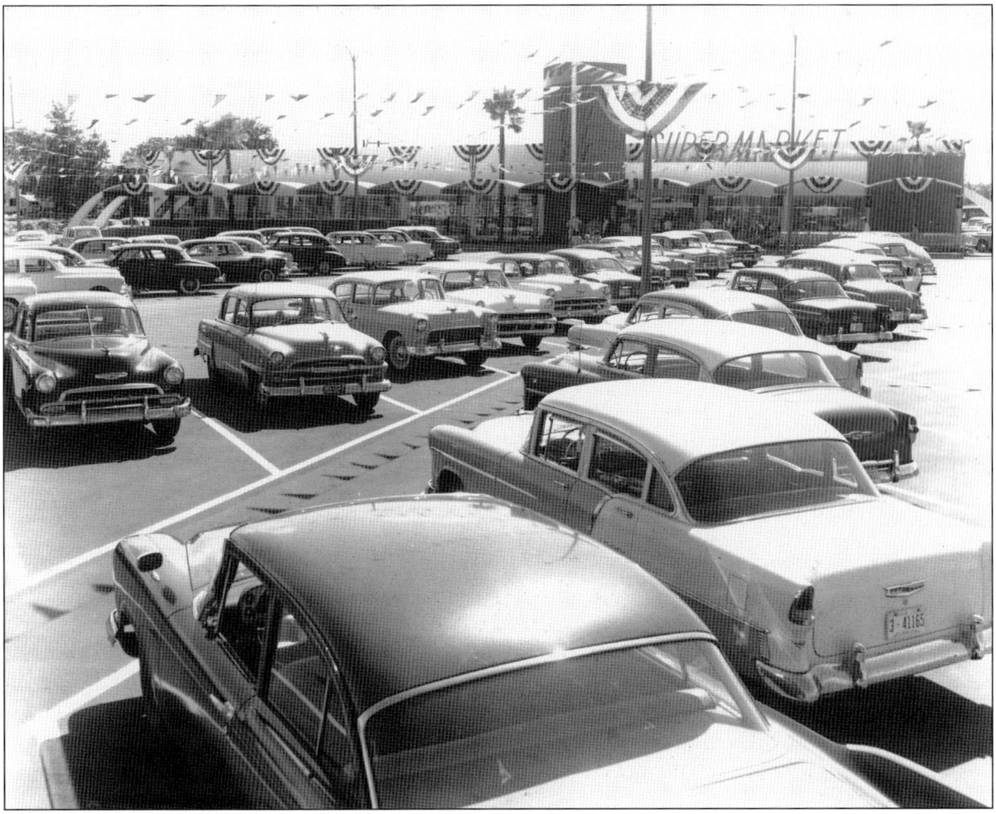

One of the first major, modern grocery stores to open in the Westshore community was Gulf Supermarket. It opened its doors to shoppers at 1705 North Dale Mabry Highway on July 16, 1957, and was quite popular, as the bustling scene below suggests. However, this location did not last long. The property was viewed as a prime spot for a new Montgomery Ward department store. Just two years after opening, the Gulf Supermarket building was demolished to make way for the new department store and was resituated on the site adjoining Montgomery Ward. (Both, courtesy of the Tampa–Hillsborough County Public Library System.)

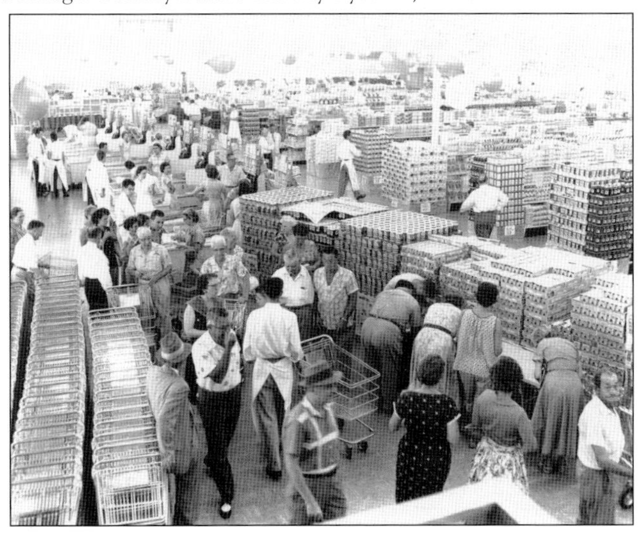

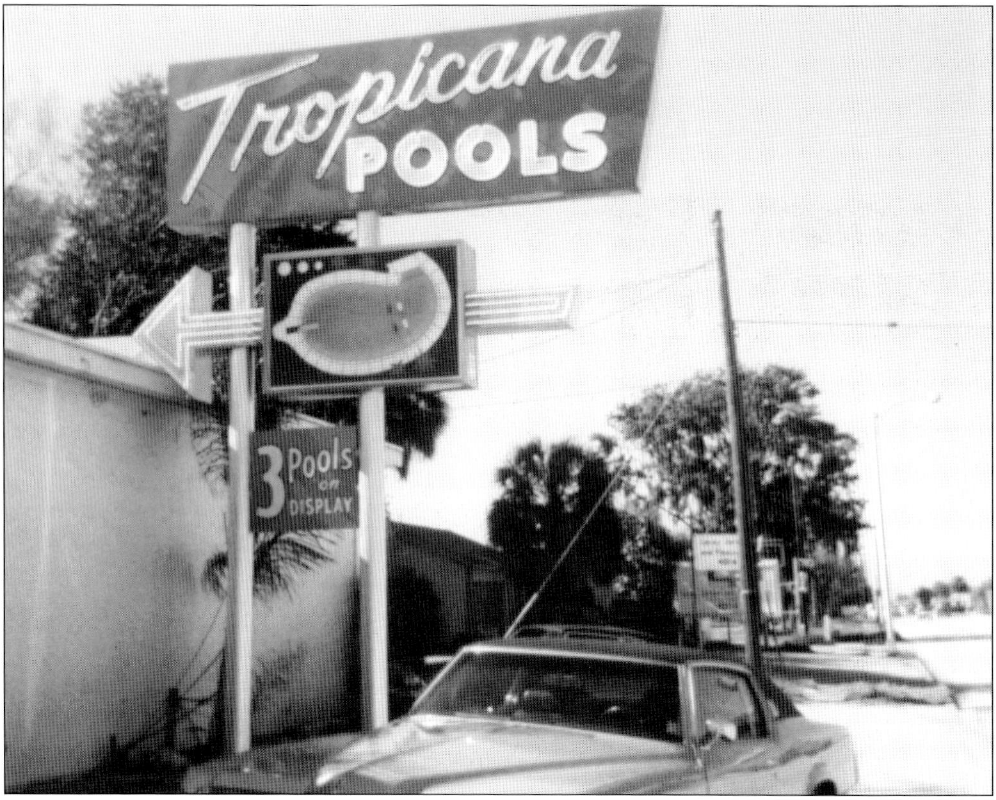

Those wanting to go big for their home could purchase a backyard oasis at Tropicana Pools. Their building at 4006 West Kennedy Boulevard is seen here in this westward-facing photograph taken in 1968. (Courtesy of John Cinchett.)

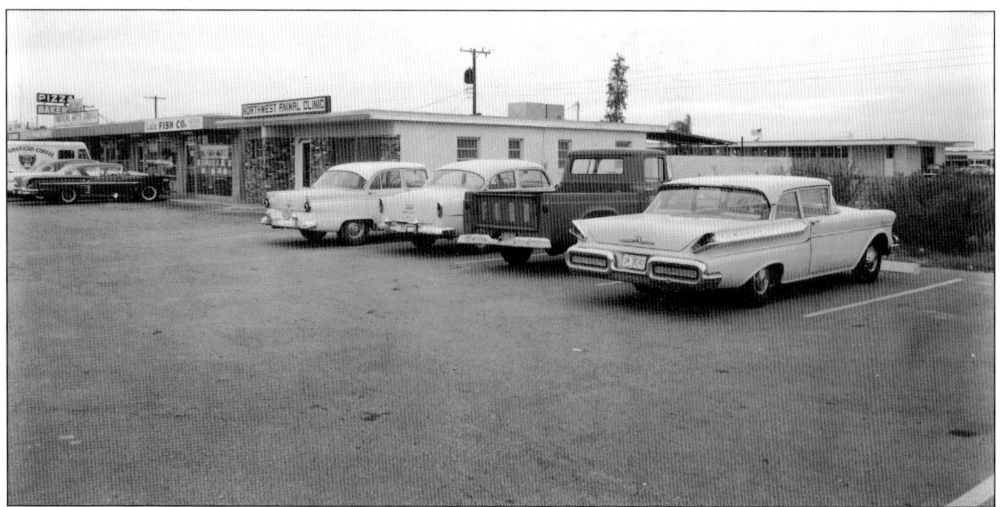

This strip mall near the northeast corner of West Hillsborough Avenue and North Hesperides Street offered a hodgepodge of retailers and restaurants, including Northwest Animal Clinic, Lala Fish Company, and Medical Arts Drugs. This small shopping center remains standing in the 21st century and is located just south of Pierce Middle School, seen in the background of this 1962 photograph. (Courtesy of the Tampa–Hillsborough County Public Library System.)

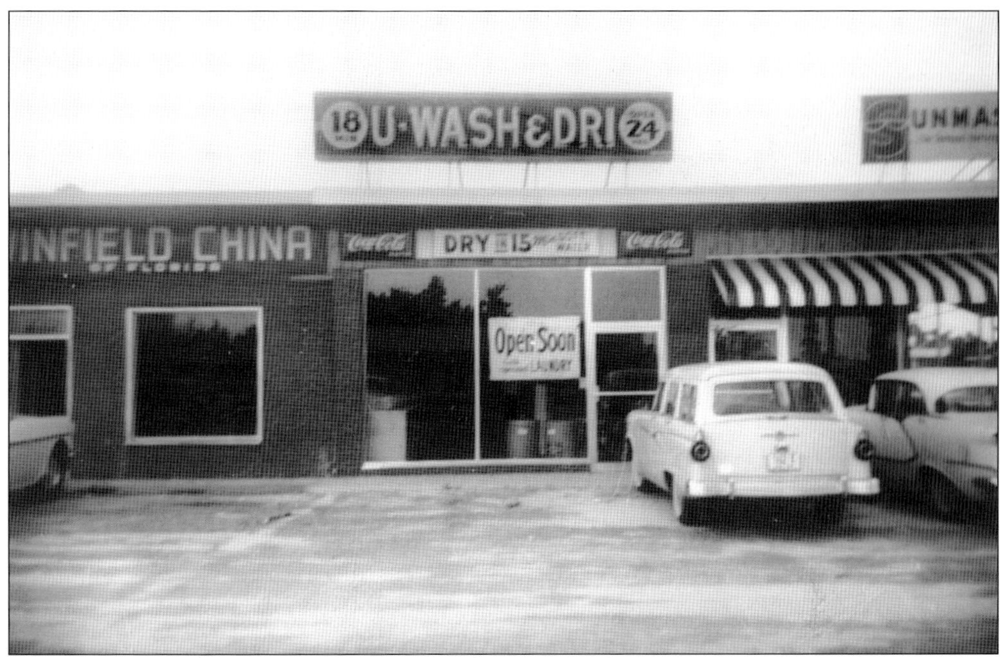

After a busy day of shopping, one's clothes are liable to get a little dusty. Those whose clothes needed laundering might have stopped by U-Wash & Dri, offering around-the-clock laundering at 322 North Dale Mabry Highway as seen here in 1960. (Courtesy of John Cinchett.)

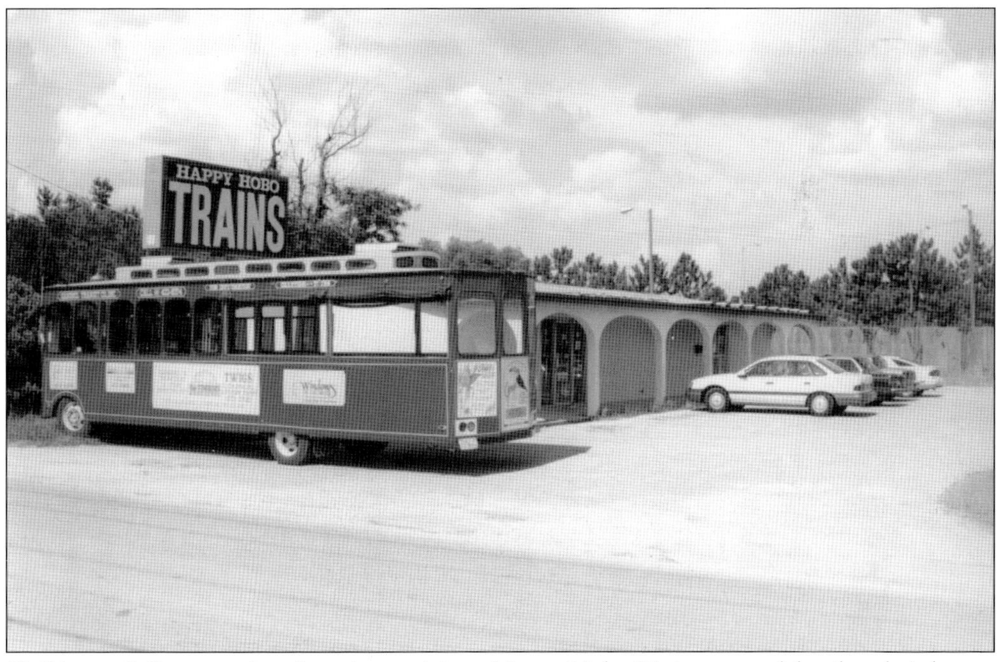

Children of all ages enjoyed paying a visit to Happy Hobo Trains, a model railroader's haven where trains, rolling stock, tracks, and lifelike accessories of all scale sizes could be found. The store was located on Church Avenue just north of West Hillsborough Avenue until 1991, when it moved to a shopping plaza on West Waters Avenue. The former Happy Hobo Trains property is today occupied by a motel. (Courtesy of Kevin Pytlak.)

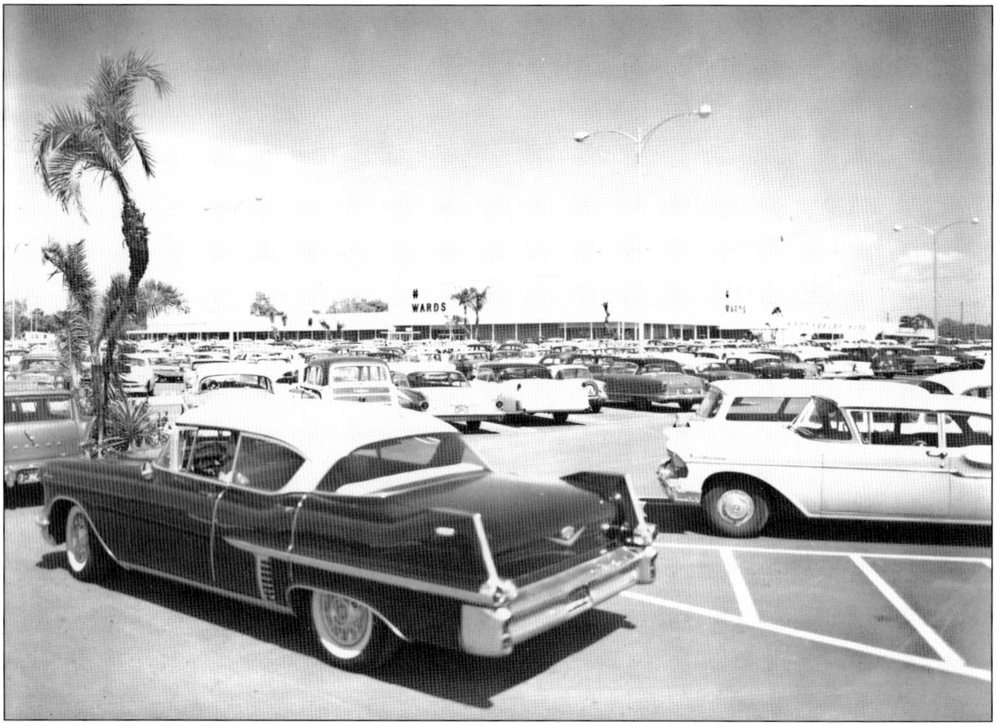

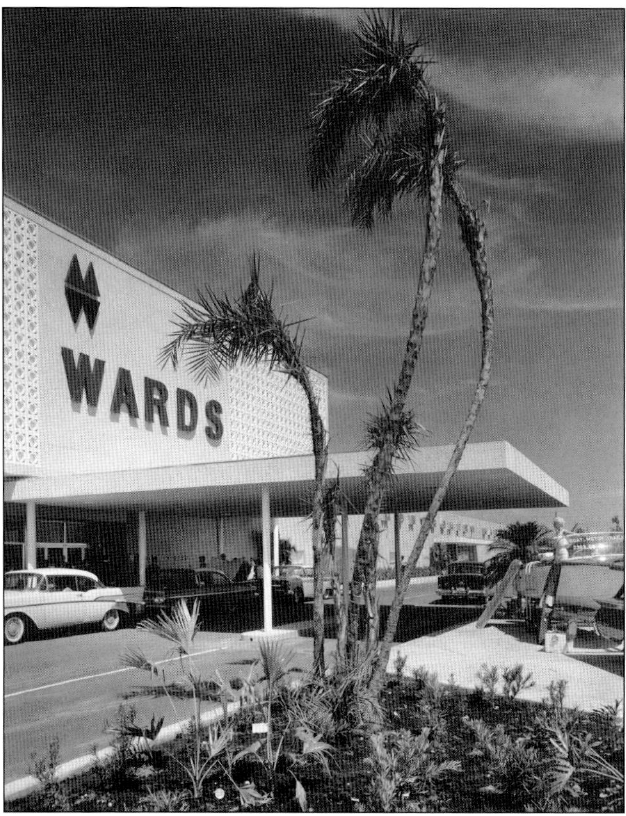

Many years before WestShore Plaza opened as Tampa's first indoor, air-conditioned mall, national chain Montgomery Ward built one of its sprawling department stores at 1701 North Dale Mabry Highway. The store opened in 1960 and replaced the Gulf Supermarket that opened at that same site just a few years earlier in 1957. Montgomery Ward operated at this location until 1980, when the store became the third anchor at nearby Tampa Bay Center. The site was redeveloped in the mid-1990s with a Walmart department store and Best Buy electronics center. (Both, courtesy of the Tampa–Hillsborough County Public Library System.)

Three

Gas, Food, and Lodging

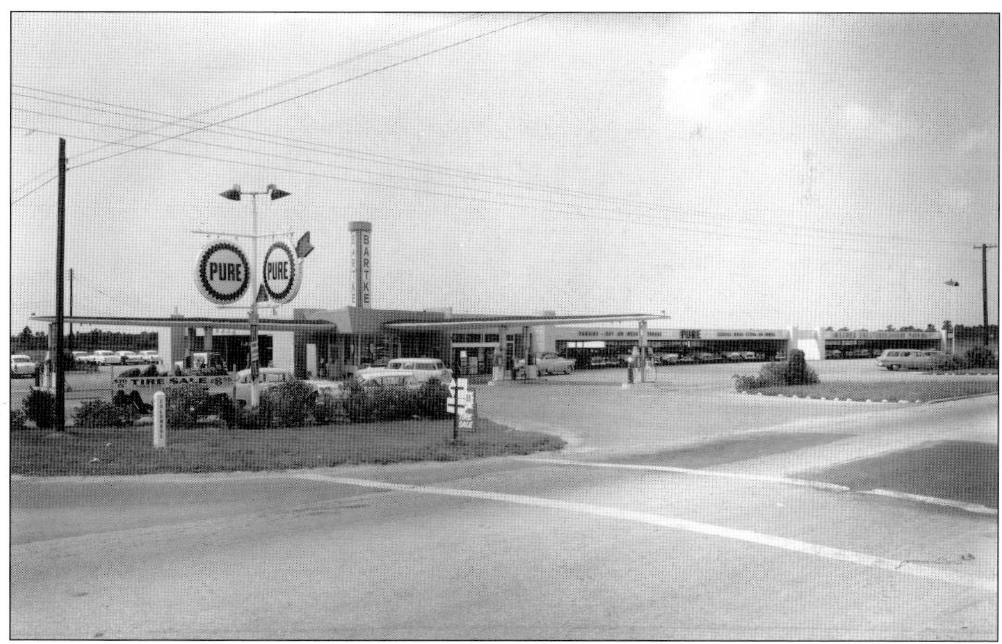

Bartke's Airport Service Station was located at the southwest corner of North West Shore Boulevard and West Columbus Drive and is seen here on August 27, 1957. At this time, the main terminal of Tampa International Airport would have been located across the street from this location, making this gas station one of the busiest in town. (Courtesy of the Tampa–Hillsborough County Public Library System.)

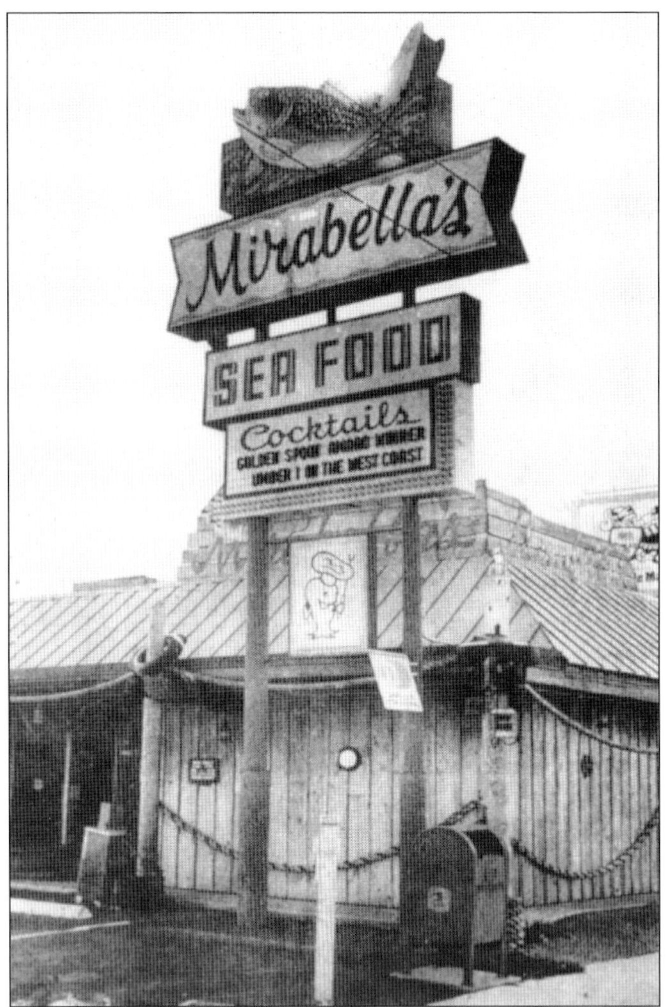

Mirabella's seafood restaurant opened its doors at 327 North Dale Mabry Highway in 1952, many decades after the Mirabella family established its name in Tampa locally as offering among the finest and freshest seafood. Mirabella's closed in 1988, and four years later, it was the site of Hops Grill and Bar, a restaurant concept that was part of a brewpub chain operated by David Mason and Tom Schelldorf. Today, the property is occupied by a bank. (Courtesy of John Cinchett.)

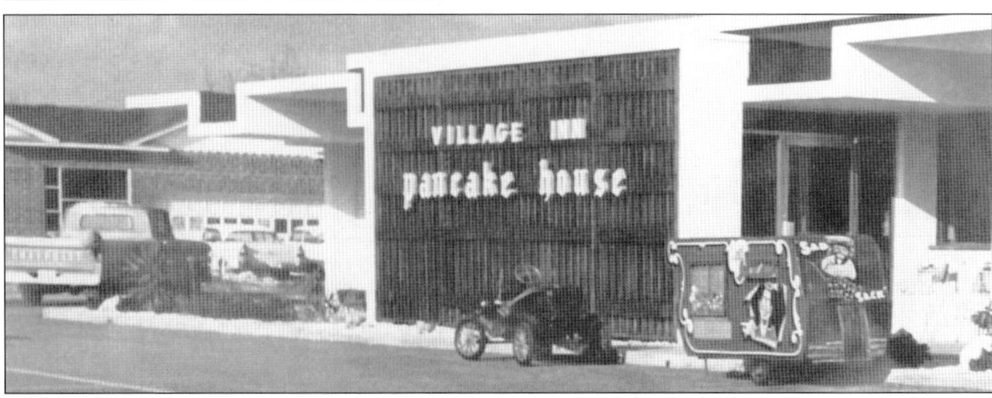

Dow Sherwood opened the Village Inn Pancake House in 1961 at 215 North Dale Mabry Highway, a location that almost always sees packed booths and bustling tables. Located a short drive from Interstate 275, Raymond James Stadium, downtown Tampa, and South Tampa, the restaurant, seen here in the 1960s, has been a favorite of locals and tourists alike for generations. (Courtesy of James Walker.)

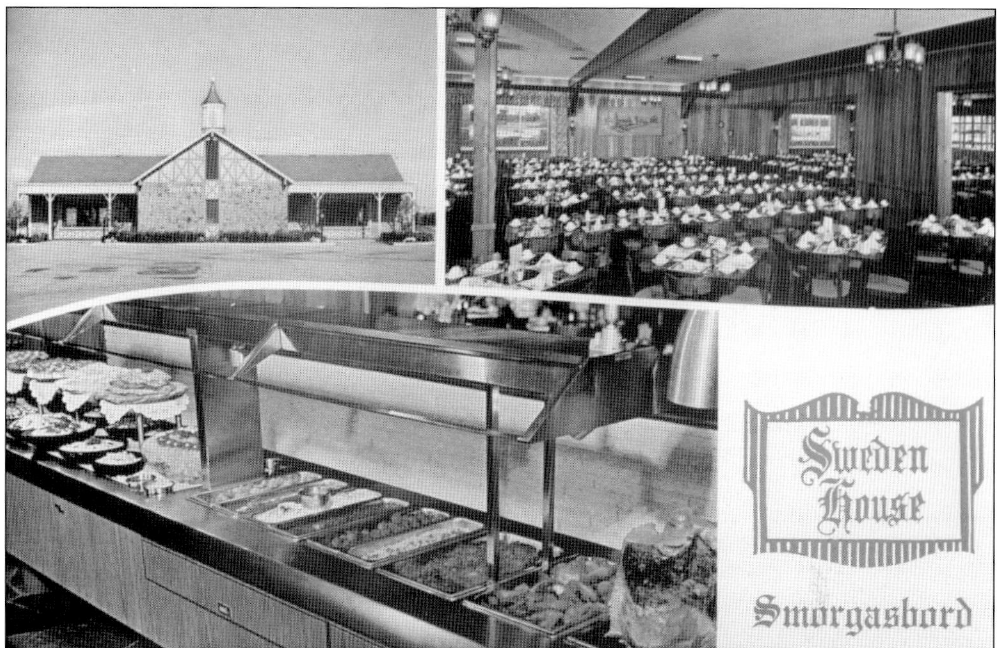

Sweden House Smorgasbord operated at 2720 North Dale Mabry Highway from 1965 through 1980 with its "all you care to eat" buffet filled with delights inspired by Sweden and other European nations as well as plentiful American fare. The restaurant also had a popular bakery and occasionally hosted live entertainment. The property went through several hands after Sweden House closed shop there; at one point, it fielded a Circuit City electronics store, and today, it is incorporated into the massive Jerry Ulm Dodge car dealership.

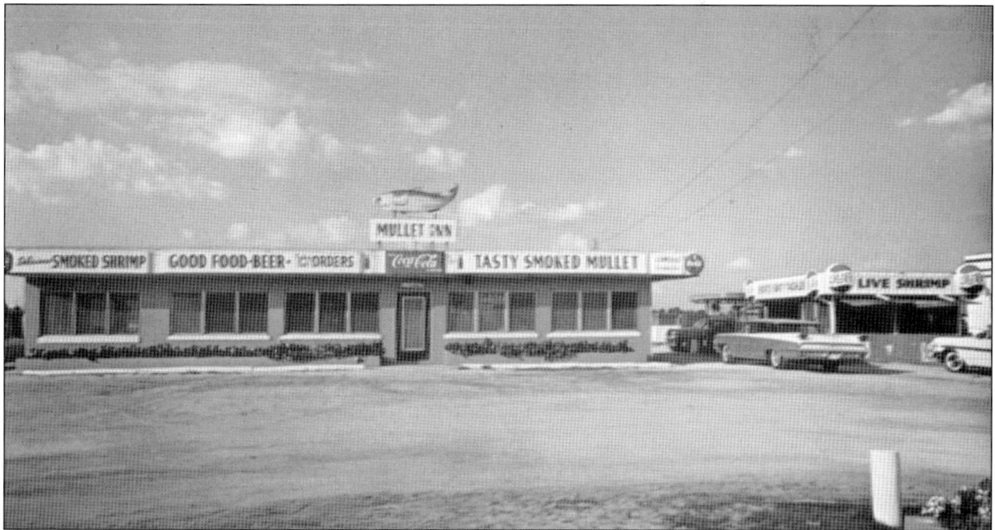

The Mullet Inn was a popular restaurant on the east end of the Courtney Campbell Causeway on Rocky Point. Billed as the "Home of Famous Zipper-Deveined Smoke Shrimp," among the restaurant's menu selections were smoked seafood, shrimp spreads, and a variety of other catches so fresh the eatery's motto was "The fish we serve today slept last night in Tampa Bay."

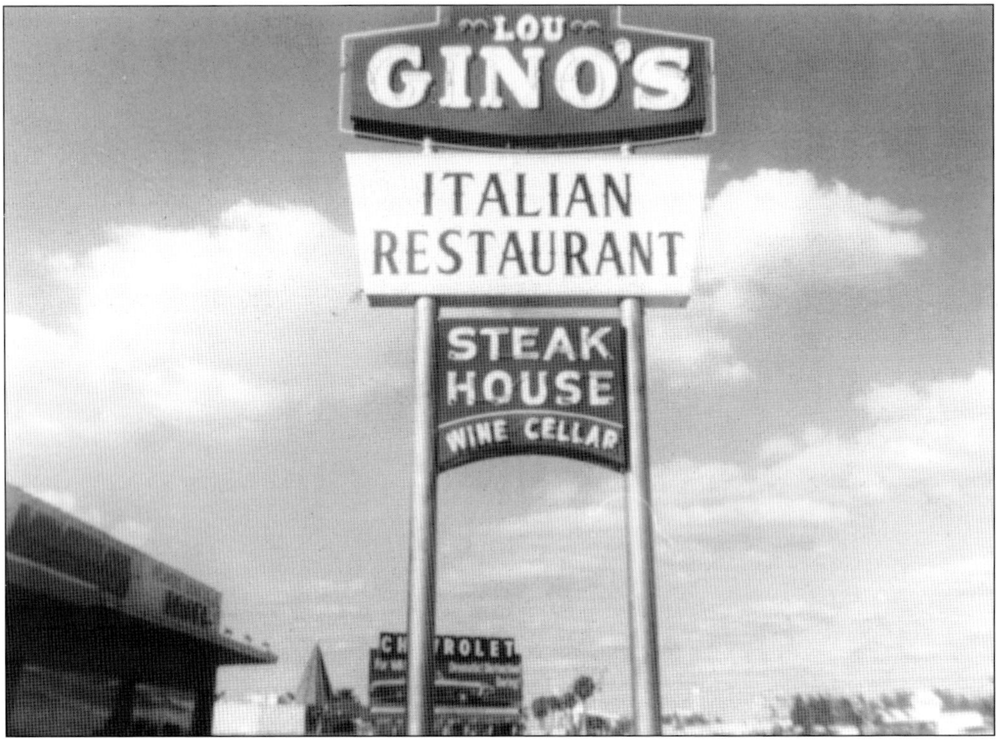

Lou Gino's Italian Restaurant is seen here in 1966 at 1202 North Dale Mabry Highway. It was one of several popular Italian restaurants in Tampa, a city which, at that time, still had large numbers of residents who originally hailed from Italy. Below is an advertisement for Lorello's Pasta & Prime, which opened in 1947 and served generations of Tampans. The property where Lorello's Pasta & Prime stood for decades is now part of the Midtown Tampa mixed-use development. (Above, courtesy of John Cinchett; below, © *Tampa Bay Times* via ZUMA Press.)

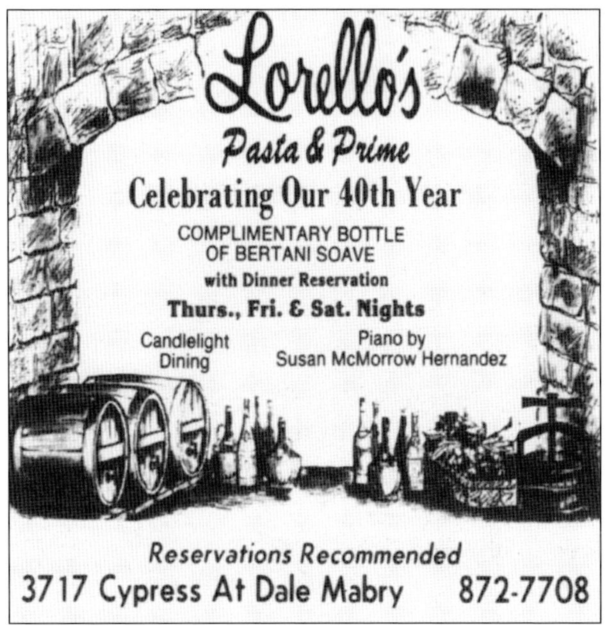

"Gourmet Seafood Dinners"

The New England Oyster House serves the biggest variety of seafare . . . 67 savory specialties from around the world! Delicacies from local Gulf waters to the Pacific . . . even from far-off Alaska, South America, South Africa. If you're not always in the mood for seafare, popular additions to the New England Oyster House menu include your favorite landlubber dishes, too. From juicy-thick prime steaks to crispy, golden-fried Maryland chicken. Whatever your mood, the lavish menu at New England Oyster House reflects a sumptuous choice of delicious food . . . always meticulously prepared and served by well-trained staffs. New England Oyster House is located at 1902 North Dale Mabry in Tampa, the new telephone number (make a note) is (813) 872-6080.

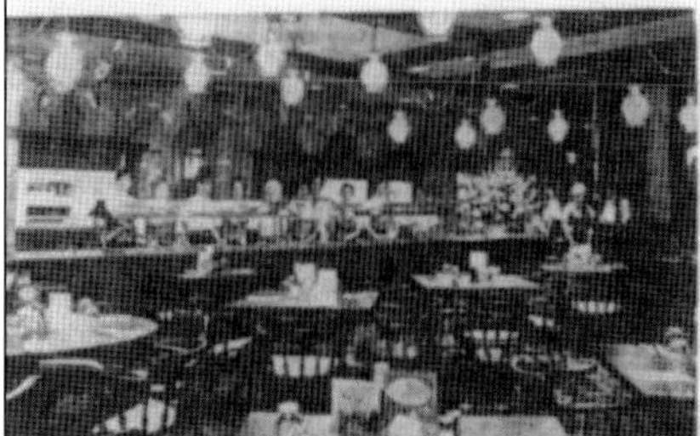

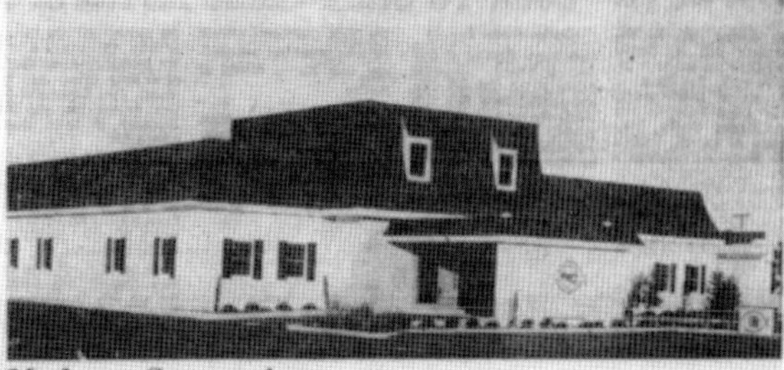

Mathews Corporation, 5644 North Dale Mabry, in Tampa, were the Designers, Engineers and Constructors of the luxurious New England Oyster House located at 1902 North Dale Mabry in Tampa. For a satisfactory solution of your building problems Dial (813) 884-8478.

George J. Harris Roofing of Tampa installed a 20 year bonded type built-up gravel roof on the New England Oyster House and a 25 year class A fire shingle roof was used for the Mansard roof. George J. Harris Roofing has been operating in Tampa since 1928.

Seafood dining options have always been many in Tampa. Two chains that offered their own brands of seafood specialties in the Westshore community were the New England Oyster House and Red Lobster. The New England Oyster House, seen above, opened in 1968 at 1902 North Dale Mabry Highway in a building that eventually served as a Sweet Tomatoes restaurant. Meanwhile, Red Lobster opened its doors to diners in 1969. It stood on the east side of the Courtney Campbell Causeway, where it operated into the mid-2000s alongside a host of restaurants and nightclubs until an expanded interchange connecting the Courtney Campbell Causeway with the nearby Veterans Expressway leveled all those businesses. (Both, © *Tampa Bay Times* via ZUMA Press.)

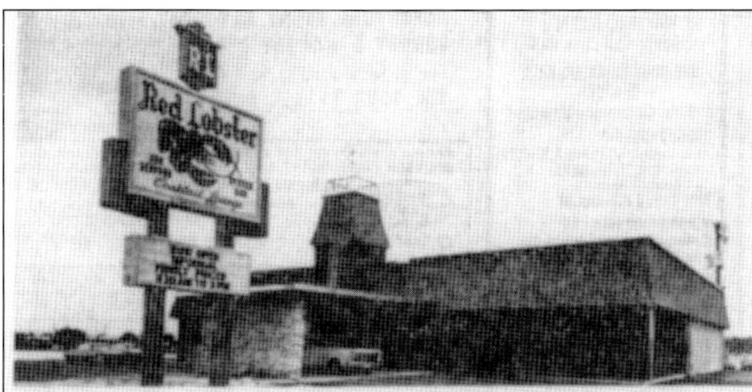

ADCO Sign Company of Clearwater fabricated and erected the Red Lobster sign

ADCO Sign Co., 6140 Ulmerton Rd., Clearwater, primarily fabricates and installs large custom built signs for chain and franchise type installations, as well as individual local customers.

The officials of the Red Lobster Restaurant and Cocktail Lounge commend the general contractor and the sub-contractors on their cooperative spirit and fine display of craftsmanship.

The Red Lobster is a haven for seafood lovers. Florida lobster is served year 'round, as well as, oysters and clams on the half shell. Shrimp are temptingly served in seven different ways and you will be delighted with the broiled or fried fish dinners. Tender, juicy steaks and galley fried chicken are for the landlubbers.

A businessman's luncheon is served daily with cocktails (if desired); however, if you are in a rush use the Red Lobster take-out service. . . . immediate service . . . no waiting. The Red Lobster is open daily from 11:30 a.m. to 11 p.m. and is located on Courtney Campbell Causeway between Tampa International Airport and the Municipal Beach.

Dial (813)884-7549 for additional information.

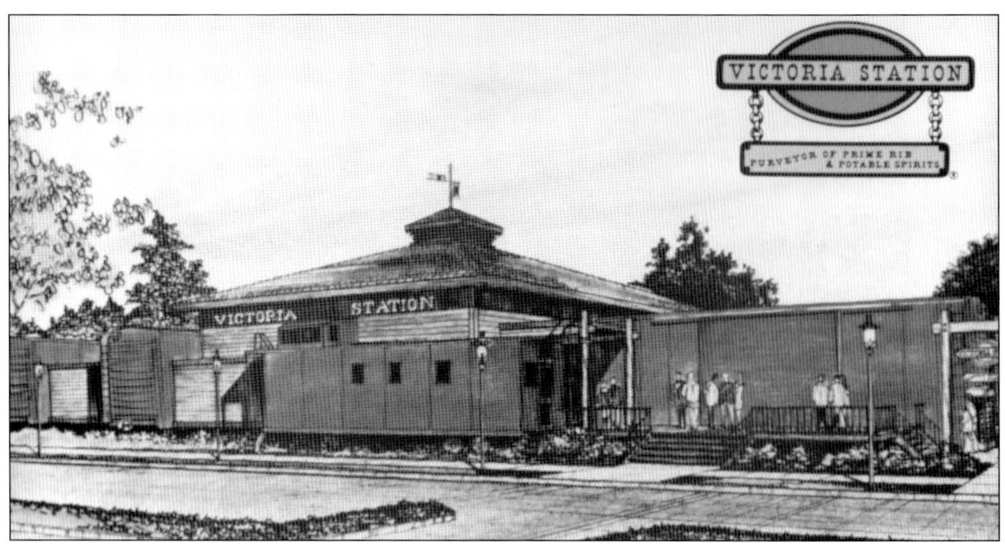

Victoria Station was a national restaurant chain based in San Francisco and featuring an antique British train-themed setting based around London's Victoria Station. The restaurant, serving up prime rib, steaks, shrimp, and other favorites, featured actual boxcars and cabooses in and around the main dining building and operated a location at 2903 North Dale Mabry Highway during the late 1970s and into the 1980s. The site today now operates as a Chili's Grill and Bar.

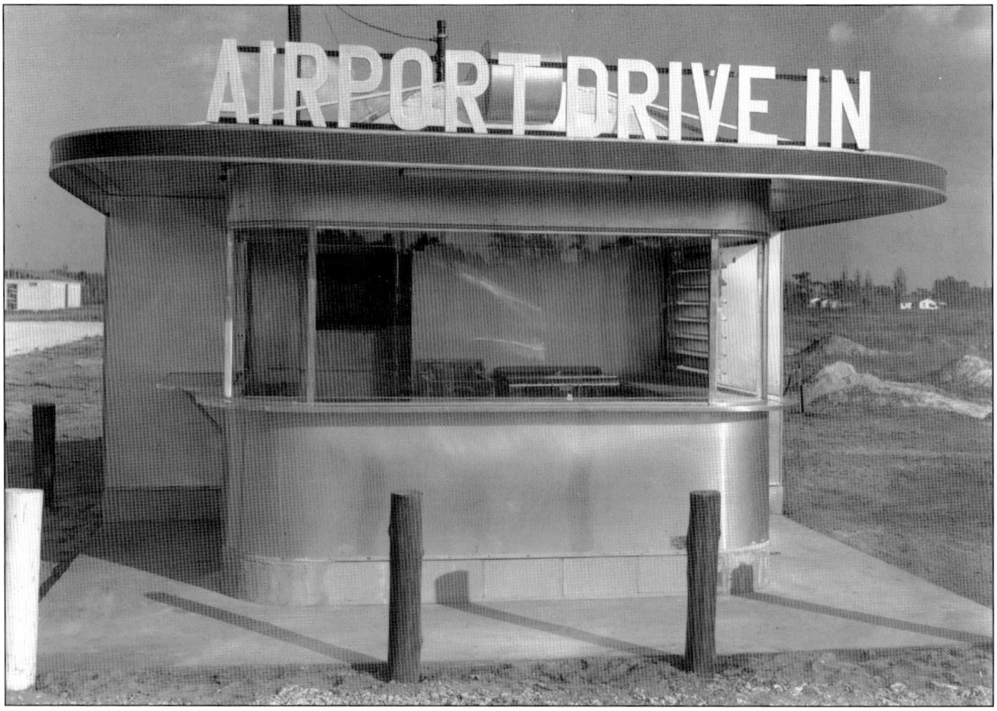

Those needing to grab a quick bite to eat on their way from or to nearby Tampa International Airport might have stopped by Airport Drive-In. The restaurant, which stood near the intersection of North Dale Mabry Highway and West Columbus Drive, is seen here in 1950, just as the nearby airport was acquiring its international status, surely driving even more traffic to this small eatery. (Courtesy of the Tampa–Hillsborough County Public Library System.)

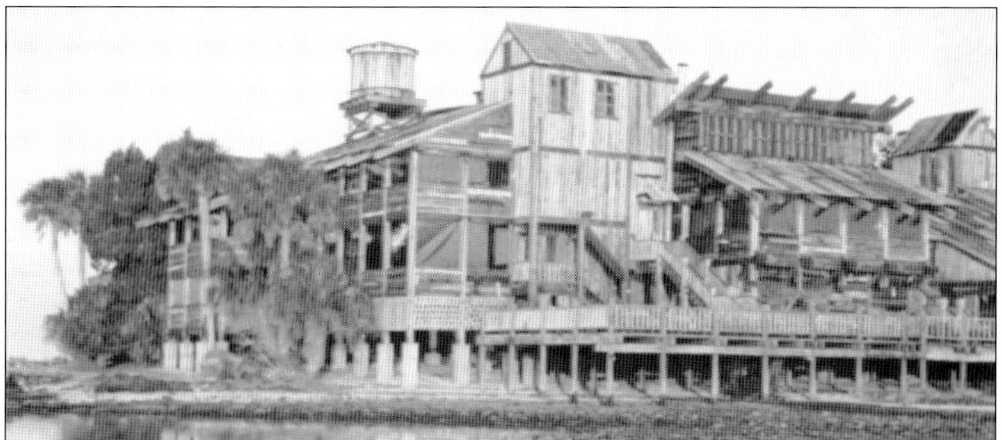

Crawdaddy's stood on the south side of Rocky Point in this rustic, multistory building modeled after a ramshackle early-20th-century wharf. The seafood restaurant operated from 1978 through 2001 and was among several landmark destinations on the southern end of Rocky Point, including Bartke's Dinner Theater, Rusty Pelican, and Whiskey Joe's, the latter now located where The Castaway restaurant was situated on the east end of the Courtney Campbell Causeway. (Courtesy of the Florida State Archive.)

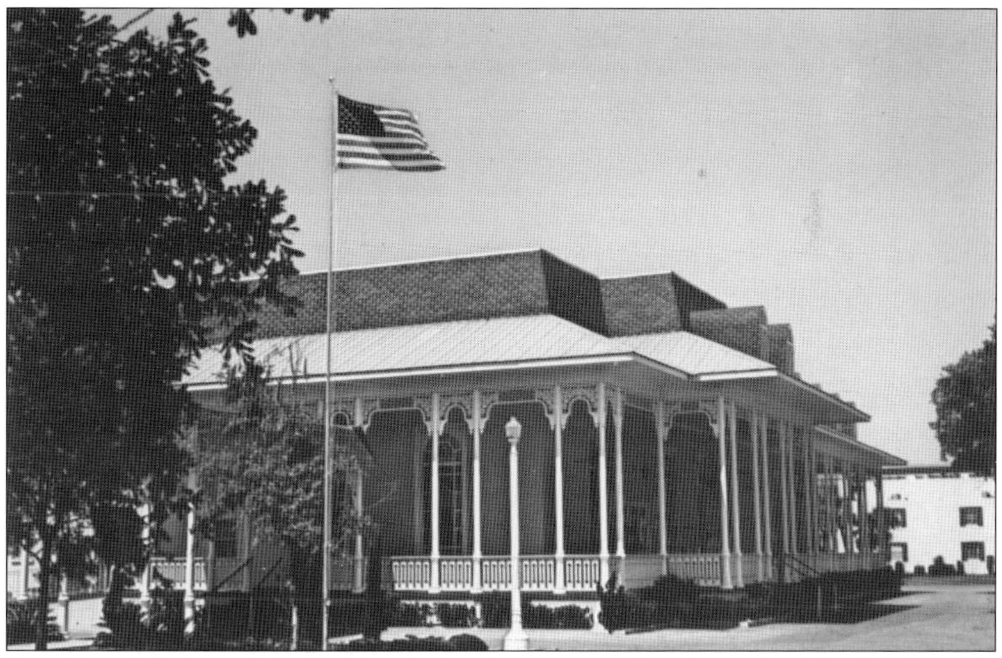

Aunt Hattie's Victorian Restaurant opened in this ornate building located at 5250 West Kennedy Boulevard in 1973. Offering an atmosphere from yesteryear, one could dine on classic fare, visit the restaurant's nickelodeon or penny arcade, and take home a nostalgic souvenir from the gift shop. In 1980, Aunt Hattie's Victorian Restaurant gave way to The Verandah, an upscale café serving steak and seafood. In the years since, this property just steps from WestShore Plaza has been developed into a condominium community.

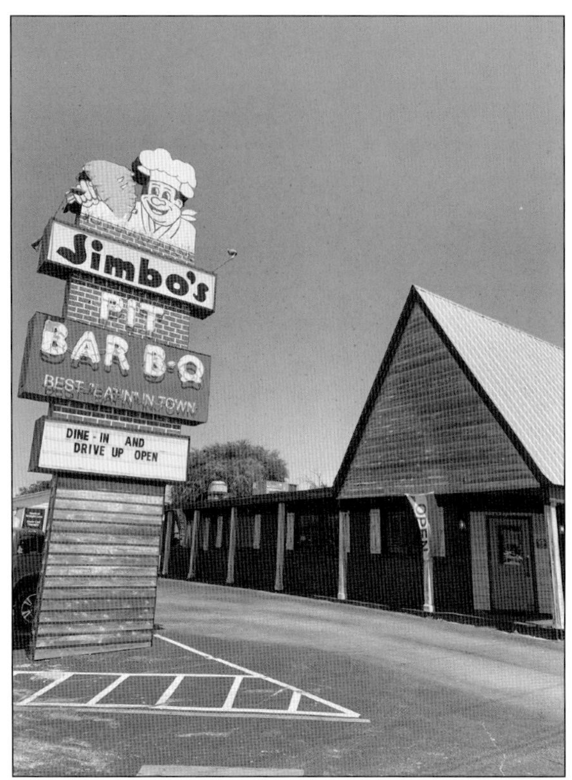

Jimbo's Pit Bar B-Q has stood at this spot at 4103 West Kennedy Boulevard since 1970. Jim Neff opened this popular eatery offering delicious smoked fare, including barbecued meat sandwiches, ribs, and chicken, as well as a full array of mouth-watering sides.

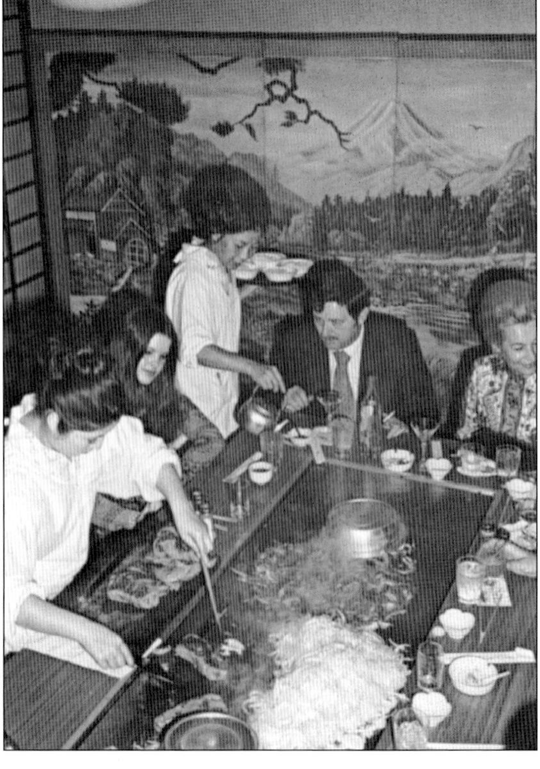

Fuji Japanese Steak House operated during the 1970s and 1980s alongside many well-traveled restaurants and clubs on the east side of the Courtney Campbell Causeway between Tampa International Airport and Rocky Point. The restaurant served up a variety of delicious Asian-inspired meals on table-side hibachis.

Brewmaster's was one of the busiest steakhouses in the Westshore area with its location at 3711 West Grace Street, where Skateland roller rink operated previously. Serving up plenty of beer, fresh bread, big steaks, and a self-serve salad bar, this location lured diners from all around. The restaurant operated at that location from 1971 through 1985 and was the first of a local chain of 13 founded by John Christen, who later launched the popular Tampa-based Shell's seafood restaurants. (Courtesy of John Christen.)

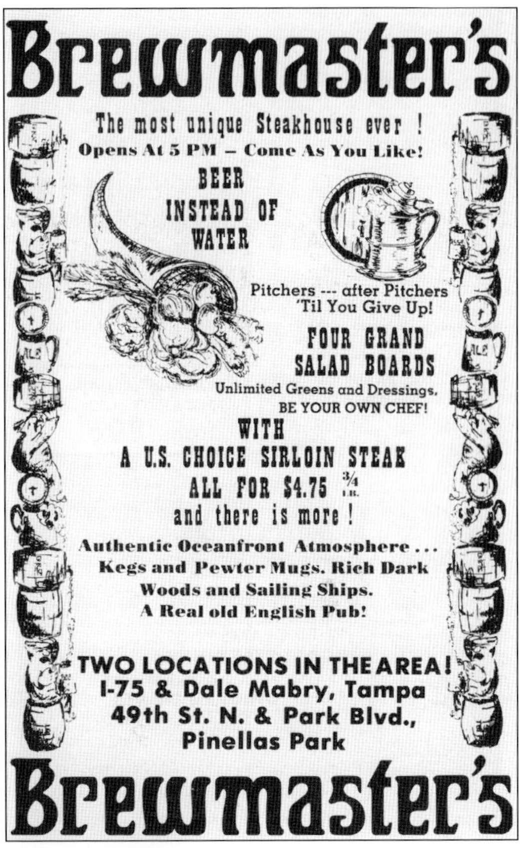

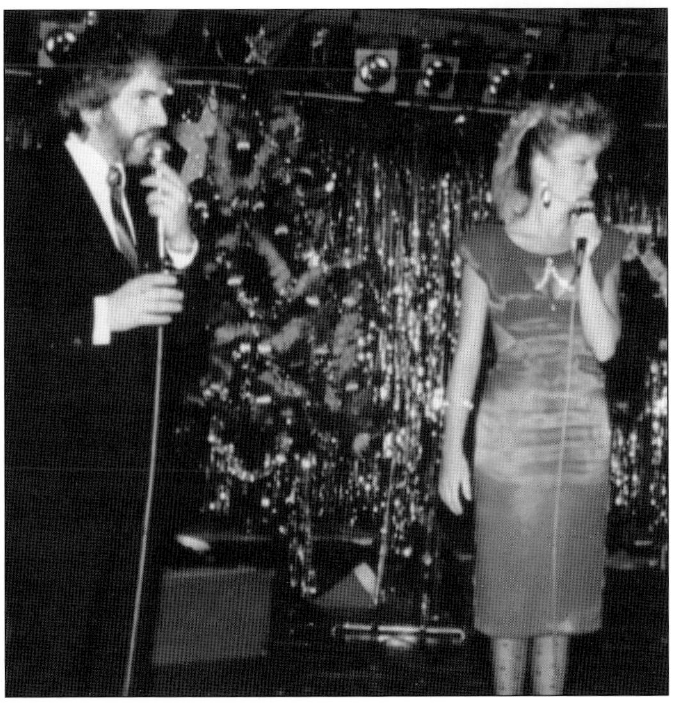

The Westshore community has long been known as the hub of entertainment, and among the most popular of all nightclubs was Robiconti's, which operated at 4444 West Cypress Street in the mid-1980s. The namesake James Robiconti, who operated several nightclubs and restaurants, is seen on stage there with locally born model and actress Lynne Austin around 1985. The building later became Charley's Steak House. (Courtesy of James Robiconti.)

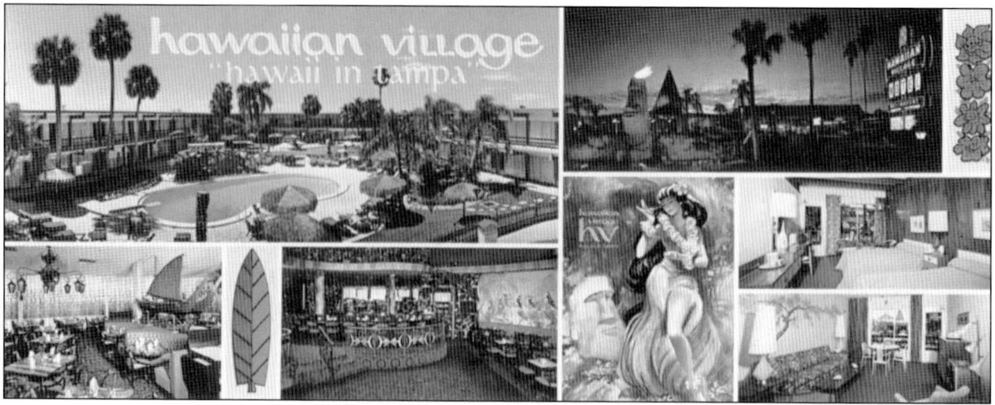

Hawaiian Village was located at 2522 North Dale Mabry Highway and billed itself as "Hawaii in Tampa." Capitalizing on a Polynesian theme that was popular in the 1960s, the luxuriant 296-room motel offered two pools, convention and meeting spaces, and a restaurant and lounge serving up various Asian- and Pacific-inspired fare as well as live entertainment on select nights. Hawaiian Village opened in 1961 and continued operating under that name into the early 1990s, when the property was assumed by Days Inn and remained under that nameplate until around 2011. The motel was razed shortly thereafter, and the location now sports a car dealership.

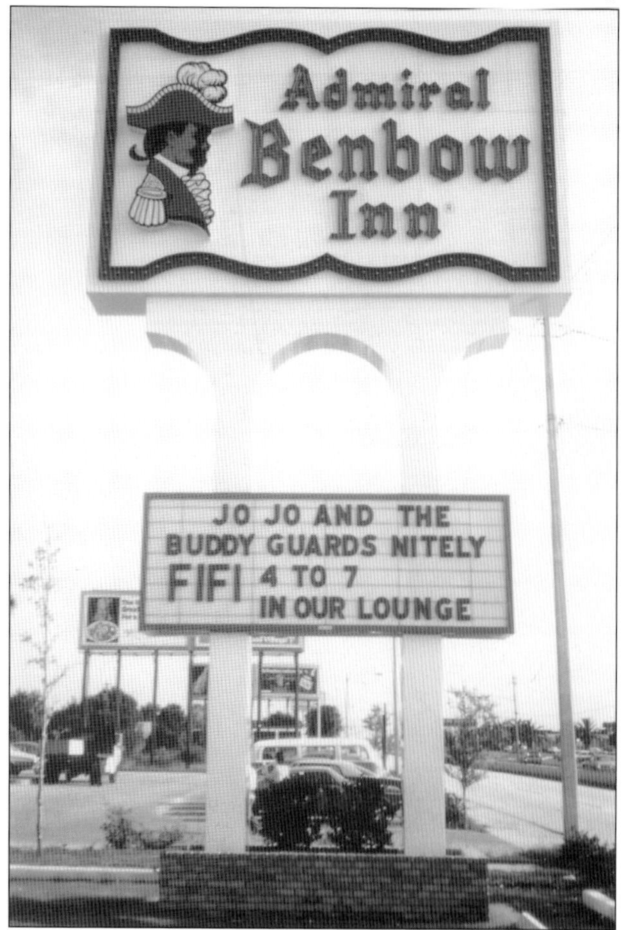

Admiral Benbow Inn opened at 1200 North West Shore Boulevard in 1973 and quickly became a top lodging destination near Tampa International Airport and offering a short drive or taxicab ride to Tampa Stadium, WestShore Plaza, and many other Tampa landmarks. The hotel still stands but has operated in more recent years as a Ramada. (Courtesy of John Cinchett.)

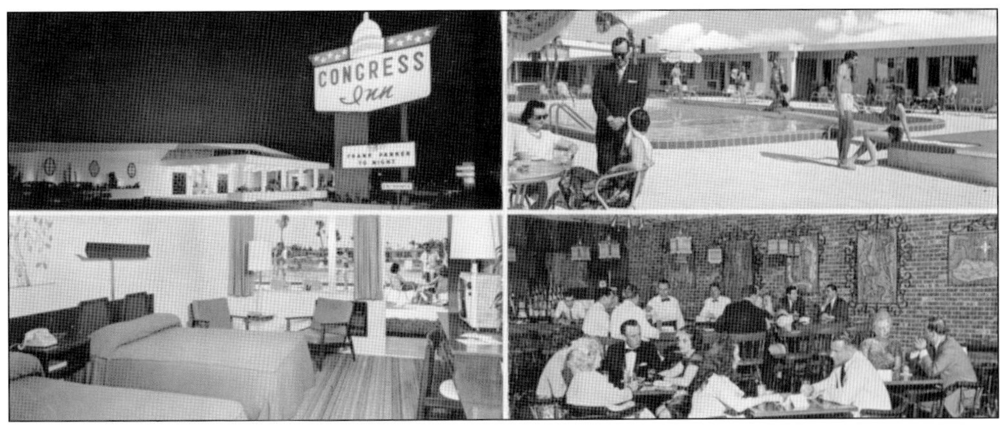

Congress Inn (above) was located at 4636 North Dale Mabry Highway and was one of several larger hotel properties near Tampa International Airport as it rapidly expanded during the jet age. As did so many hotels at the time, Congress Inn offered a popular lounge and plenty of live entertainment, which continued after the property received a drastic remodel in 1967 to become King Arthur's Inn (below). The property was later overtaken by a car dealership.

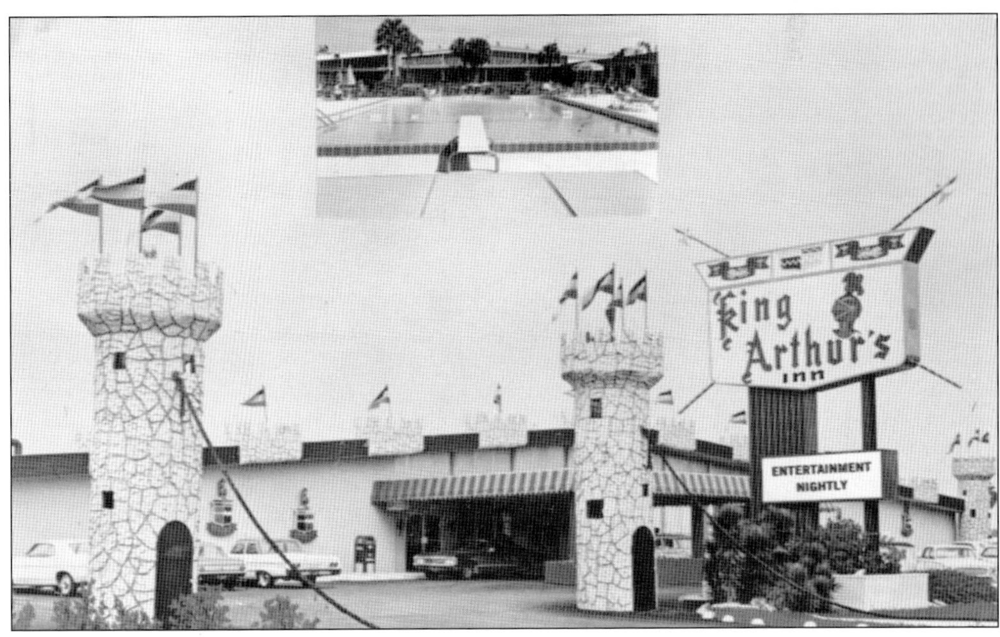

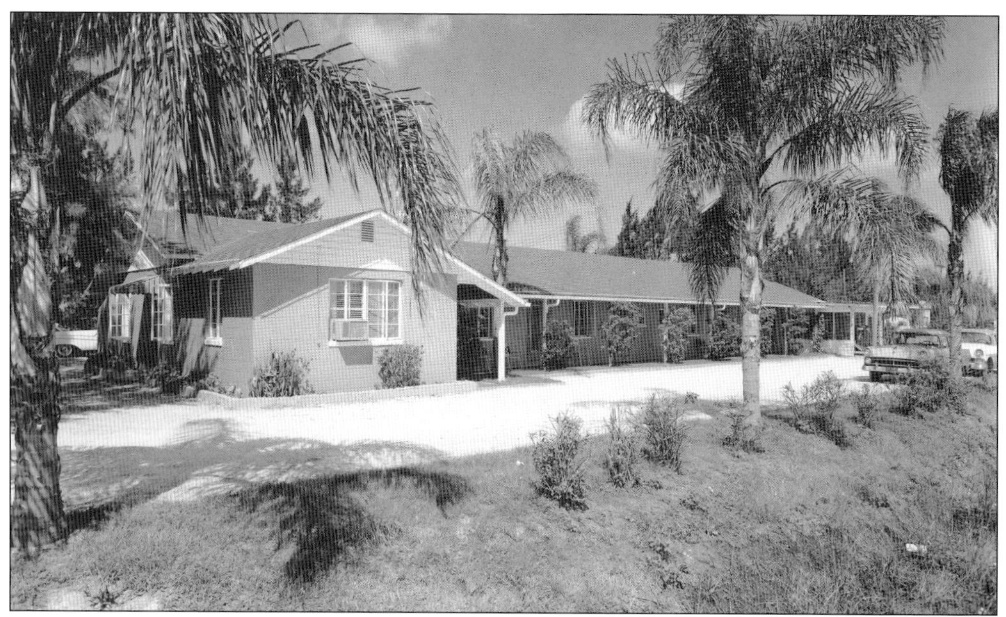

Drew Park Motel was located at 4430 North Dale Mabry Highway and is pictured here from its rear on March 20, 1957. It represents a time when many smaller motor inns proliferated in the Westshore community during the mid-20th century, when traveling by car was the most convenient, affordable alternative to paying relatively high ticket prices and getting dressed up to take a flight into nearby Tampa International Airport. (Courtesy of the Tampa–Hillsborough County Public Library System.)

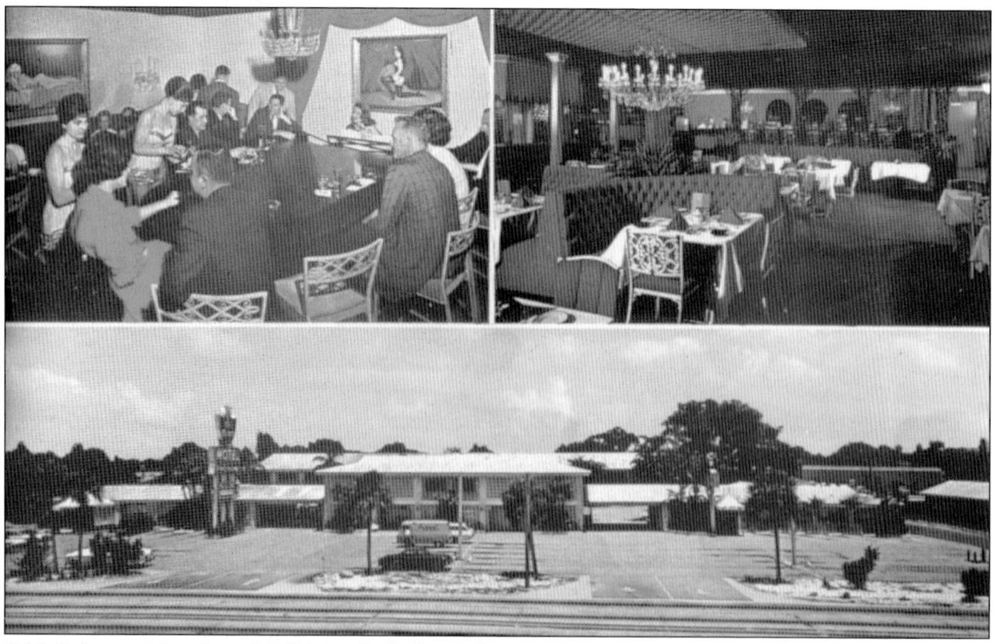

Old Orleans Motel, at 2055 North Dale Mabry Highway, offered 140 rooms with luxurious accommodations of air-conditioning, color televisions, and 24-hour direct-dial phone service. The property's Mardi Gras Lounge and Maison Rouge Restaurant were popular with guests as well as in-town residents.

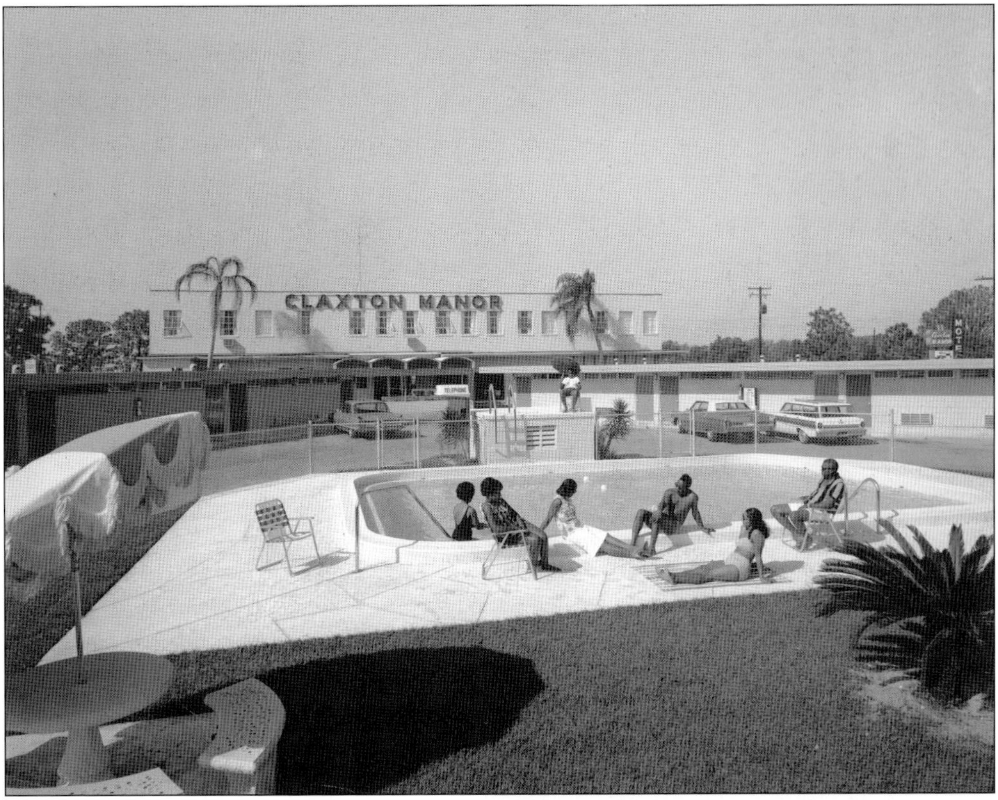

The Claxton Manor hotel was built by American vaudeville performer Leon Dunkins Claxton. The African American impresario produced his *Harlem in Havana* shows featuring a variety of performances ranging from dance to comedy. He retired from show business in Tampa, where he won a Citizen of the Year Award in 1959, and opened his posh 32-room Claxton Manor hotel to people of all races, creeds, and colors in December 1964 at 4308 West Cypress Street. (Courtesy of the Harlem in Havana Project.)

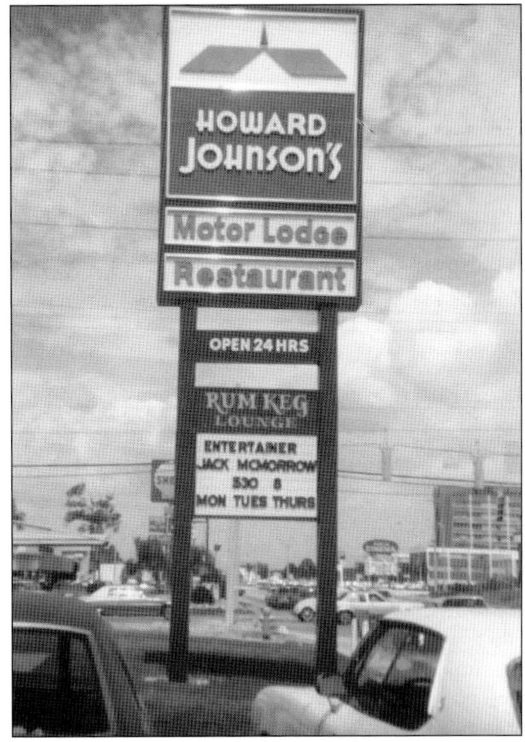

Howard Johnson's motor lodge is a name familiar to countless millions of Americans who took road trips during the second half of the 20th century. The Tampa Bay area boasted several "Hojos" during the mid-1970s, when this photograph was taken of the Howard Johnson's location at the southwest corner of North West Shore Boulevard and West Cypress Street. In the background, the Austin Cinema and the Austin Center office complex are visible.

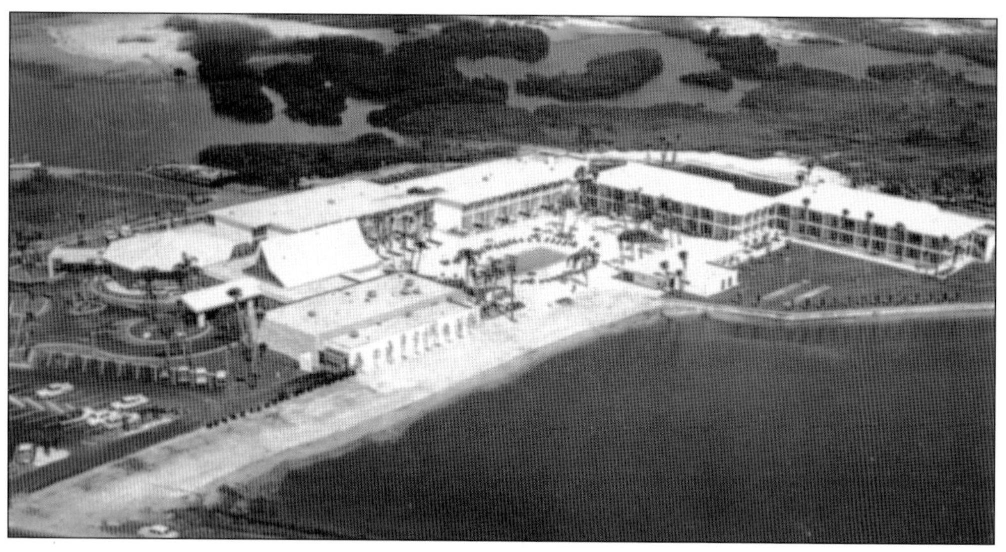

Causeway Inn (above) and the Rocky Point Beach Motel (below) flanked the Courtney Campbell Causeway for decades, both serving as popular destinations for tourists. Causeway Inn offered 152 rooms, while the Rocky Point Beach Motel had 107 rooms. Both properties sported pools, lounges, and other recreational amenities and were conveniently located near Tampa International Airport and the best that the region had to offer. The Rocky Point Beach Motel, which underwent many name changes over the years, fell to the wrecking ball by the mid-1990s, and the property today is a condominium community. Causeway Inn spent its last years as a Days Inn property before being converted to the Westin Tampa Bay in 2008.

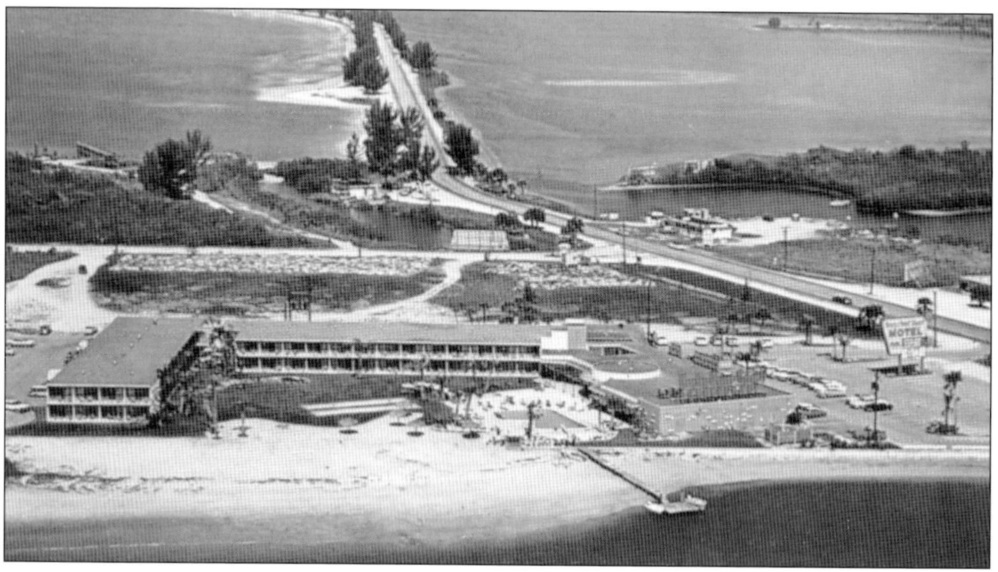

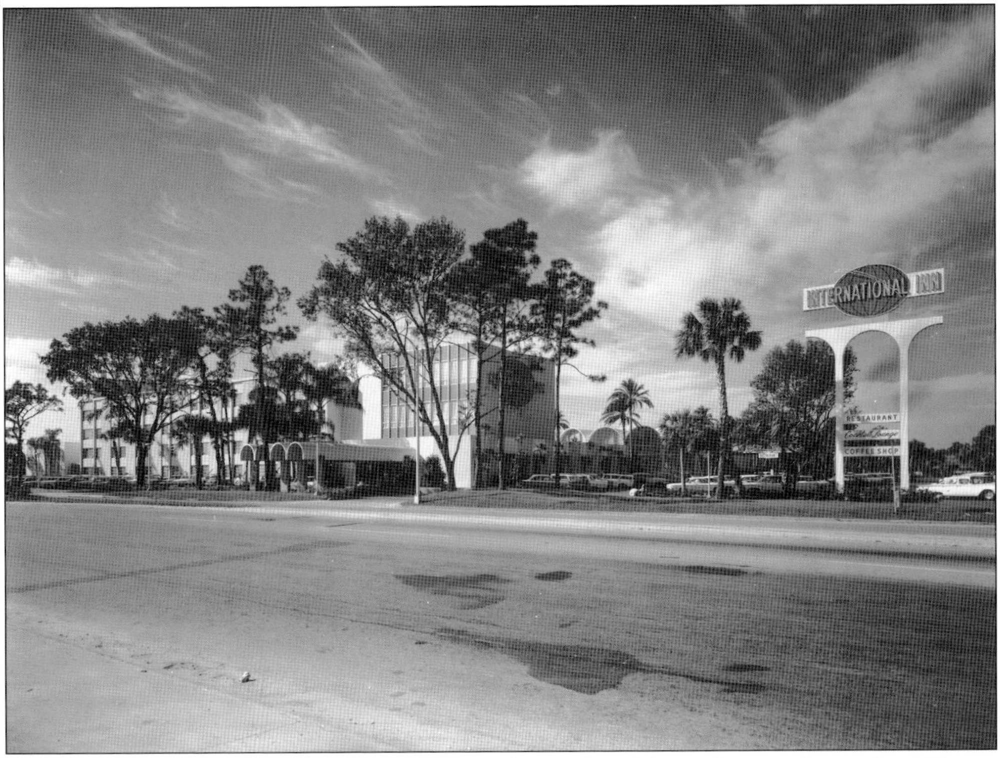

International Inn opened in 1962 as a modern luxury hotel located one mile south of Tampa International Airport at the southwest corner of Grand Central Avenue (now Kennedy Boulevard) and West Shore Boulevard. The tropically landscaped resort boasted 172 rooms, a convention center capable of hosting 600, a lounge, a coffee shop, a heated pool, a sauna, and tennis courts. International Inn operated until 1982, when it was demolished and later replaced by the Urban Centre complex. (Courtesy of the Tampa–Hillsborough County Public Library System.)

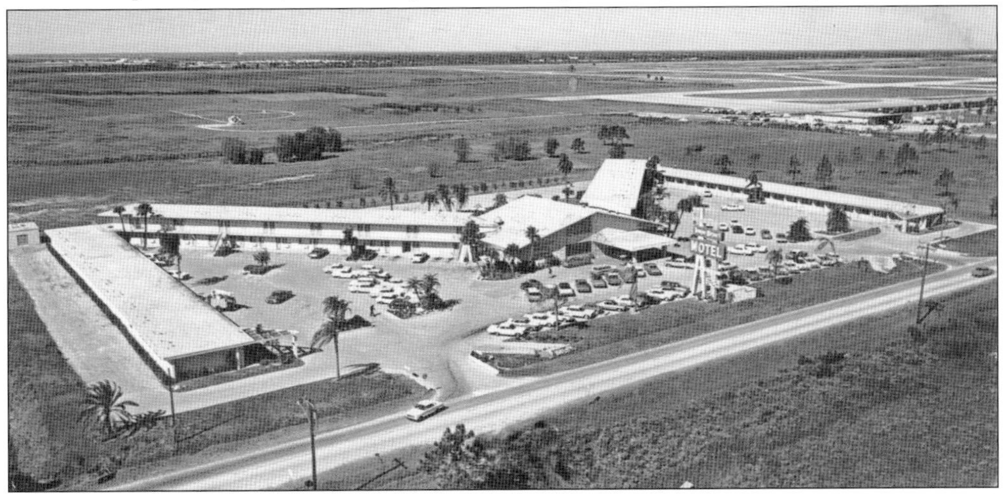

Tampa Airport Motel was convenient to the neighboring Tampa International Airport. Located at 2222 North West Shore Boulevard, it was billed as "60 seconds south of the airport" and offered a rental car facility on its premises, in addition to air-conditioned rooms, a swimming pool, a lounge, a spacious convention facility, and the popular Four Winds Restaurant.

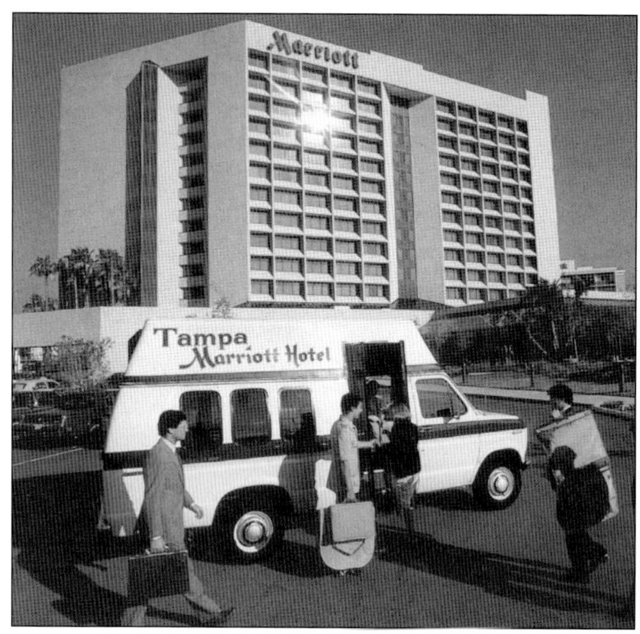

The Marriott Tampa Westshore opened on June 8, 1981, at 1001 North West Shore Boulevard on the former site of the Loew's Tampa Theater, later Austin Cinema. The hotel opened with 310 rooms and what was Tampa's only indoor-outdoor pool. Other amenities included a hydrotherapy pool, sauna, game room, and bar and grill. The opening of the high-end resort helped usher in a wave of swanky hotel options in the Westshore community and led the way for a new generation of luxury lodging to cater to Tampa's increasing number of business and international travelers. (Courtesy of the Marriott Corporate Archives.)

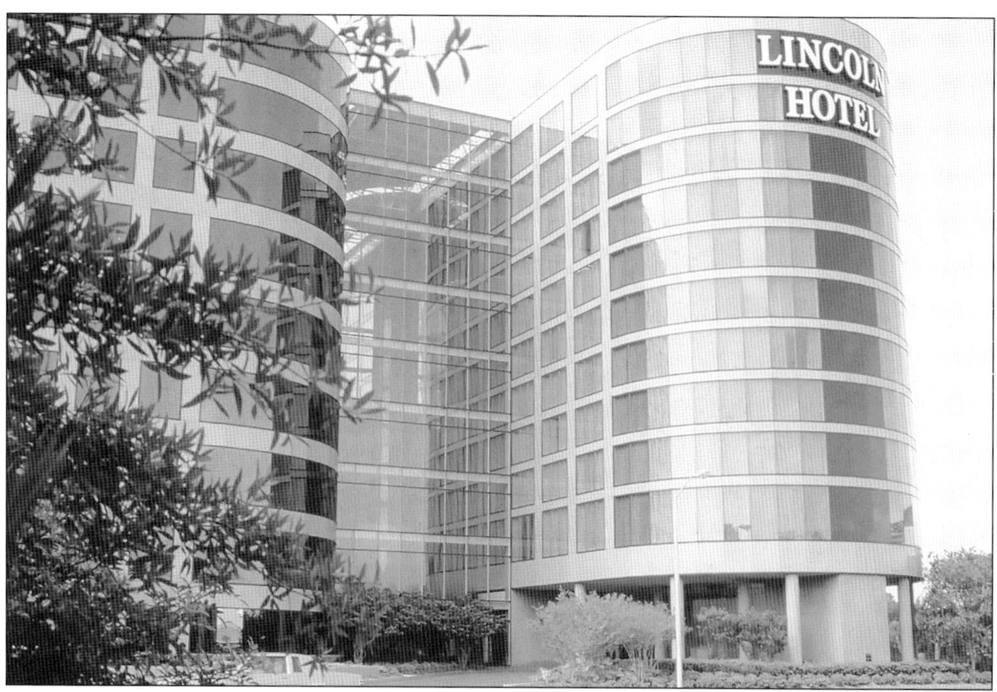

The Lincoln Hotel, at 4860 West Kennedy Boulevard, was one of Tampa's hottest hotels as Westshore rose ever skyward in the 1980s. Built in 1984 in conjunction with the neighboring Urban Centre complex, the hotel was in close range of Tampa International Airport, Tampa Stadium, downtown Tampa, and St. Petersburg. More recently, the luxury property operates as the Westshore Grand. (Courtesy of the University of South Florida Special Collections Department.)

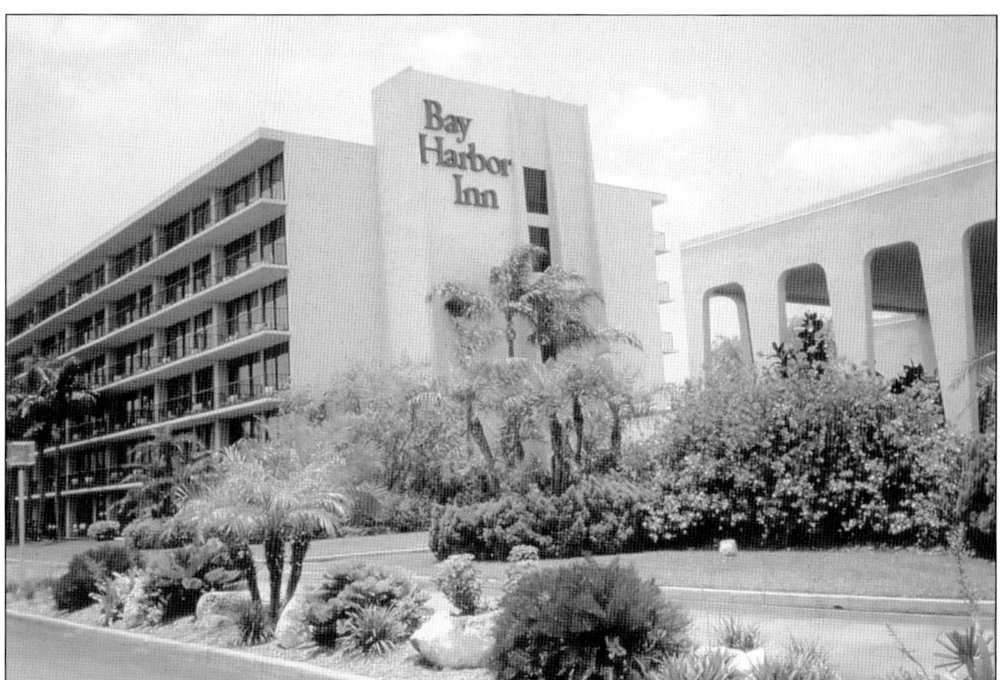

Bay Harbor Inn was a well-traveled mid-rise hotel on the south side of Rocky Point near the Courtney Campbell Causeway. Its onshore location assured plenty of rooms with excellent views as well as private beach access, along with a restaurant, a lounge, and a suite of other amenities. (Both, courtesy of the City of Tampa Archives.)

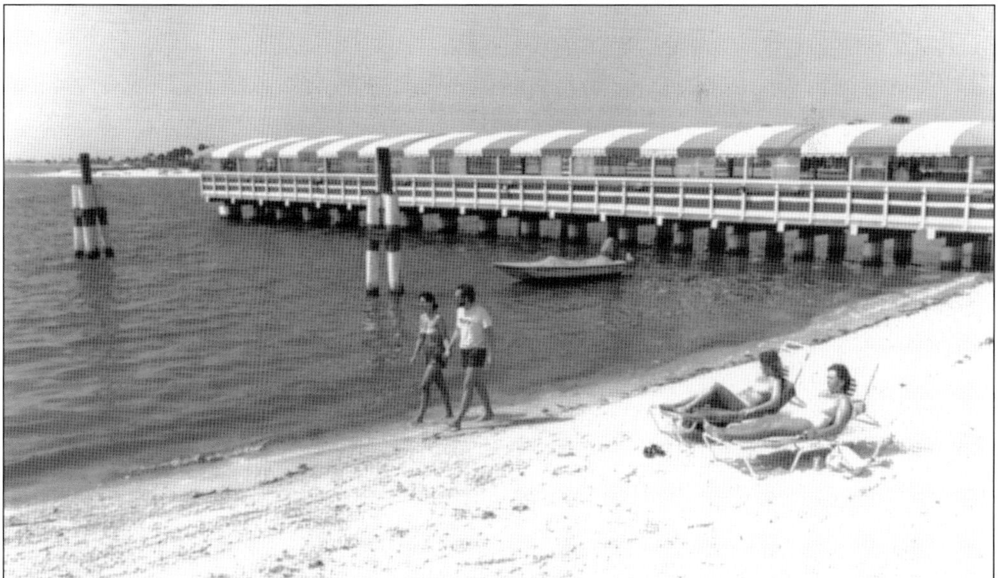

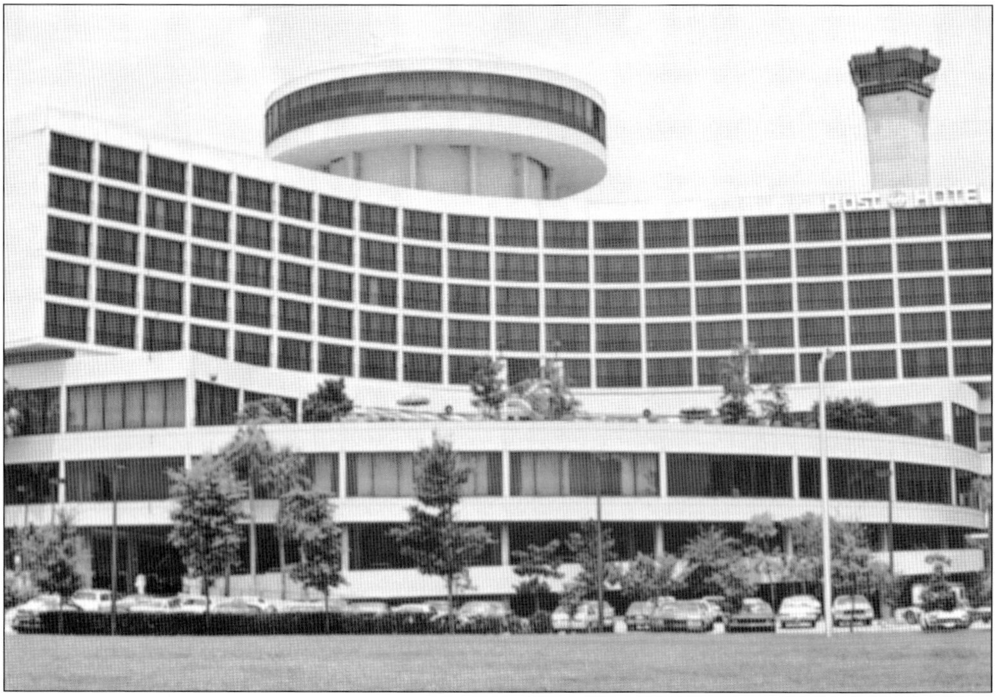

Host Hotel and its accompanying rotating rooftop restaurant, known as CK's, opened in 1973 as the crowning project at Tampa International Airport, which opened two years earlier. The 300-room hotel complex was one of the best in the Tampa Bay area and was just steps from any arriving or disembarking plane at the airport. Meanwhile, CK's was a destination itself for both travelers and local Tampans wanting to eat a fine dinner that was a true cut above the rest. Host Hotel was converted to a Marriott property in 1982, the banner under which the airport resort continued operating into the 2020s. (Above, courtesy of the University of South Florida Special Collections Department; below, courtesy of Tampa International Airport.)

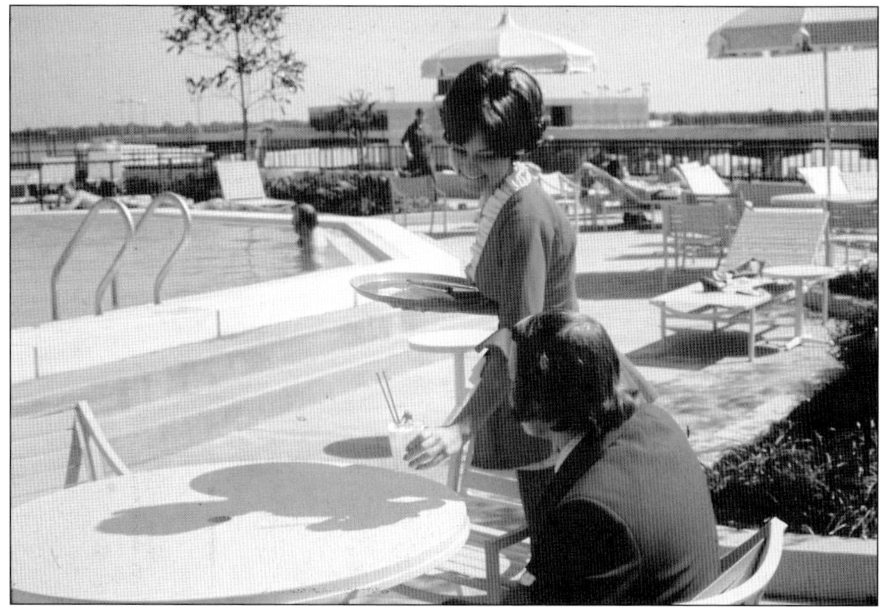

Four

Scenes and Views

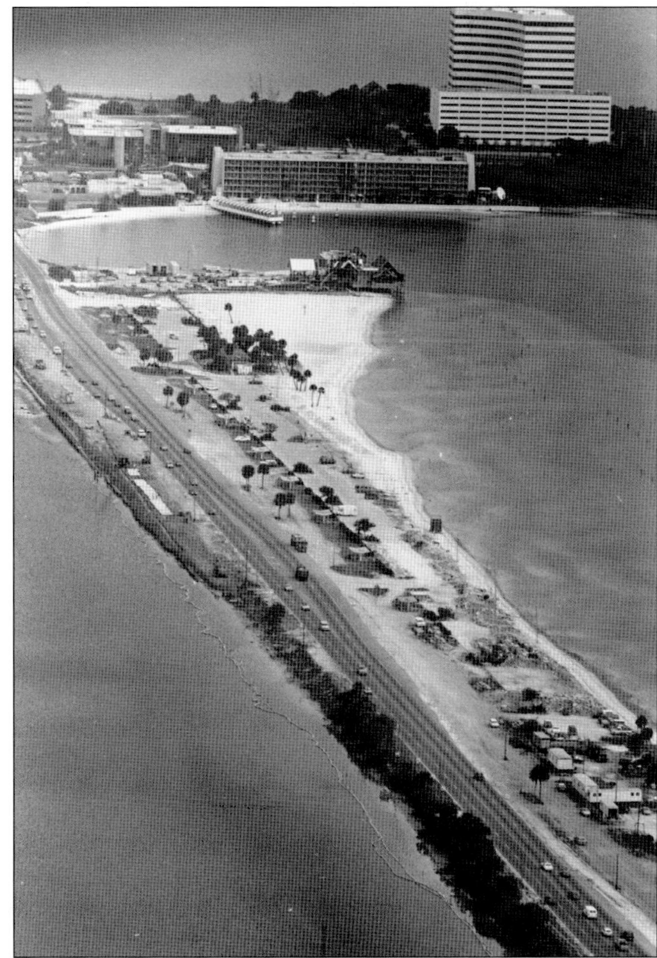

This view looks east down the Courtney Campbell Causeway in January 1988, when the scenic byway connecting Tampa to Clearwater was undergoing some enhancements on the Tampa side. This view shows many landmarks, including Ben T. Davis Beach in the foreground and the building that became The Castaway (and later Whiskey Joe's) under construction in the mid-ground. In the background are Bay Harbor Inn (upper center), the Shriners International Headquarters (upper left), and Island Center office tower (upper right), with the latter first piercing the skyline in 1986. (© Jim Stem/*Tampa Bay Times* via ZUMA Wire.)

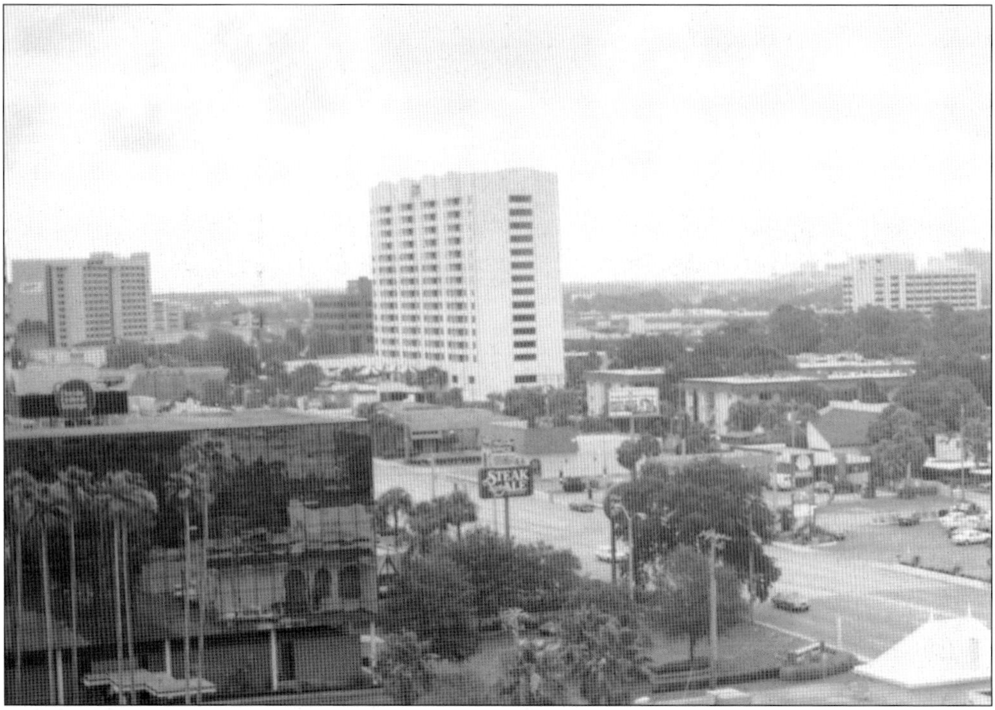

These two views show how the area near WestShore Plaza looked in the mid-1980s. The upper image looks northeast toward a Steak & Ale restaurant and the 16-story Guest Quarters in the mid-ground, while Westshore Marriott and Embassy Suites rise in the background to the left and right, respectively. The lower image reveals a parade of businesses marching eastward along Kennedy Boulevard between West Shore Boulevard and Himes Avenue, with the 13-story Tampa Commons at 1 North Dale Mabry Highway in the background. (Both, courtesy of the City of Tampa Archives.)

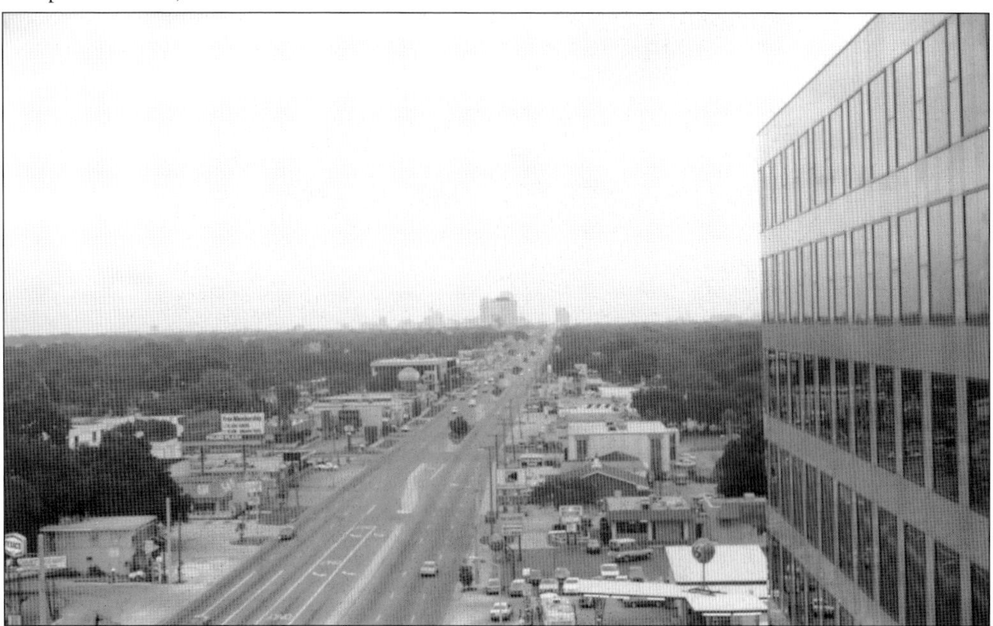

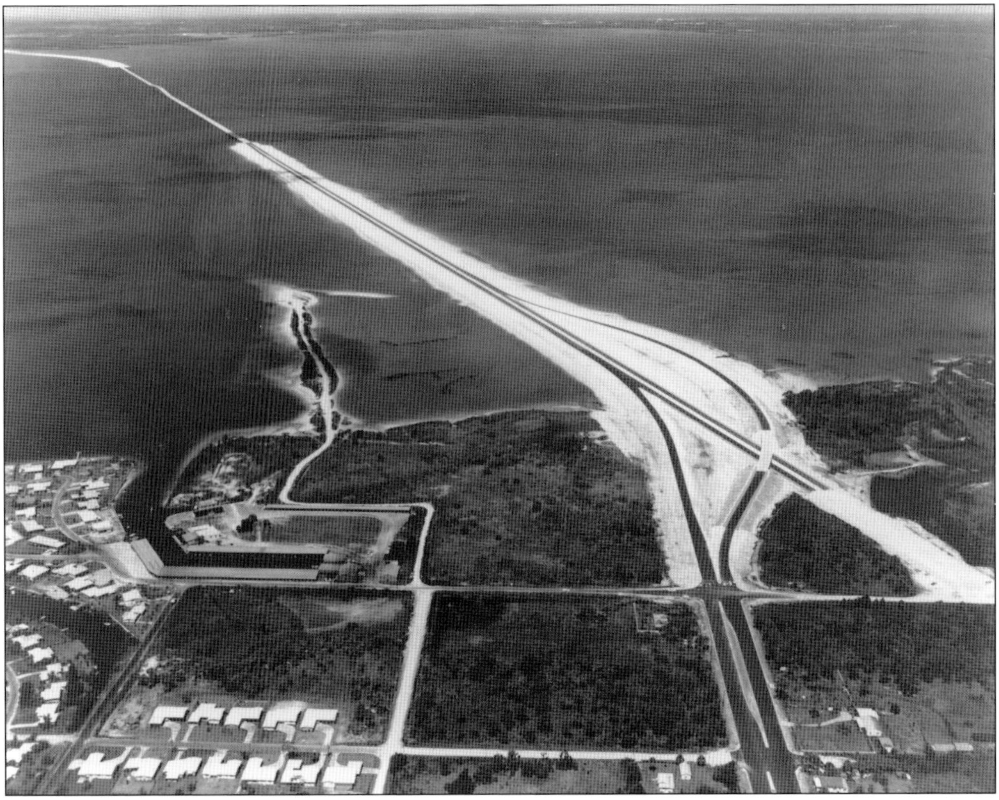

The upper image, looking west, shows the 11-mile-long link between Tampa and St. Petersburg as it appeared on July 20, 1959, about six months before the original four-lane bridge opened to traffic and when the Tampa approach connected to Grand Central Avenue. The lower photograph, from April 7, 1977, shows a new overpass (center) from the Howard Frankland Bridge to Tampa International Airport promising to bring traffic relief on Kennedy Boulevard, seen along the bottom of the photograph. (Above, courtesy of the Tampa–Hillsborough County Public Library System; below, © *Tampa Bay Times* via ZUMA Press.)

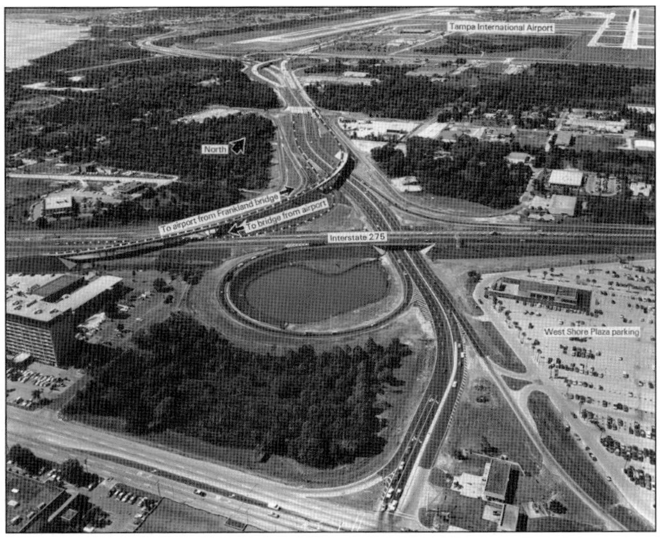

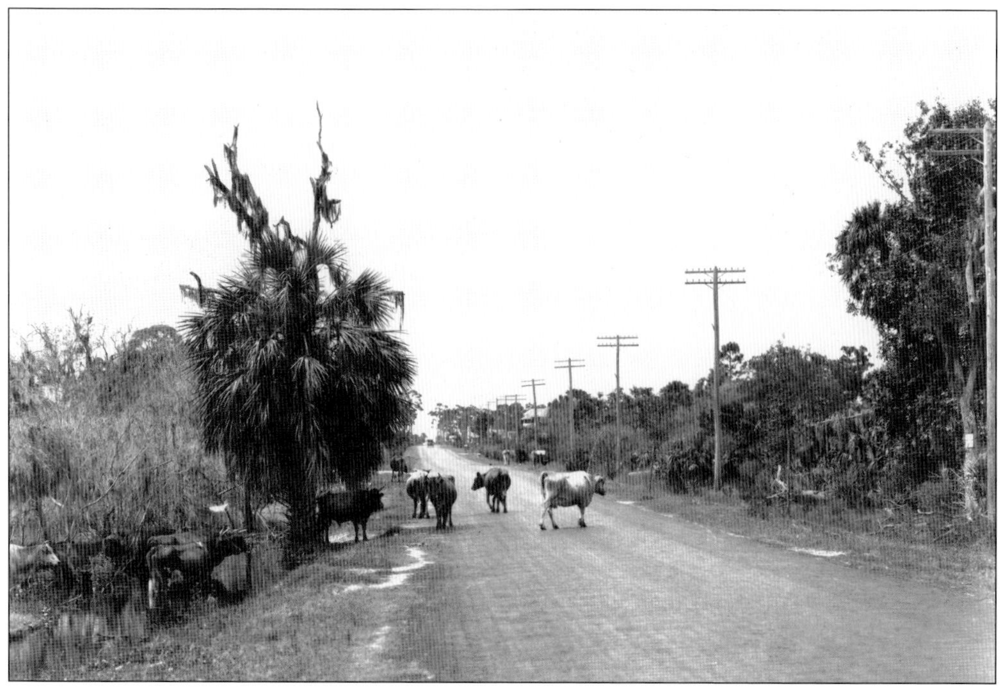

These two images date to the early 1920s, when the Westshore community was still largely agrarian and untamed. The 1922 photograph above shows cows crossing the road near Memorial Highway and West Shore Boulevard, while the 1921 image below reveals great expanses of undeveloped land along Memorial Highway in the Westshore area. Memorial Highway in this area of Tampa was later called Grand Central Avenue, followed by official renaming to Kennedy Boulevard in 1964 in honor of Pres. John F. Kennedy, who visited Tampa just a few days before being assassinated in Dallas, Texas, in 1963 and whose motorcade proceeded down that Tampa roadway. (Both, courtesy of the Tampa–Hillsborough County Public Library System.)

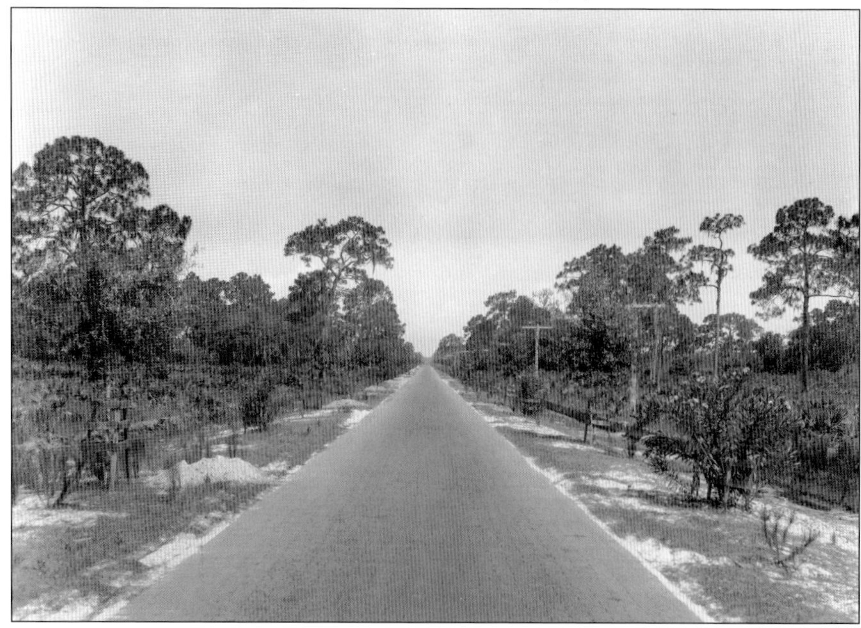

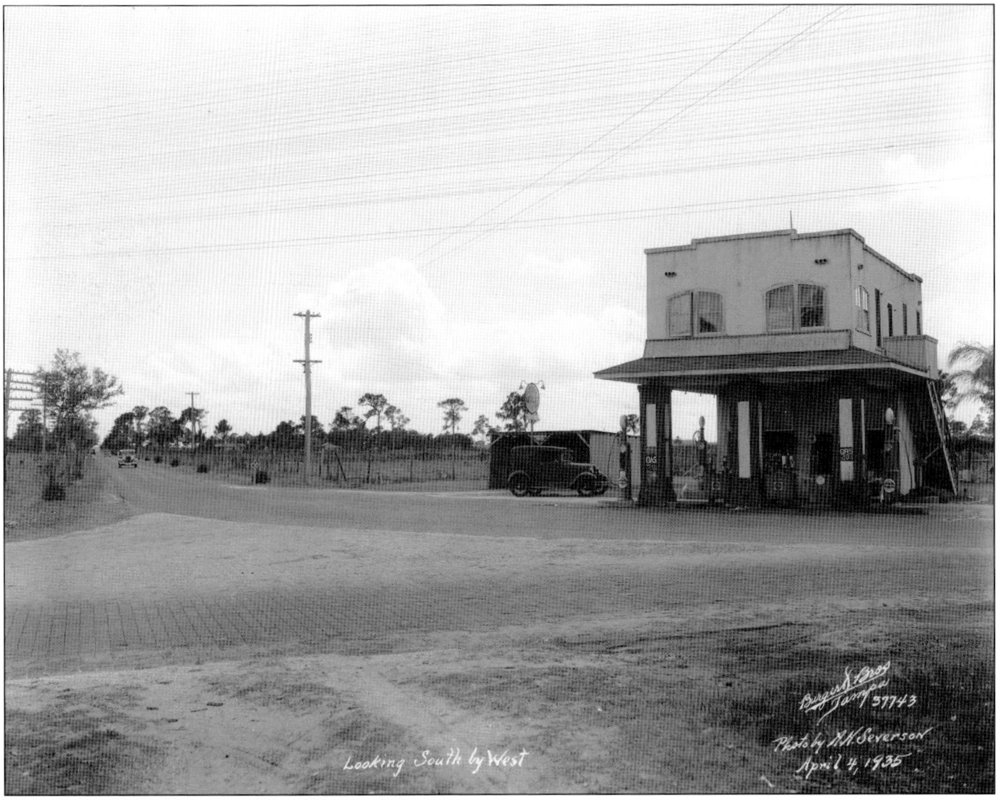

Above, a Gulf gas station stands sentinel not far from the intersection of Columbus Drive and Memorial Highway below. Both photographs were taken in 1935 and exhibit the character of the Westshore community before the office towers, high-rise hotels, Tampa International Airport, and Tampa sports complexes that helped put the region on the map. (Both, courtesy of the Tampa–Hillsborough County Public Library System.)

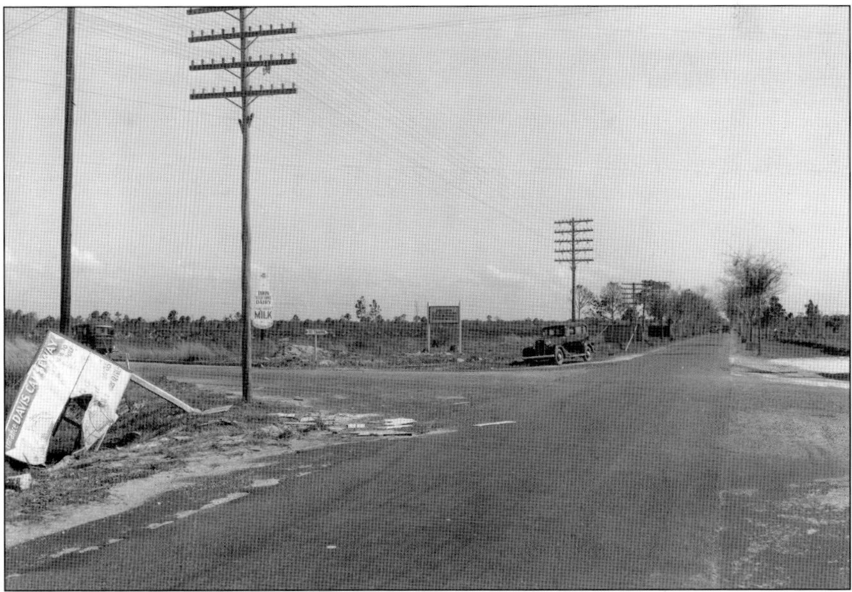

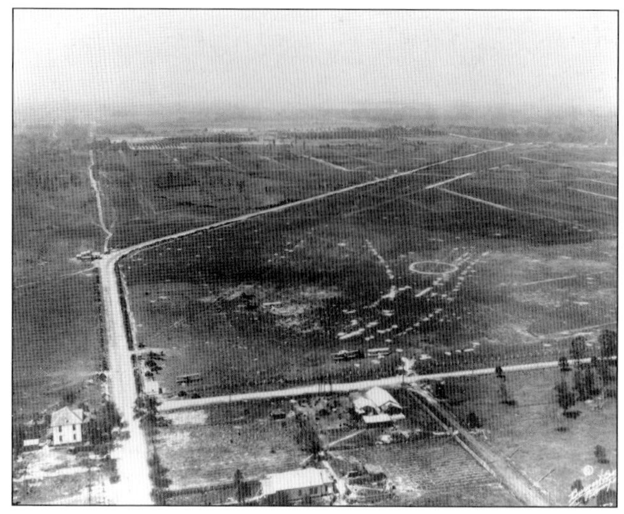

This 1926 photograph looks westward from the approximate vantage point of modern-day Himes Avenue (crossing left to right in the foreground) and Tampa Bay Boulevard, which bends northwest to the right in the mid-ground. The two-story house in the lower-left portion of the image stood for many decades after this image was taken. The little circle in the center-right area of the photograph is roughly where Raymond James Stadium stands today. (Courtesy of the University of South Florida Special Collections Department.)

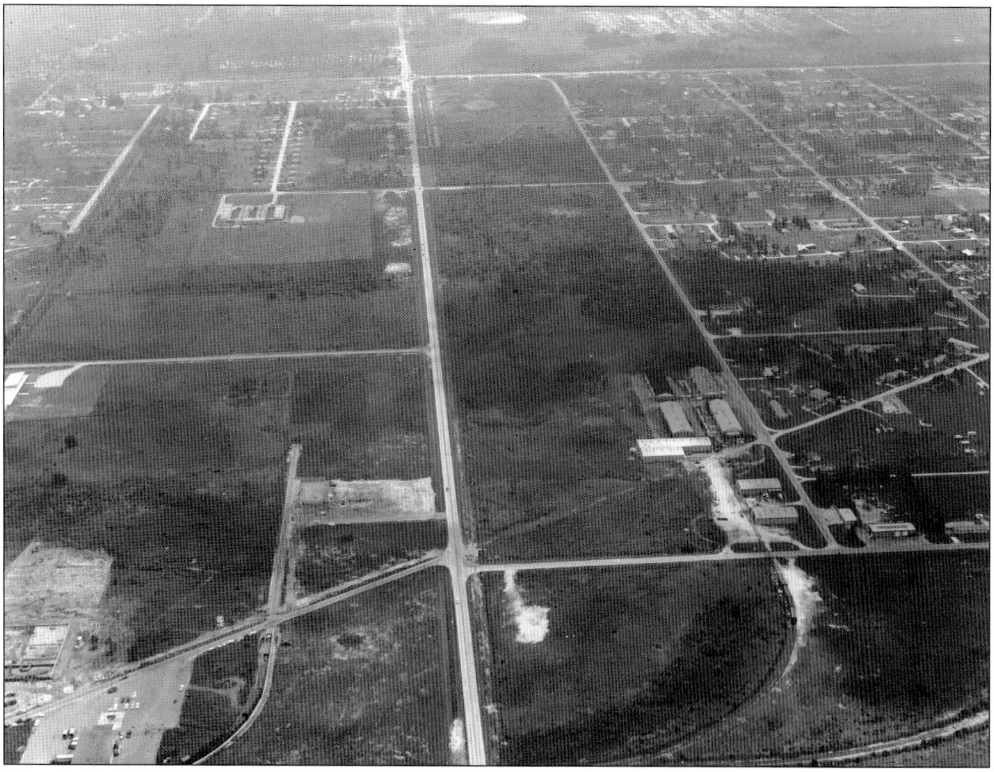

This August 1, 1958, image looks eastward down Hillsborough Avenue with West Shore Boulevard seen to the lower right and Anderson Road cutting diagonally to the lower left. Beyond that, the crossroads seen here in progression from front to back are Hesperides Street, Lois Avenue, and Church Avenue. In the background, North Dale Mabry Highway cuts from left to right, with the large, diamond-shaped patch of light-colored land in the upper background belonging to Hillsboro Drive-In. (Courtesy of the Tampa–Hillsborough County Public Library System.)

This July 1984 photograph shows West Hillsborough Avenue looking west from near Anderson Road. At the time, this four-lane stretch north of Tampa International Airport fielded a handful of businesses, including Lindsley Lumber and Crown Lanes at 5015 and 5555 West Hillsborough Avenue, respectively. In the background is seen a one-lane flyover ramp taking southbound motorists to Eisenhower Boulevard, an un-tolled highway connecting West Hillsborough Avenue to Memorial Highway and the Courtney Campbell Causeway to the south. Eisenhower Boulevard was significantly realigned to accommodate the Veterans Expressway, a tolled turnpike reaching north to Lutz that opened in 1994. (Courtesy of George Youdal.)

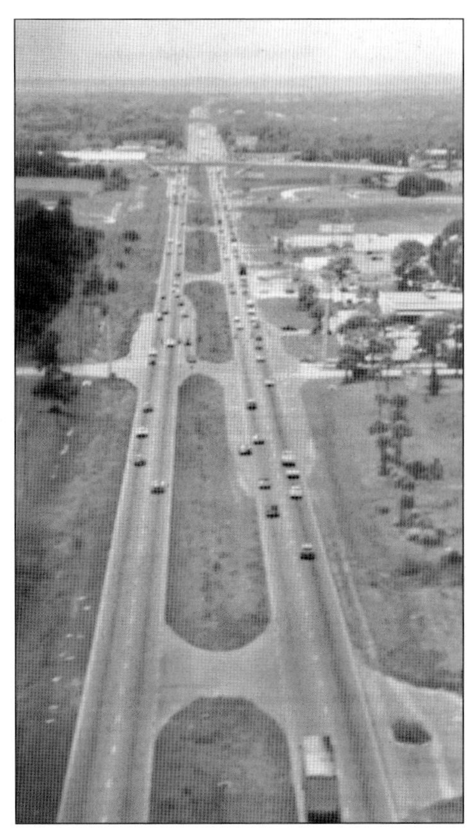

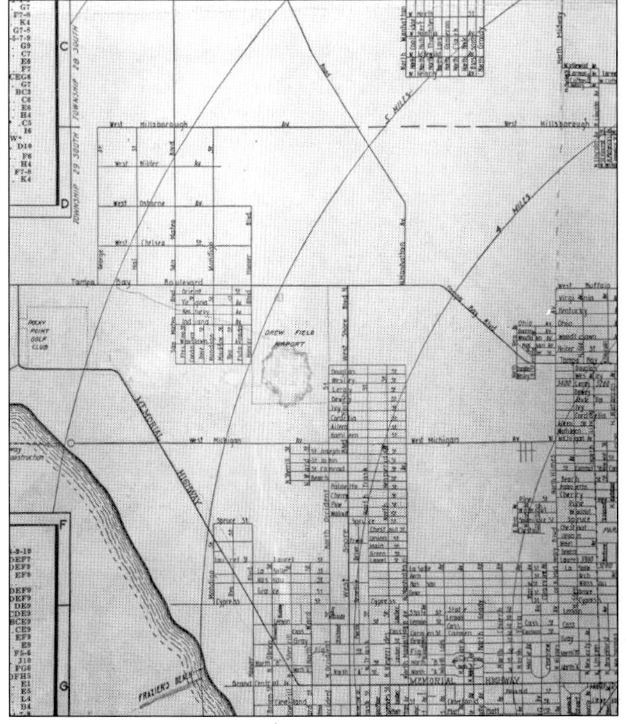

This 1932 road map shows the lay of Westshore in earlier decades, with many streets that have since been removed or entirely renamed. Notably absent is North Dale Mabry Highway, which was first built in 1943 to connect Drew Field to MacDill Air Force Base in South Tampa during World War II. Columbus Drive, once named Michigan Avenue, served as a straight shot from the Ben T. Davis Causeway (now Courtney Campbell Causeway) to Tampa; that path is now bent around Tampa International Airport via Boy Scout Boulevard, the latter an homage to the Boy Scouts of America Gulf Ridge Council, which built its headquarters at 4410 Boy Scout Boulevard in 1966. (Courtesy of the University of South Florida Special Collections Department.)

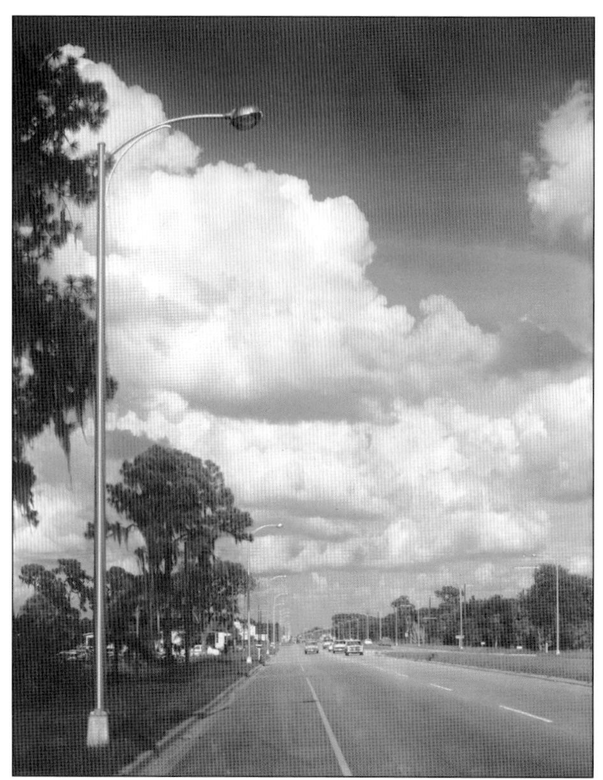

These two August 6, 1960, views reveal Grand Central Avenue in the vicinity of where WestShore Plaza would stand within a decade. The image to the left is an eastward-looking perspective down Grand Central Avenue with the approach for the Howard Frankland Bridge behind the photographer. The image below was taken at the intersection of Grand Central Avenue and West Shore Boulevard and looks west, toward the Howard Frankland Bridge. (Both, courtesy of the Tampa–Hillsborough County Public Library System.)

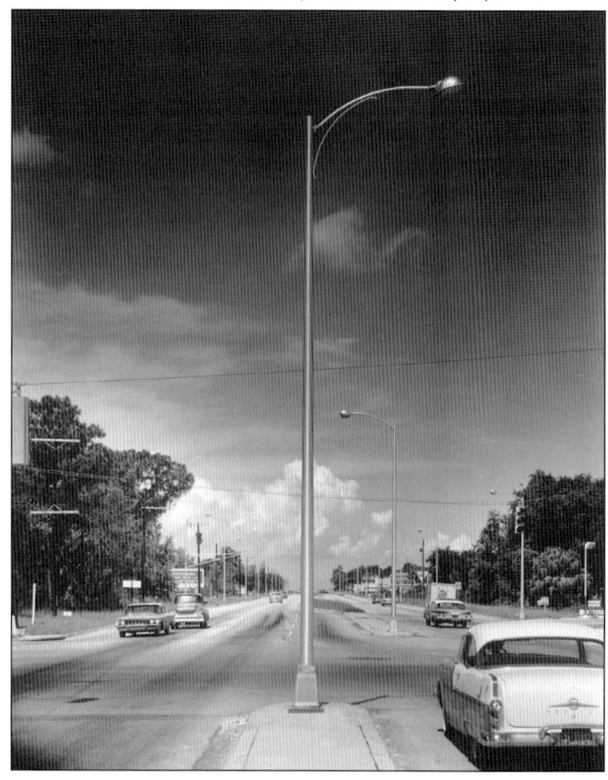

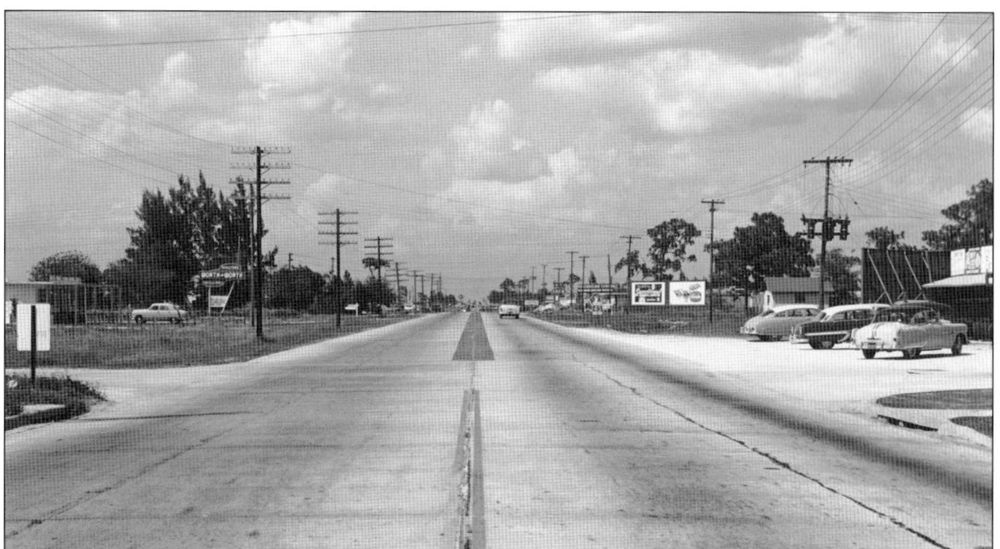

This 1954 photograph taken on North Dale Mabry Highway at its intersection with West Gray Street looks north along the four-lane highway toward a strip mall to the right, Worth & Worth Realtors on the left in the mid-ground, and Peninsular Lumber at right in the background. (Courtesy of the Florida State Archive.)

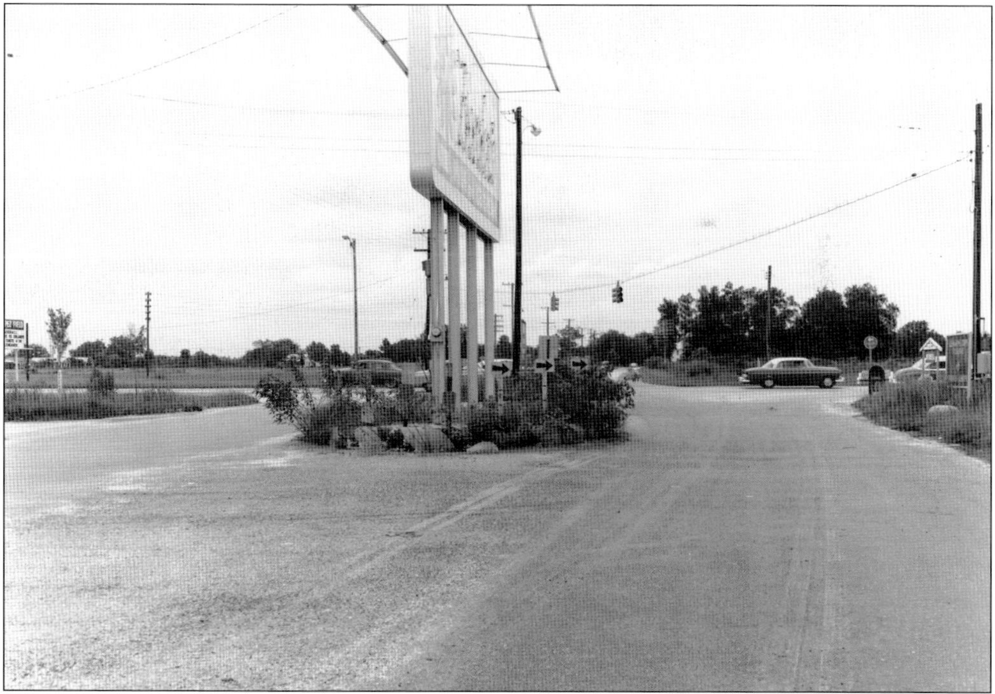

The large, light-up sign for the Borden Dairy Company and its congenial bovine mascot, Elsie the Cow, is seen in the foreground of this photograph taken near the plant's entrance at the corner of North Dale Mabry Highway and Tampa Bay Boulevard. This eastward-facing image, taken on August 11, 1959, would look much different today, with Raymond James Stadium dominating most of the left half of this photograph. (Courtesy of the Tampa–Hillsborough County Public Library System.)

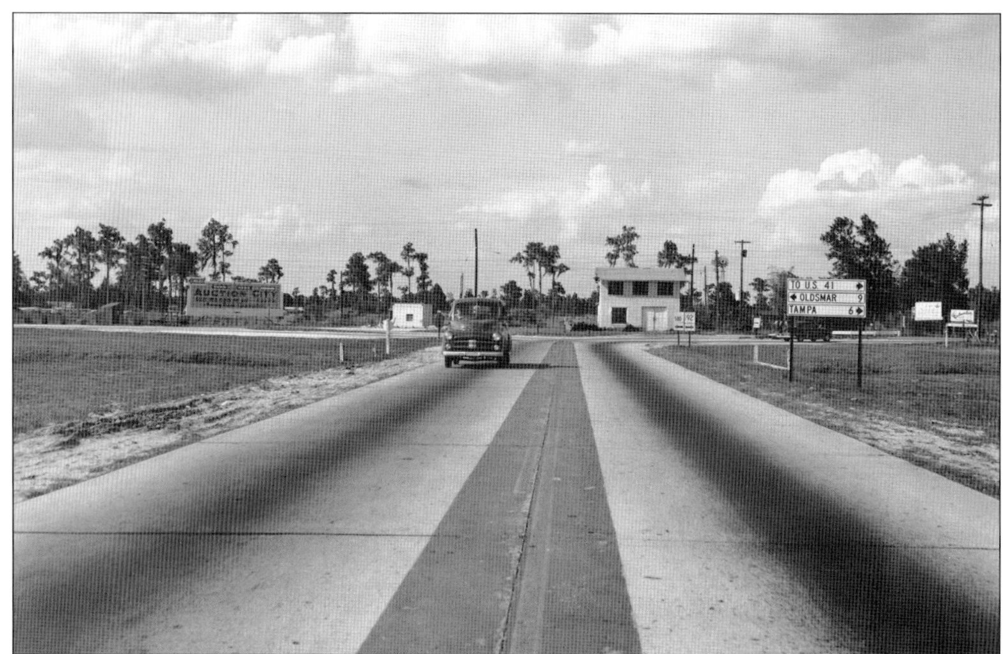

Prior to 1955, North Dale Mabry Highway terminated on its north side at West Hillsborough Avenue, seen in the upper image. A small building stands in this 1954 photograph where North Dale Mabry Highway soon leaped across Hillsborough Avenue toward Carrollwood, which was yet to be built in the mid-1950s. Much has changed by 1959, when the lower artistic night scene was shot looking south toward the four-way intersection of Hillsborough Avenue and North Dale Mabry Highway. Within a few years, an overpass relieved increasingly thick traffic at that intersection, flying North Dale Mabry Highway motorists over West Hillsborough Avenue. (Both, courtesy of the Florida State Archive.)

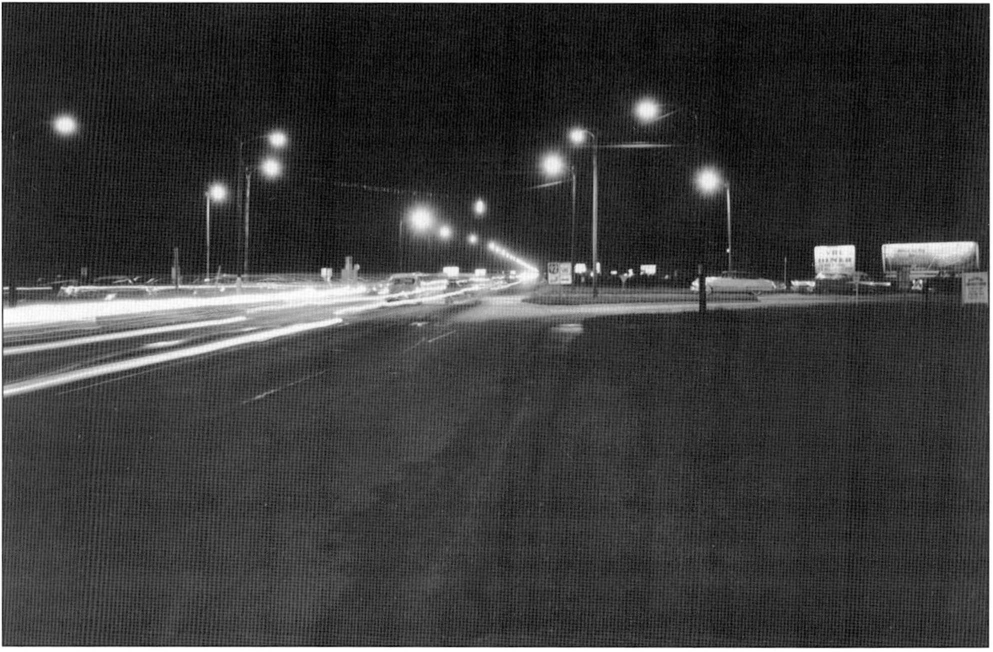

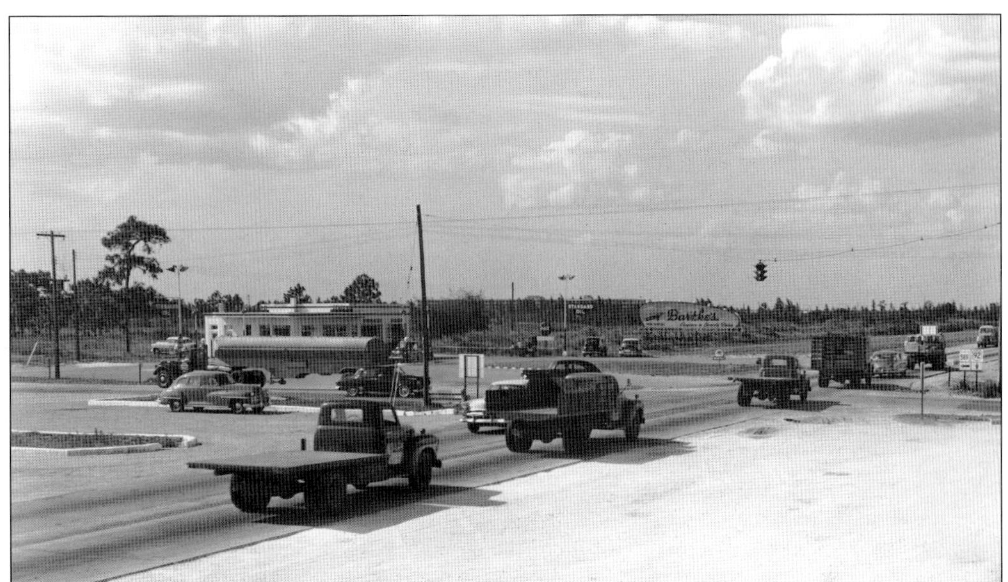

A Standard Oil service station stands at the northwest corner of North Dale Mabry Highway and West Columbus Drive in April 1954. A large billboard points west toward Bartke's, a classy restaurant at Tampa International Airport that was popular with local diners and tourists for many years. (Courtesy of the Florida State Archive.)

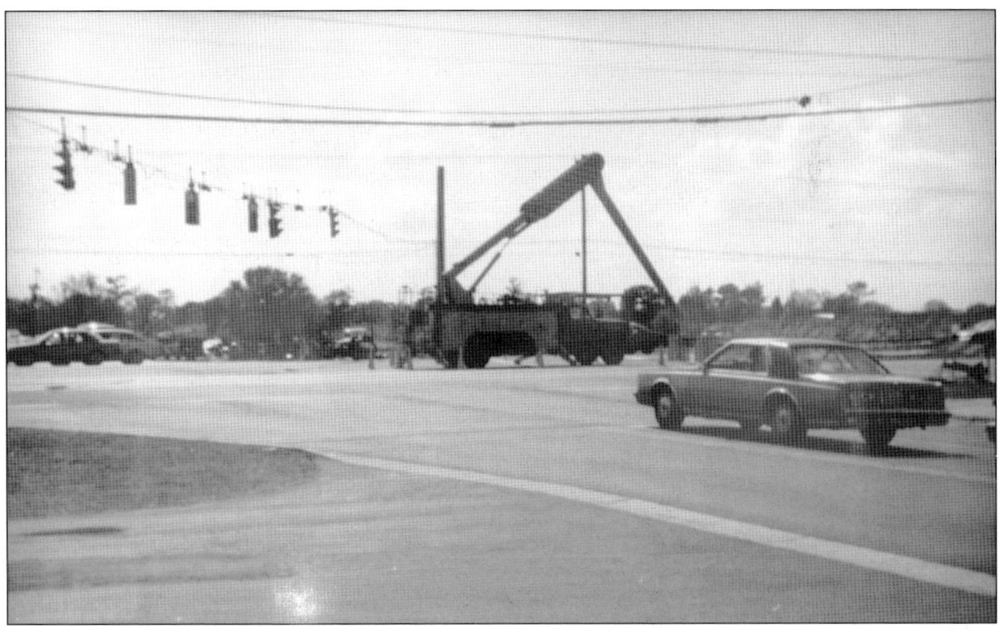

Construction ramps up around the intersection of West Hillsborough Avenue and North Lois Avenue in 1988. A signal crew works with a boom truck to install new traffic lights over the intersection ahead of a new shopping mall at the southwest corner of the crossroads that soon included Service Merchandise, Sports Authority, Zak's hobby supply store, and many other retailers alongside Bally Health Club.

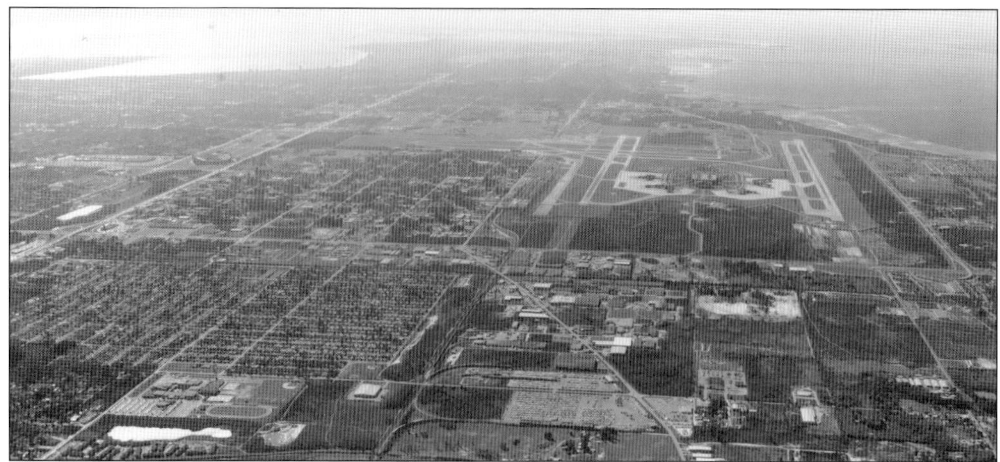

This aerial image captures virtually the entire Westshore area as it appeared on January 4, 1979. Looking south from over Waters Avenue, one sees Tampa International Airport prominently sprawling across much of the mid-ground with Horizon Park (now Al Lopez Park), Tampa Stadium, and Al Lopez Field toward the center left. The Howard Frankland Bridge reaches St. Petersburg on the right, while the peninsula of South Tampa stretches into the background. (Courtesy of Todd Keil.)

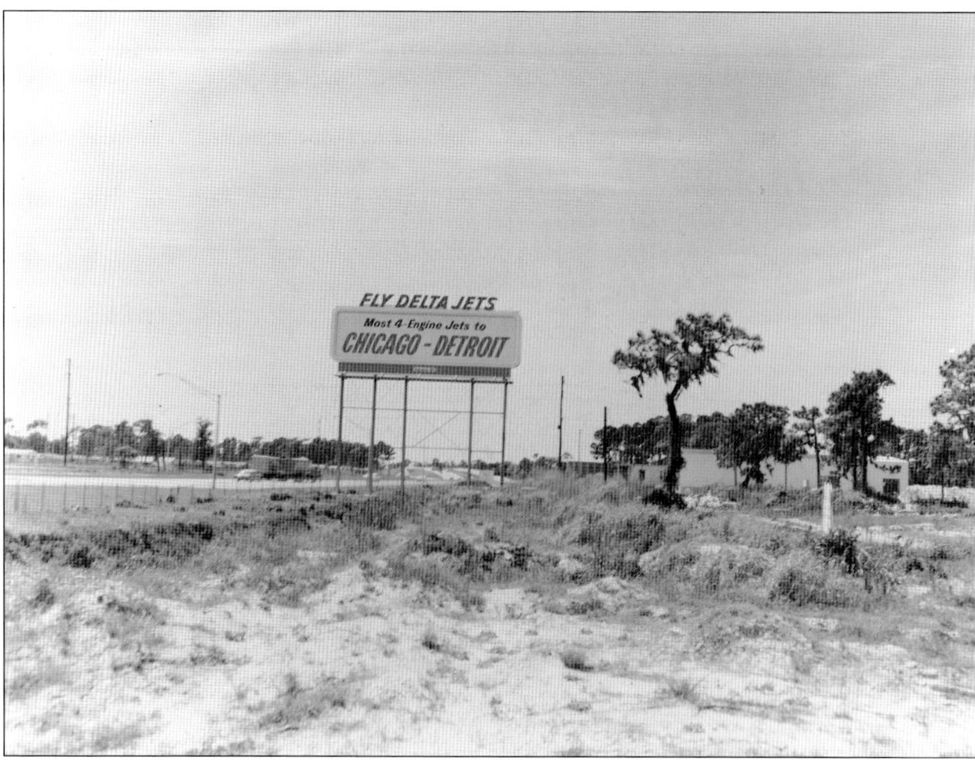

This Delta Airlines billboard tries snagging westbound motorists along Interstate 4 around 1964 between Lois Avenue and West Shore Boulevard. This stretch of interstate was redesignated as Interstate 75 in 1969 and renamed Interstate 275 in the early 1980s, as the Interstate 75 route bypassing Tampa was built in phases through eastern Hillsborough County. (Courtesy of the Tampa–Hillsborough County Public Library System.)

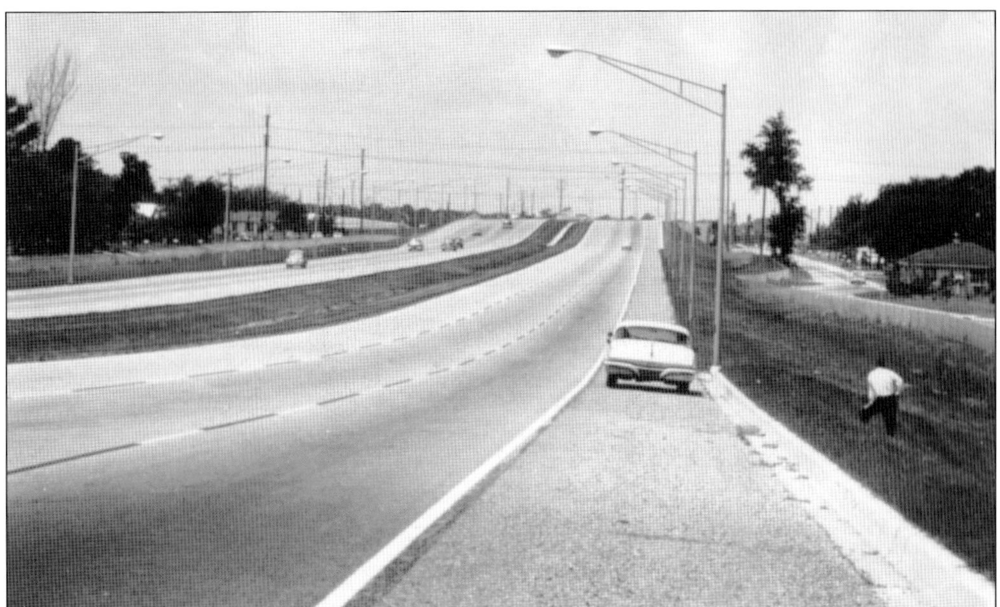

These two images progress the viewer along recently completed Interstate 4 in the Westshore community during the mid-1960s. The photograph above shows a motorist on the shoulder out of his car and looking west toward the overpasses crossing North Himes Avenue (mid-ground) and North Dale Mabry Highway (background). The lower view captures Interstate 4 crossing over North Lois Avenue, with an overpass traversing North West Shore Boulevard in the background. (Above, courtesy of the Tampa–Hillsborough County Public Library System; below, courtesy of the Florida State Archive.)

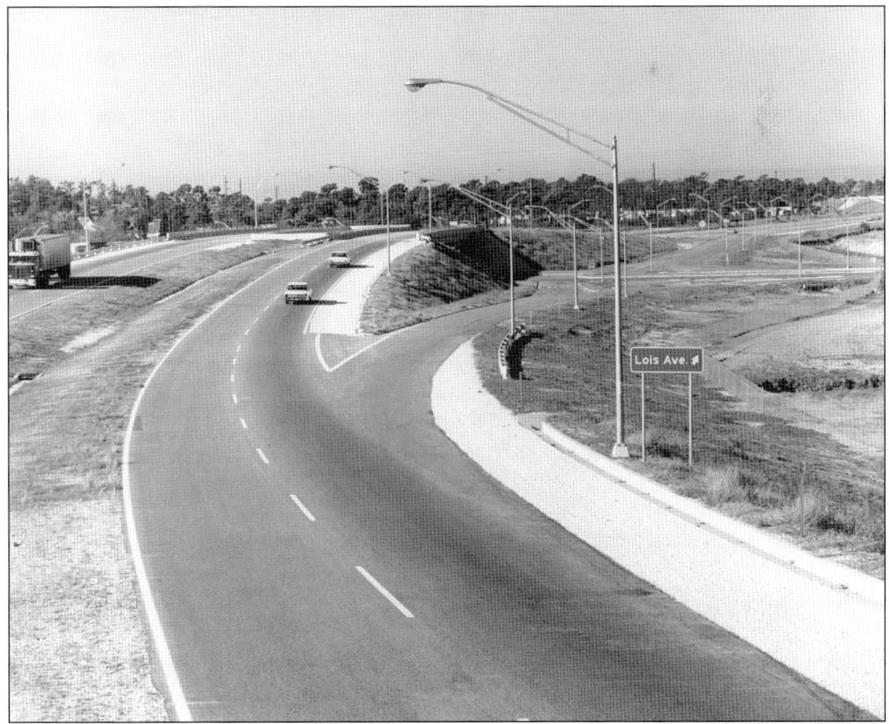

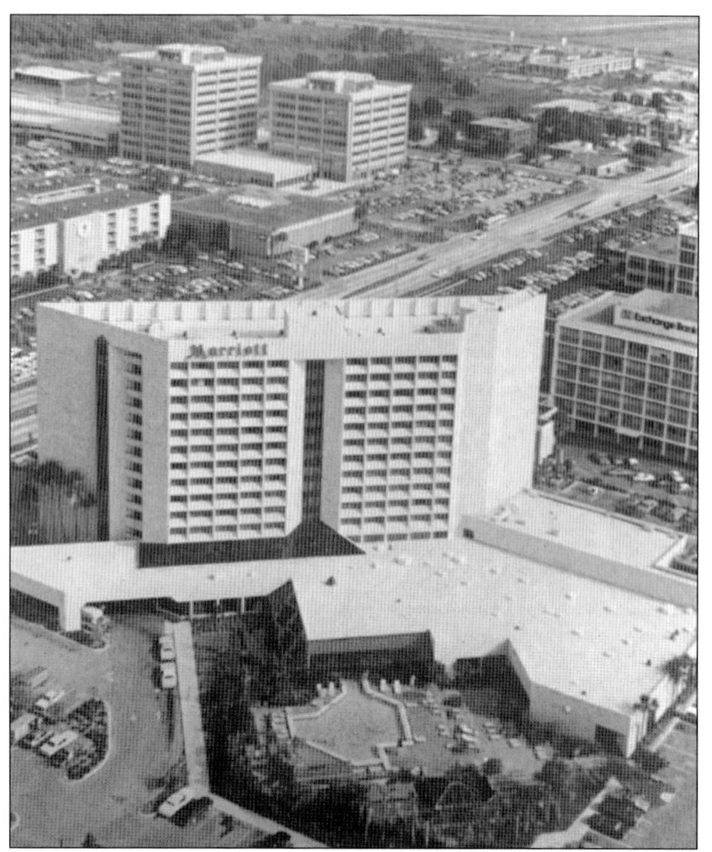

The 1983 photograph to the left centers on the Westshore Marriott and encompasses the Admiral Benbow Inn (upper left), Austin Center West Atrium Mall (top center), and Austin Center (center right), with the Exchange Bank building mostly visible. Meanwhile, the lower photograph from 1990 looks north along West Shore Boulevard with two more recently completed towers at 1511 and 1715 North West Shore Boulevard. Both images capture the explosive vertical growth in Westshore during the latter decades of the 20th century. (Left, courtesy of the Marriott Corporate Archives; below, © *Tampa Bay Times* via ZUMA Press.)

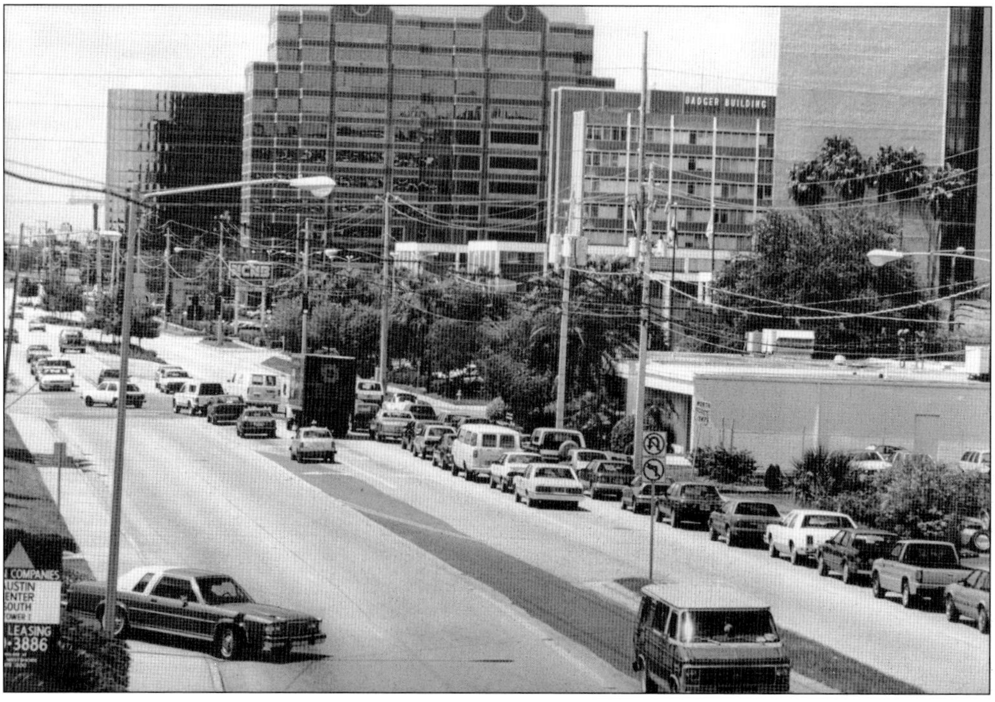

Five

Office Space

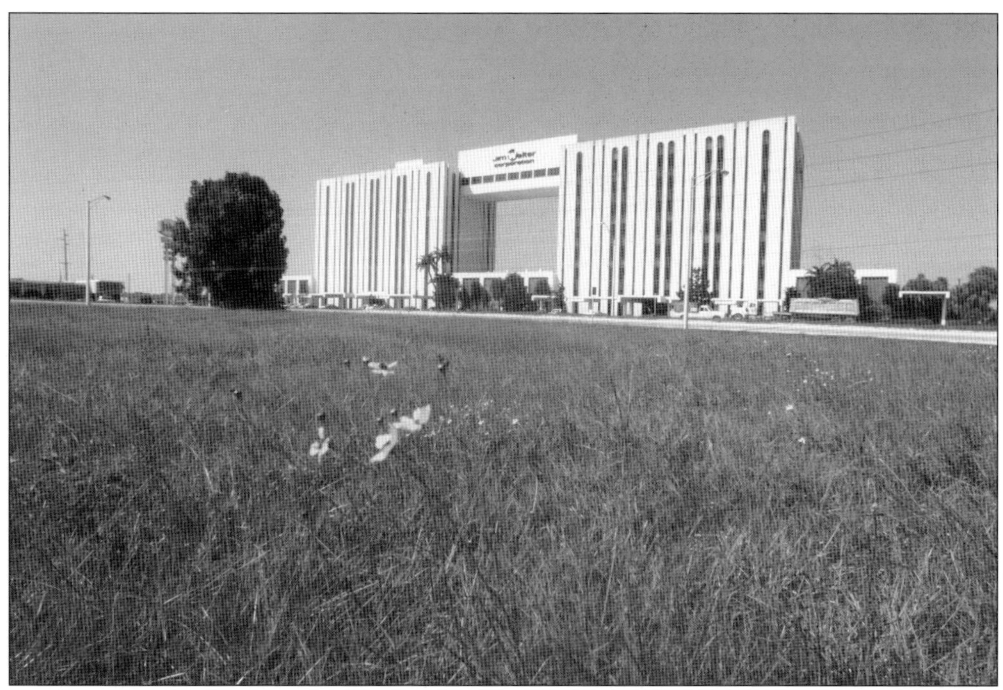

James W. Walter Sr. was a Tampa home builder who launched his highly successful Jim Walter Homes and Jim Walter Industries in 1946. Walter constructed an eight-story headquarters tower at 1500 North Dale Mabry Highway in 1966 and built a second tower in 1975, connecting the twin structures by way of a suspended pedestrian bridge. The entire 240,000-square-foot structure was demolished to make way for a retail complex anchored by a Target department store in 2003, the same year the western portion of Columbus Drive near International Plaza was renamed in honor of Walter, who died in 2000 at the age of 77. (Courtesy of the Florida State Archive.)

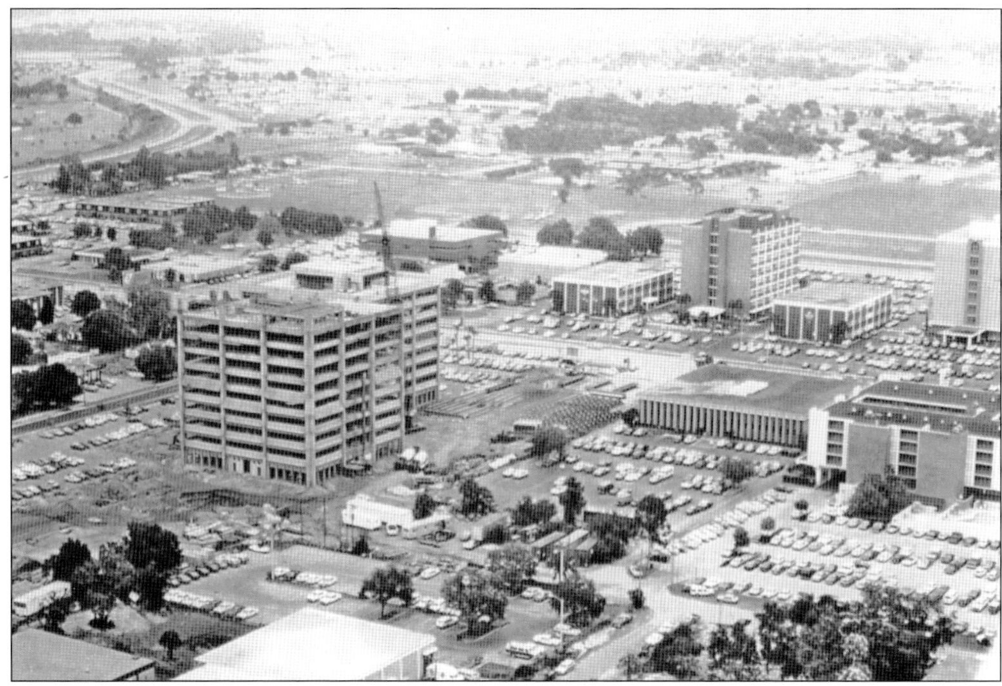

This 1981 photograph shows construction in the foreground of Austin Center West Atrium Mall, consisting of two nine-story towers at 1408 and 1410 North Westshore Boulevard. In the upper center right are the many buildings of the 1960s development known as Austin Center. These complexes, built by iconic Tampa developer Al Austin, helped drive much of the commercial growth in Westshore and are seen surrounded here by the Admiral Benbow Inn (lower right) and the 18-hole Tampa Airport Resort Golf & Racquet Club (upper left), built in 1974 by Jim Walter. (Courtesy of George Youdal.)

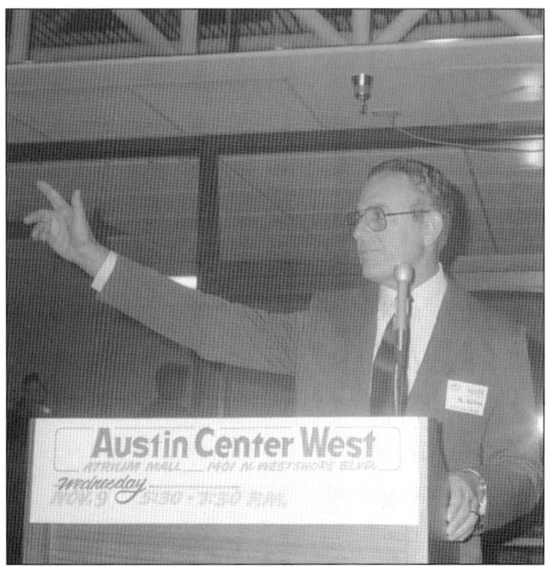

Al Austin, seen here around 1983, was one of Tampa's foremost developers and civic leaders. Born in Springfield, Massachusetts, in 1929, he attended the University of Tampa and joined his father's Davis Islands home construction business in the mid-1950s. He shifted to commercial development and transformed large swaths of Westshore land into thriving business centers throughout the 1960s, 1970s, and 1980s. His endeavors helped Westshore earn the distinction of being the largest office market in Florida, with more than 10 million square feet of commercial space. He was still planning new Westshore projects when he died at the age of 85 in 2014. (Courtesy of the City of Tampa Archives.)

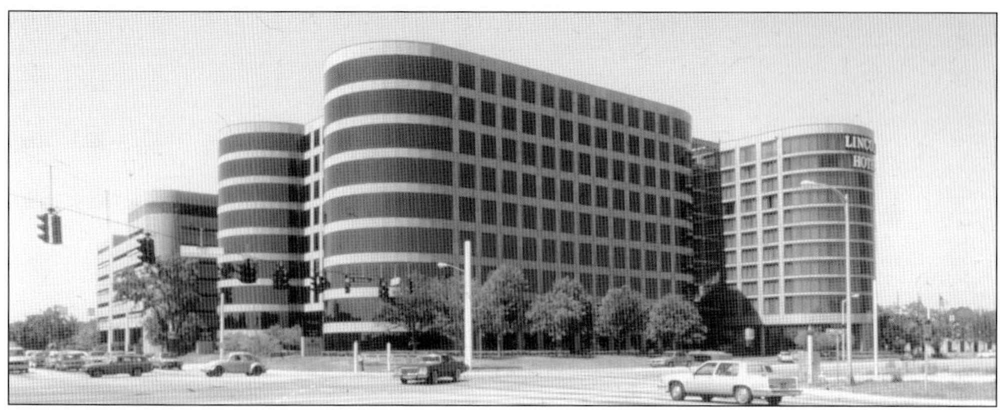

The site once occupied by the swanky International Inn was reimagined in the 1980s as a multistory business hub catering to Tampa's growing executive scene. The nine-story Urban Centre was built in 1984 at the southwest corner of West Kennedy Boulevard and West Shore Boulevard, accompanied by the prestigious Lincoln Hotel. The complex continues thriving today adjacent to a bustling WestShore Plaza and amid many other multimillion-dollar projects both long since completed and still on drawing boards. (Courtesy of the University of South Florida Special Collections Department.)

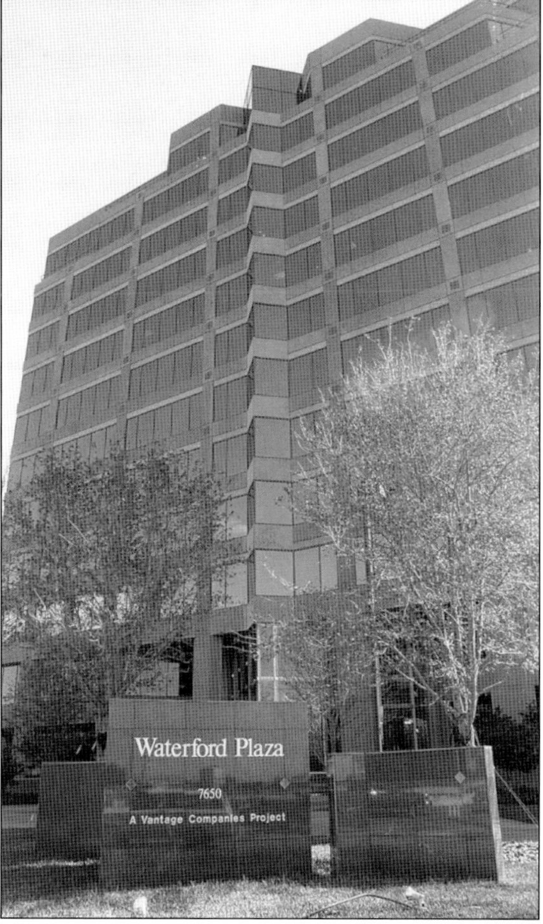

Waterford Plaza, at 7650 West Courtney Campbell Causeway, was built in 1987 during a boom of high-rise construction in and around Rocky Point. Other nearby projects from the era reaching eight stories or taller include The Pointe at 2502 North Rocky Point Drive in 1983, Rocky Pointe Centre at 3030 North Rocky Point Drive in 1985, and Island Center at 2701 North Rocky Point Drive in 1986. The latter office complex was built the same year as Pickett Suite Hotel, a seven-story resort now operating as DoubleTree by Hilton. (Courtesy of the City of Tampa Archives.)

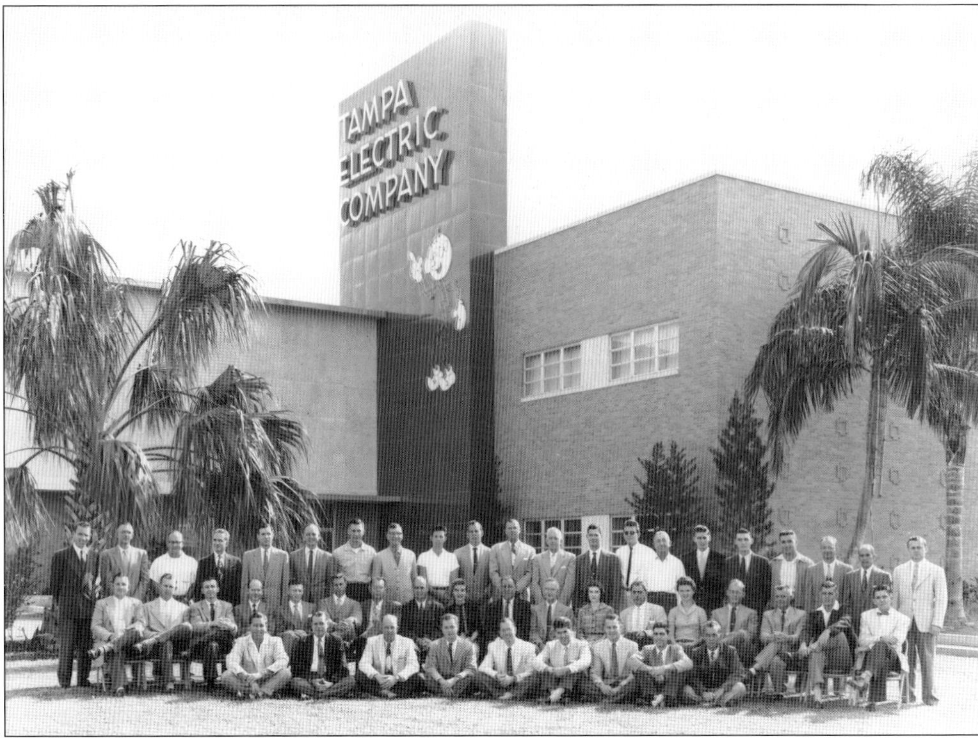

Tampa Electric Company, more popularly known as TECO, opened its headquarters building in 1956 at the northeast corner of North Dale Mabry Highway and West Grand Central Avenue. Amid the region's rapid growth, Tampa Electric moved its headquarters to an ultramodern nine-story building in downtown Tampa in 1981. The 125,000-square-foot building it left behind in Westshore briefly served as the headquarters for Freedom Savings until the former TECO site was redeveloped into the 13-story Tampa Commons high-rise (now known as One North Dale Mabry Highway) and three smaller retail buildings in the mid-1980s. (Above, courtesy of the University of South Florida Special Collections Department; below, courtesy of the Florida State Archive.)

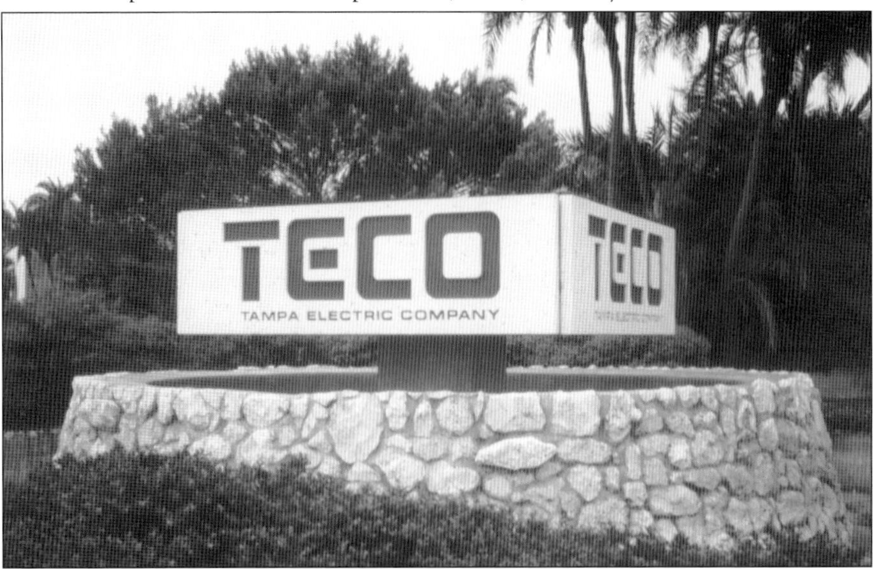

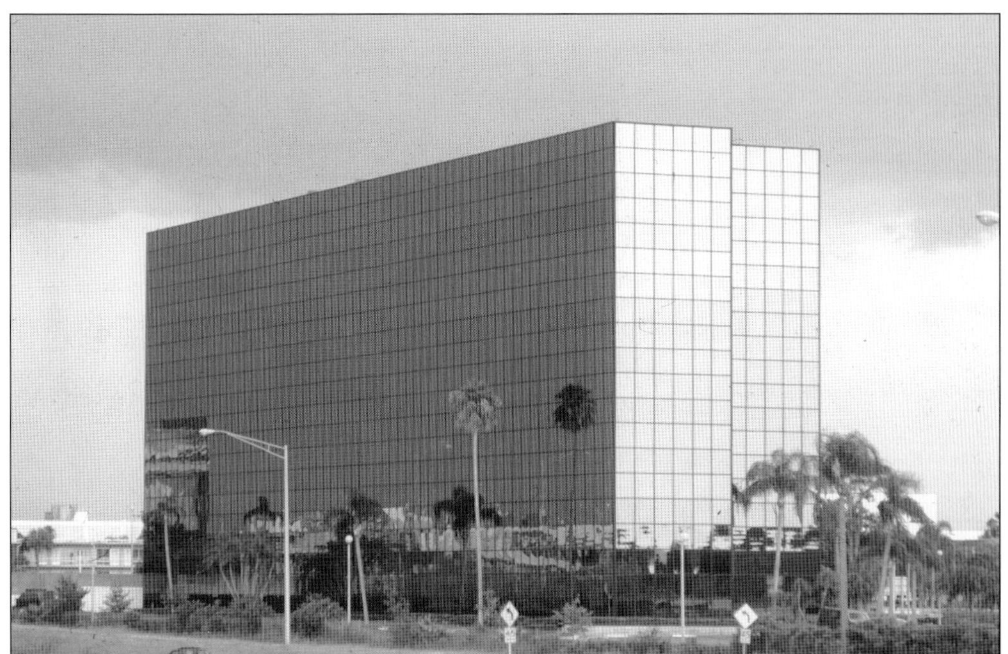

Lincoln Center was built at 5401 West Kennedy Boulevard in 1975. The 223,500-square-foot office building is situated near the modern-day interchange of Interstate 275 and the Veterans Expressway and is an earlier example of the sleek, glass-curtain commercial architecture that sprang up throughout Westshore, downtown Tampa, and other parts of the Tampa Bay area in later years. (Courtesy of the University of South Florida Special Collections Department.)

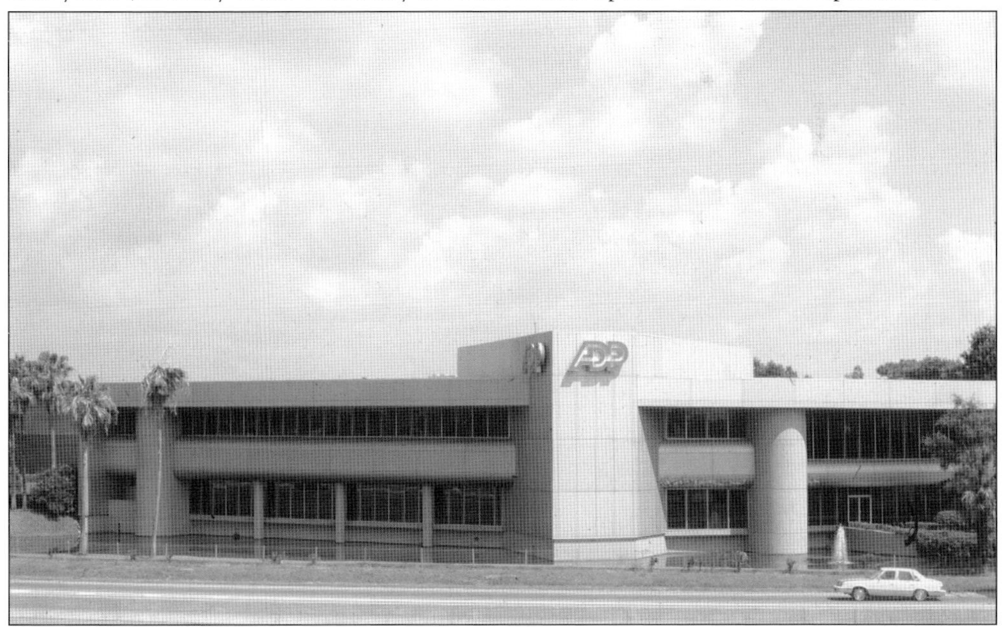

The Automatic Data Processing (ADP) Tampa payroll services building at 4900 West Lemon Street was built in 1981. ADP has since relocated its Tampa offices, and as of this writing, this building is owned by the Florida Department of Transportation, which may use the land for a future highway project. (Courtesy of the University of South Florida Special Collections Department.)

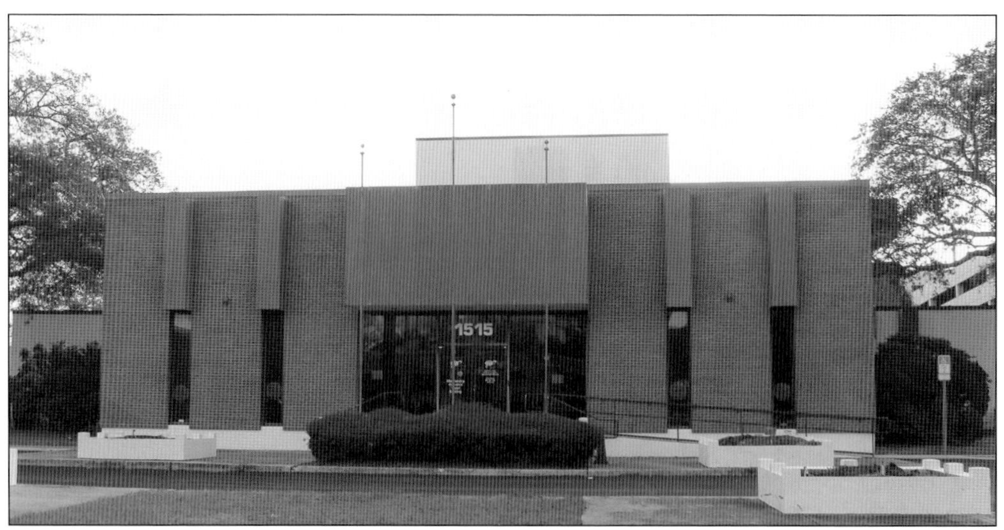

The Auto Club South division of the American Automobile Association (AAA) spent decades headquartered in this building at 1515 North West Shore Boulevard. The building, constructed in 1965, was vacated by AAA in 2020 for a new location just steps away and demolished in 2021 to make way for a new project in the Austin Center complex, renamed Westshore City Center after its purchase by Ally Capital Group in 2019.

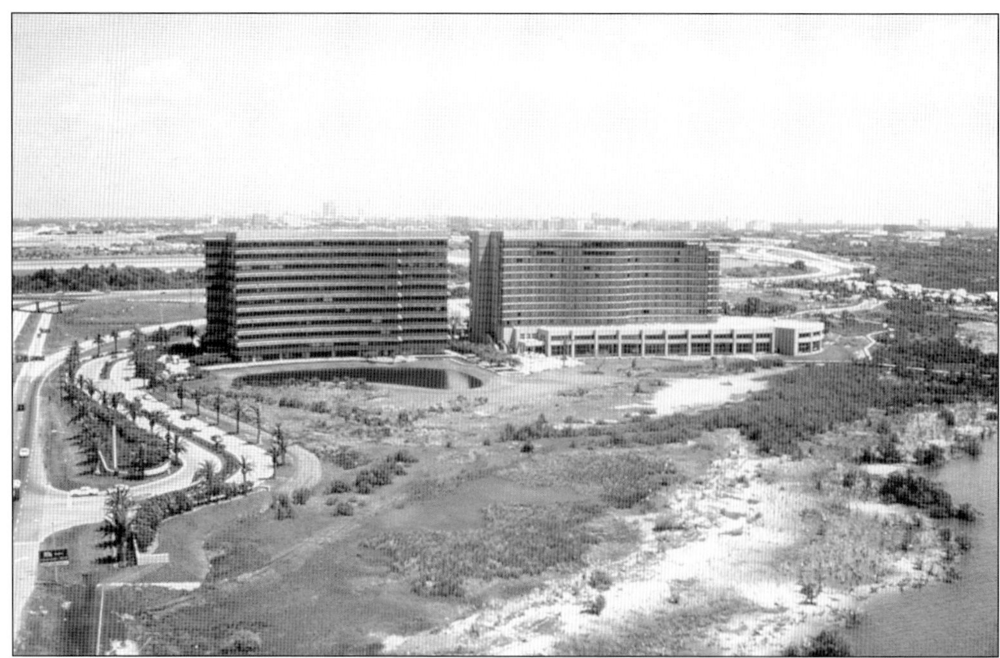

These two high rises were built in the mid-1980s on the marshy shores of Old Tampa Bay. The office building on the left in this eastward-facing photograph was constructed in 1985 as part of Bayport Plaza, while the similar-looking structure on the right belongs to the Grand Hyatt Tampa Bay. Built in 1986, Grand Hyatt Tampa Bay fields a luxurious resort experience with two restaurants, Armani's and Oystercatchers, serving up fine cuisine for both hotel patrons and locals looking for a splendid meal. (Courtesy of the City of Tampa Archives.)

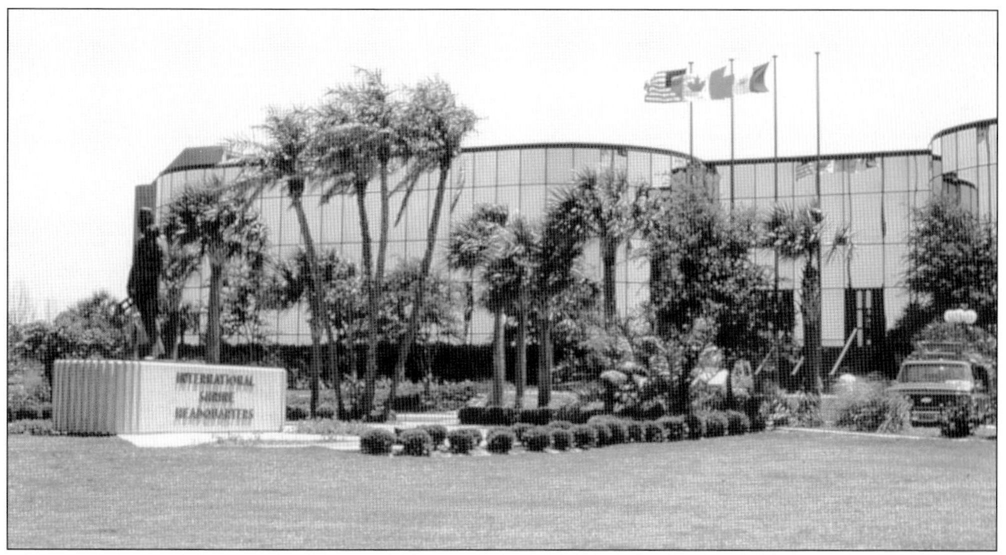

Shriners International, the good Samaritans behind the globally known Shriners Hospitals for Children, operates its headquarters at 2900 Rocky Point Drive. The organization's building, seen here soon after its opening in 1979, has been heavily remodeled in the years since as the group has continued growing to reach more children. (Courtesy of the City of Tampa Archives.)

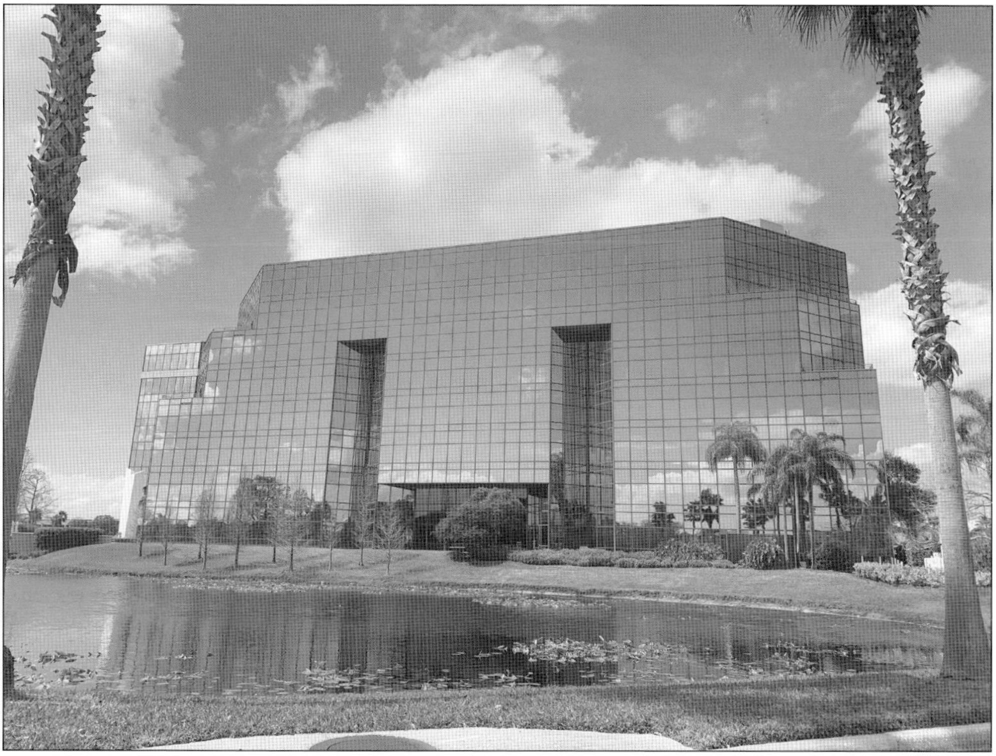

Tampa Bay Park is located along Dr. Martin Luther King Jr. Boulevard and boasts several buildings housing corporate headquarters, company regional branches, and a technical school. The building seen here is known as LakePointe One and was built in 1986 during a later phase of the office park project that originally overtook Loch Raven Golf Course in the late 1970s.

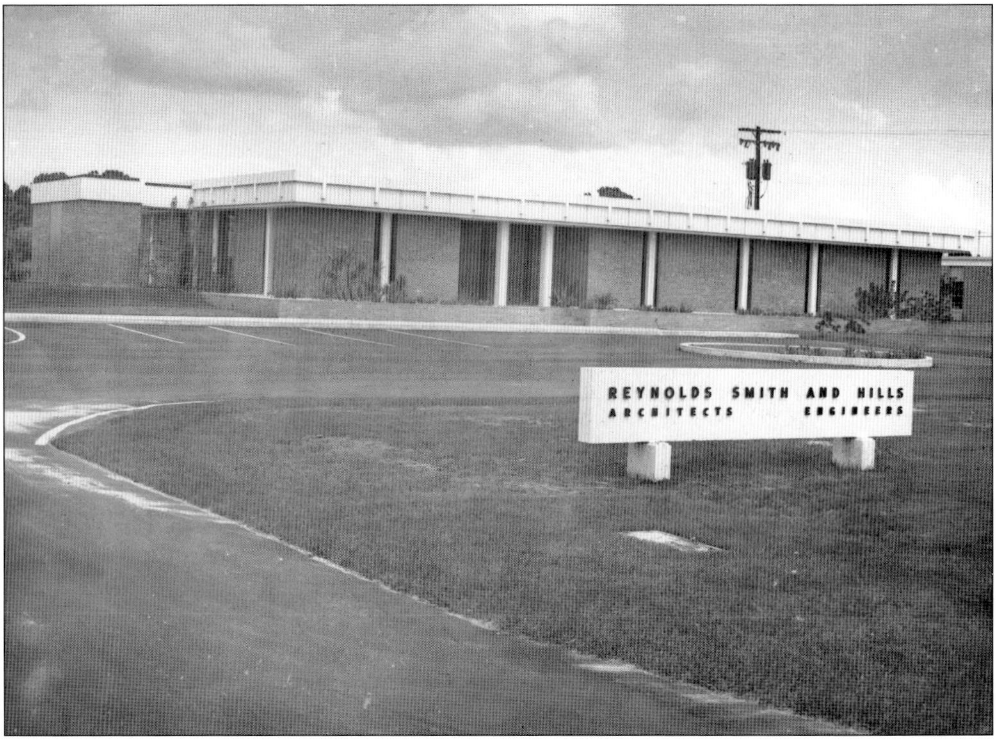

Notable architectural and engineering firm Reynolds, Smith, and Hills was located in this building at 1715 North West Shore Boulevard. Pictured here on May 21, 1964, the building was demolished for the construction of Westshore Center, a high-rise office complex that the firm designed and that was built in 1984. (Courtesy of the Tampa–Hillsborough County Public Library System.)

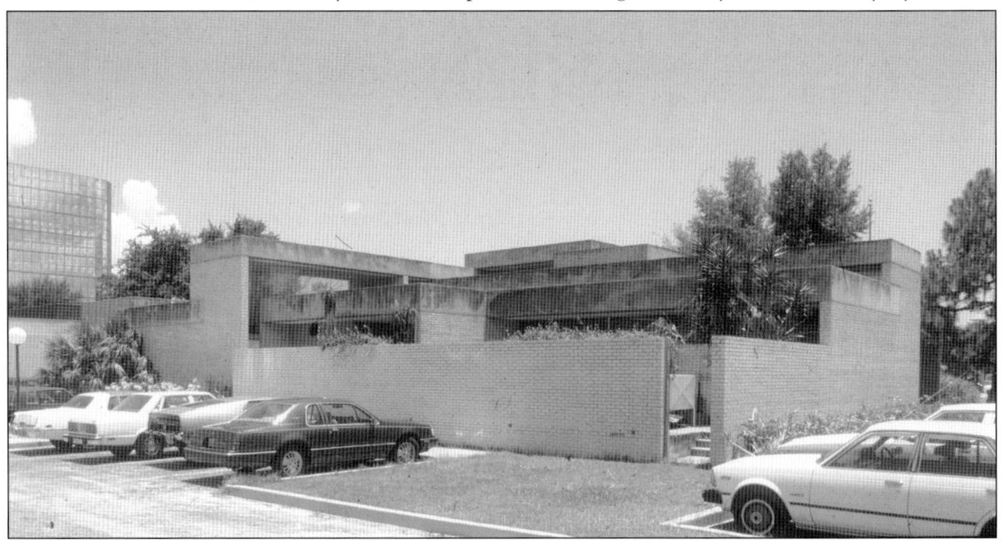

Part of the massive Westshore Center referenced above is seen on the left side of this photograph showing Associated General Contractors in the mid-1980s. This building, located at 1509 North West Shore Boulevard, was demolished to make way for Tower Place, an 11-story office tower built in 1988 and addressed as 1511 North West Shore Boulevard. (Courtesy of the University of South Florida Special Collections Department.)

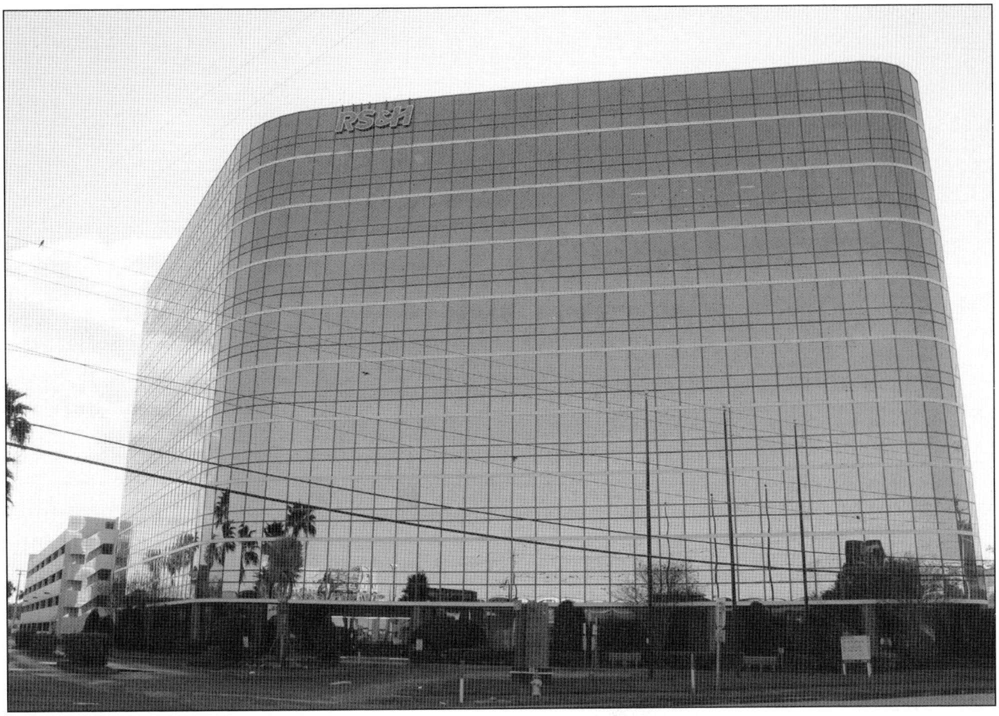

Westshore Center, built in 1984, replaced a building long occupied by Reynolds, Smith, and Hills. That firm designed this nine-story office tower, which incorporates a glass-curtain facade featured on many other office towers built throughout Tampa during the 1970s and 1980s. Westshore Center's angular parallelogram footprint makes for stunning views of nearby Tampa International Airport, the waters of Tampa Bay, and the surrounding Westshore skyline.

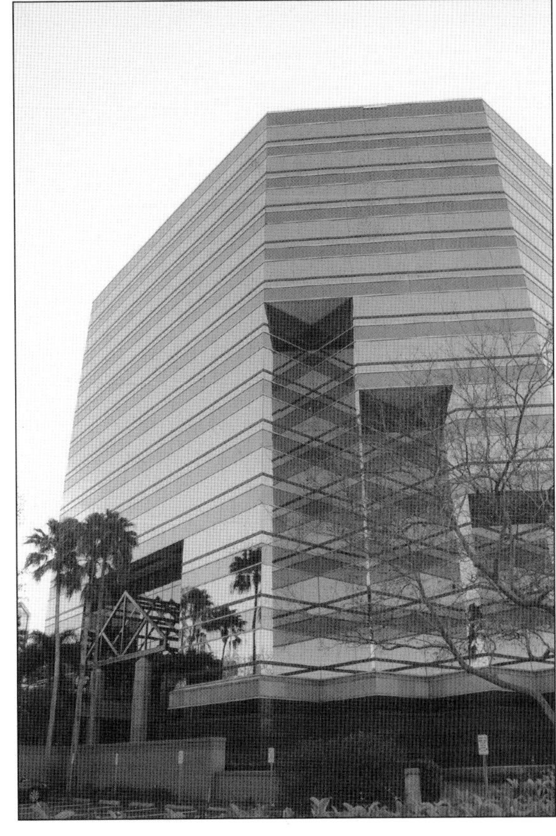

Tampa Commons opened in 1985 on a site formerly occupied by the Tampa Electric Company headquarters and, later, the main offices of Freedom Savings bank. Smaller retail buildings were constructed alongside the Tampa Commons project, including parcels long occupied by Barnes & Noble bookstore and Office Depot.

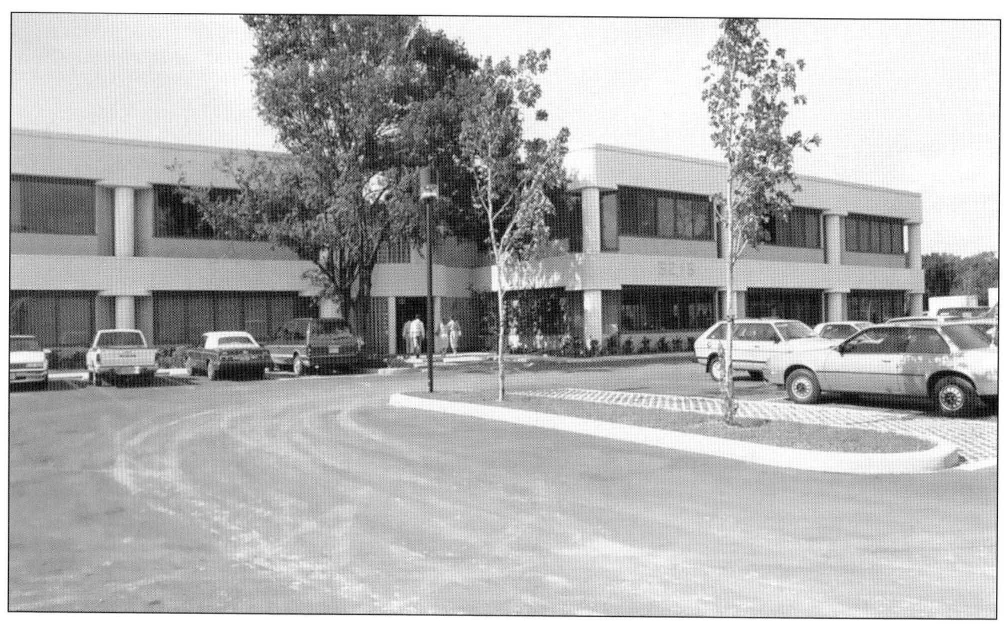

While Westshore saw several notable high-rise projects in the 1980s, there were also many classy office buildings more closely sized to the modest human scale. These include the two-story complex at 5215 West Laurel Street (above) built in 1988 and the three-story building at 5405 West Cypress Street (below), which came along as part of the Corporate Oaks office park in 1983. (Both, courtesy of the City of Tampa Archives.)

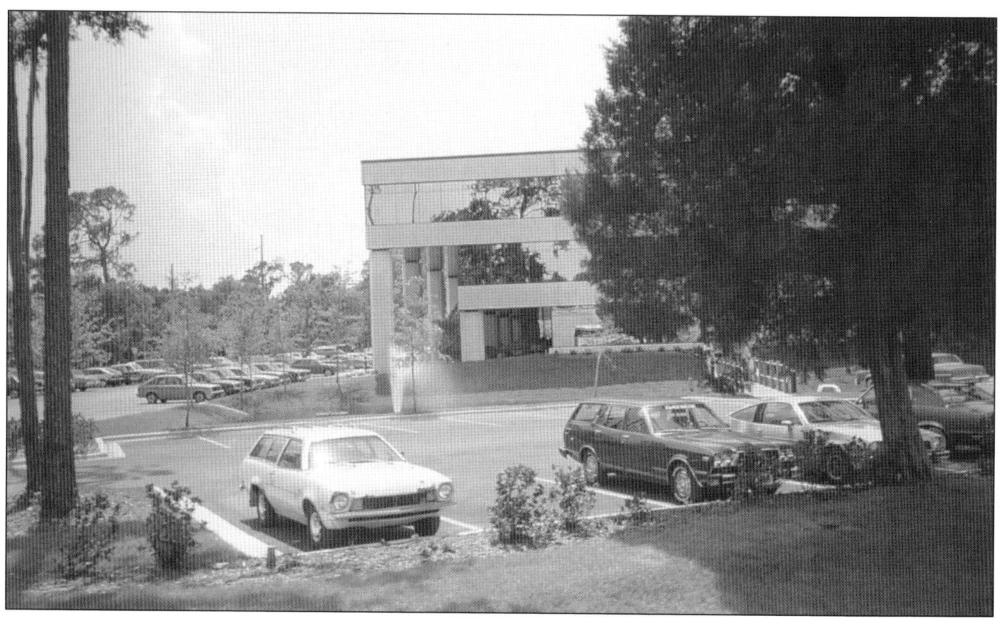

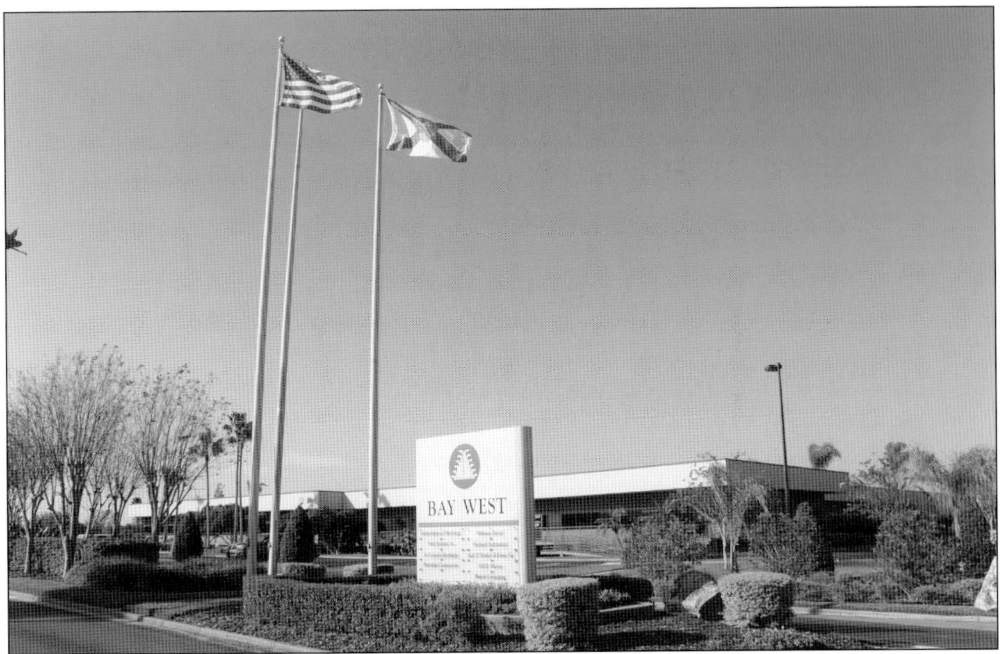

Sprawling near the picturesque shores of Cypress Point Park is Bay West, an office park consisting of mainly one-story buildings constructed between 1983 and 1985. Many of the spaces here serve as corporate headquarters and regional offices for smaller to mid-size companies.

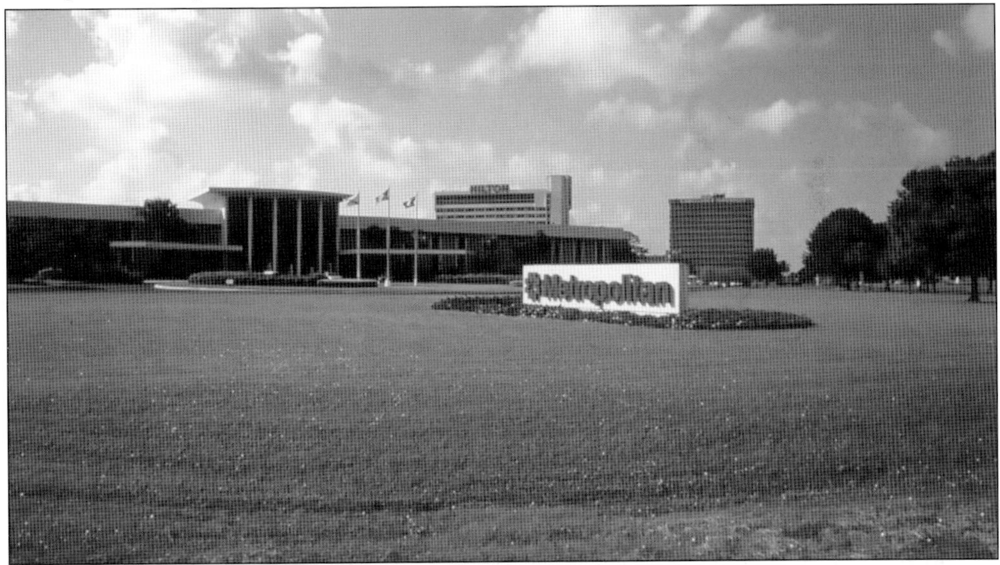

Metropolitan Life Insurance built its $4.5-million regional service center on a 32-acre campus at 4100 West Boy Scout Boulevard in 1971. The building was home to the corporation's Southeast operations until 2007, when the site was reimagined as a mixed-use development called MetWest International. The 185,000-square-foot building erected decades earlier was razed to develop new offices, apartments, retail units, and a hotel. Also seen in this image are other Westshore landmarks, including a Hilton (left background) at 2225 North Lois Avenue, built in 1982, and a 13-story office complex (right foreground) that rose at 2203 North Lois Avenue in 1985. (Courtesy of the City of Tampa Archives.)

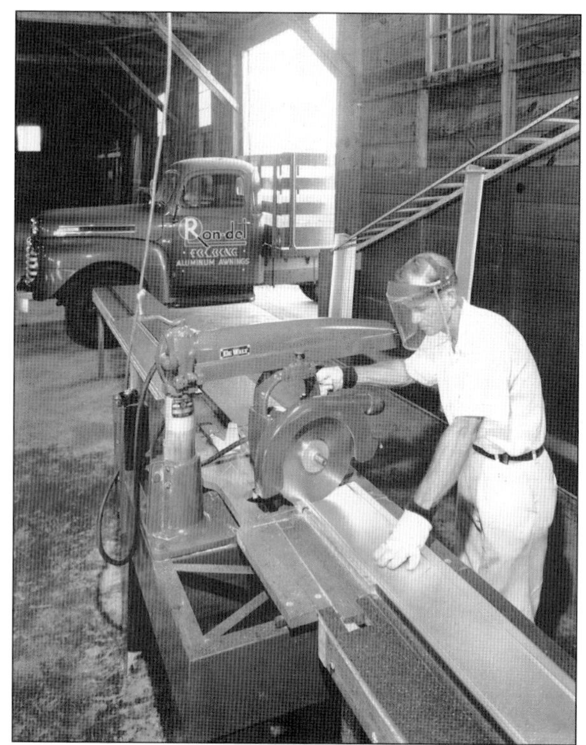

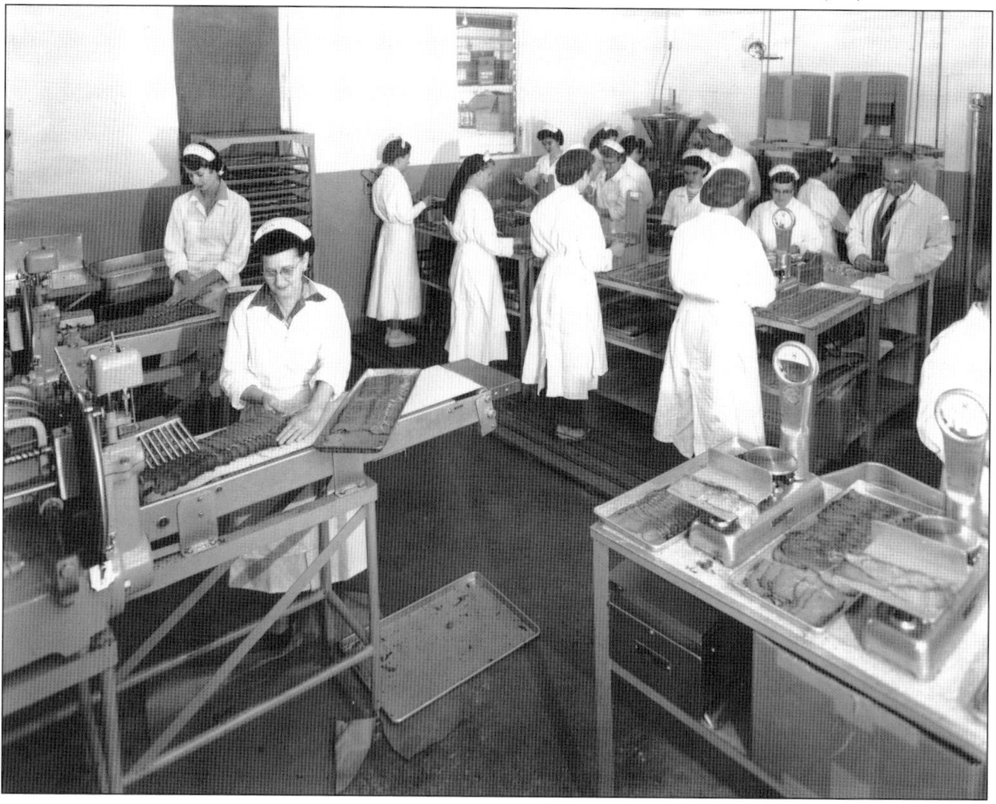

For some, the phrase "going to the office" does not necessarily mean commuting to a desk or cubicle in a shiny high-rise building. For many in Westshore, the "office" refers to workbenches, conveyor belts, and warehouses. To the left, a man cuts aluminum at Ron-Del Florida Inc. in Drew Park on October 19, 1950, while the people below prepare meals in the Cook-Quik kitchen at 4822 Anderson Road on February 28, 1957. (Both, courtesy of the Tampa–Hillsborough County Public Library System.)

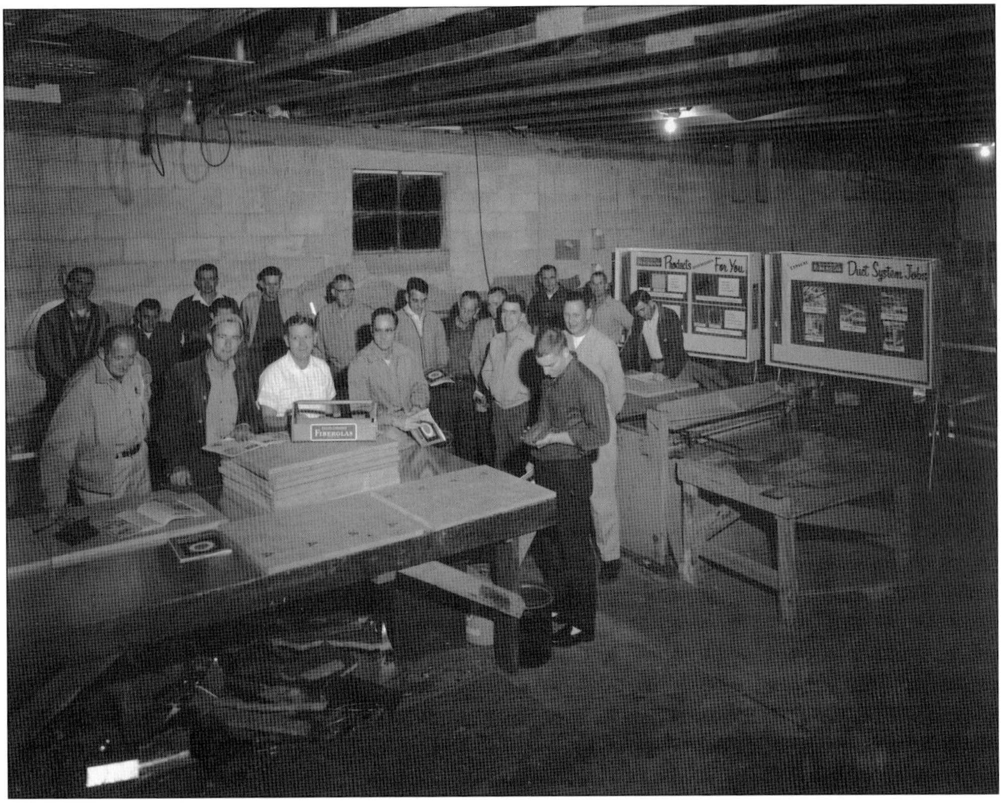

These men above at JW Metals, located at 4713 North Clark Avenue, pose for a photograph on February 6, 1964, during a presentation of Owens-Corning fiberglass duct products and sheet insulation. Below is the Borden Dairy Company, seen here in 1960. Located at the northwest corner of Lois Avenue and Tampa Bay Boulevard, the Borden Dairy Company plant employed hundreds of workers and produced millions of gallons of milk and ice cream every year to operate as one of the largest industrial outfits in Drew Park. (Above, courtesy of the Tampa–Hillsborough County Public Library System; below, © *Tampa Bay Times* via ZUMA Press.)

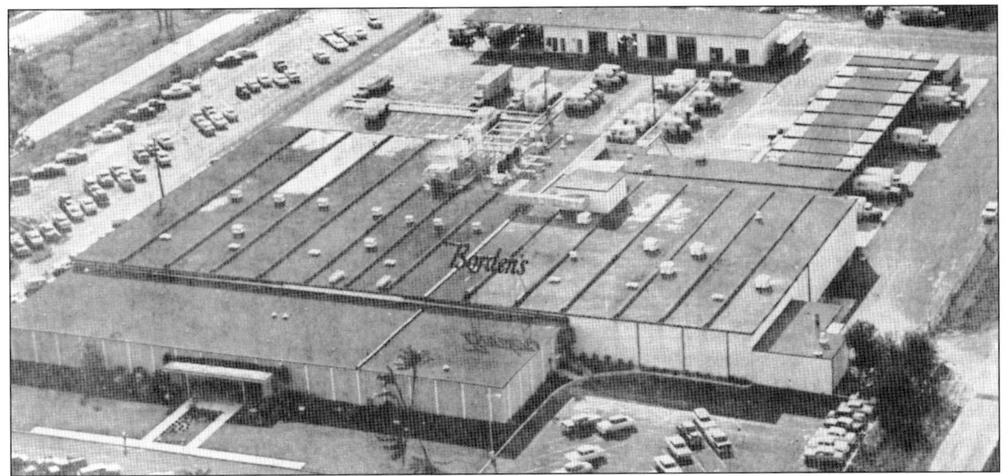

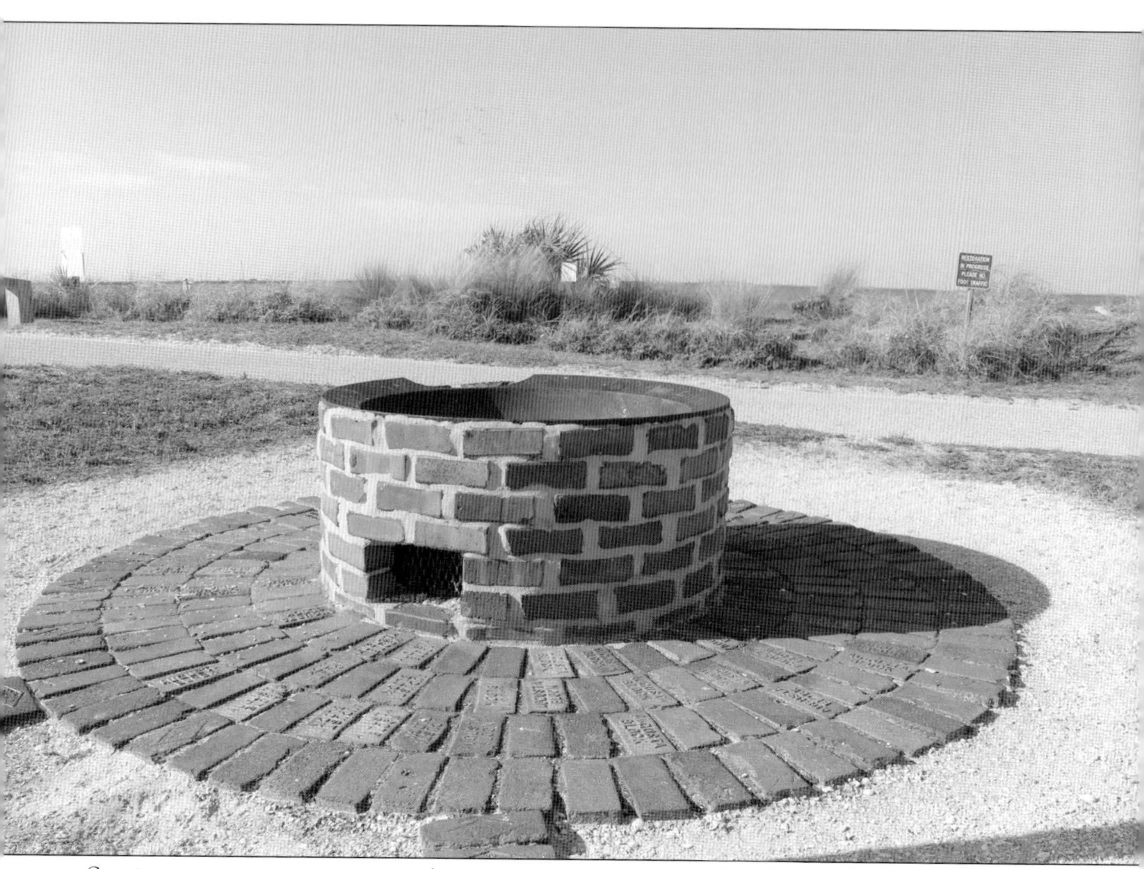

Serving as a meat preservative, salt was an important commodity during the Civil War. Florida's seemingly endless coastlines ensured plentiful access to saltwater, which could be boiled to leave behind salty residues. One of these salt works was located on Frazier's Beach, in the vicinity of modern-day Cypress Point Park. That is where a replica of a boiler stands as a reminder of Tampa Confederate Salt Works, the location where one of the most significant Civil War skirmishes in the Tampa area occurred in the fall of 1864. The salt works, run by Capt. James McKay Sr., was overrun by Union soldiers from the USS *Nita* and USS *Hendrick Hudson*. The only person staffing the salt boiler at that moment was Tampa pioneer Joseph Robles, who, armed with a double-barreled rifle, fired upon the party and caused it to retreat. Eight soldiers were left behind. They surrendered to Robles, who took his empty rifle and marched the eight into town.

Six

Let's Fly Away

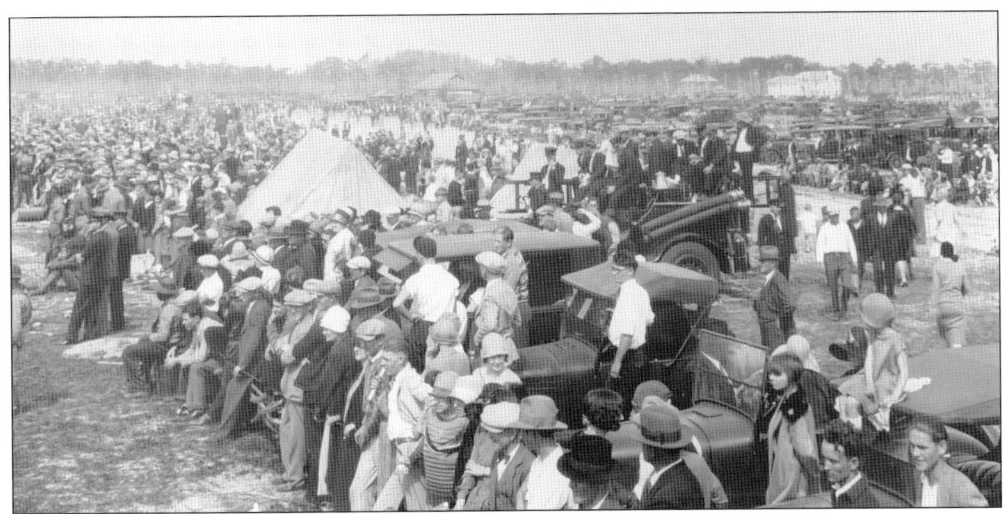

A crowd of 100,000 attend the first Southeastern Air Meet on February 22, 1928, to mark the formal opening of Drew Field. The 160-acre airfield traced back to a private airstrip built by local developer and aviation aficionado John H. Drew and Tampa cigar mogul Hugh C. MacFarlane. Originally leasing the property from Drew, the City of Tampa bought the property from him for $11,654, and its eventual improvement as a modern commercial airport became an important Works Progress Administration project in the 1930s. (Courtesy of the University of South Florida Special Collections Department.)

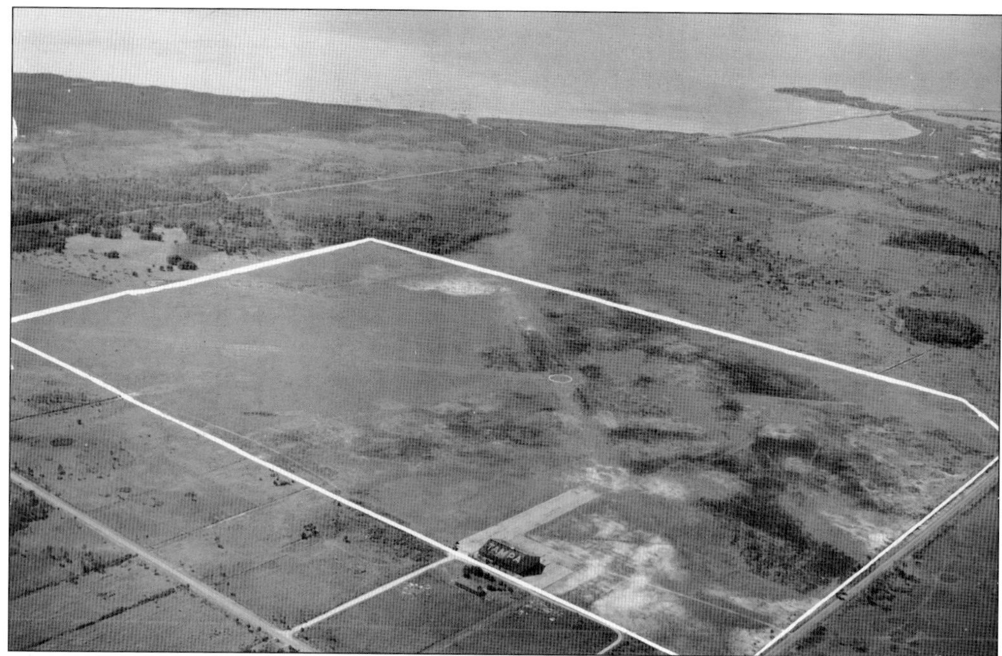

This is Drew Field as seen from the air in 1939. The long, straight road running from left to right toward Rocky Point (upper right) is Columbus Drive, which was known as Michigan Avenue until 1933. The road offered motorists a straight drive from Tampa to Clearwater via the Ben T. Davis Causeway, which was completed in 1934 and had a toll of 25¢ per car. The bridge was renamed in 1948 for Clearwater resident and US congressman Courtney W. Campbell, who led efforts to beautify the causeway connecting the two cities. (Courtesy of the Tampa–Hillsborough County Public Library System.)

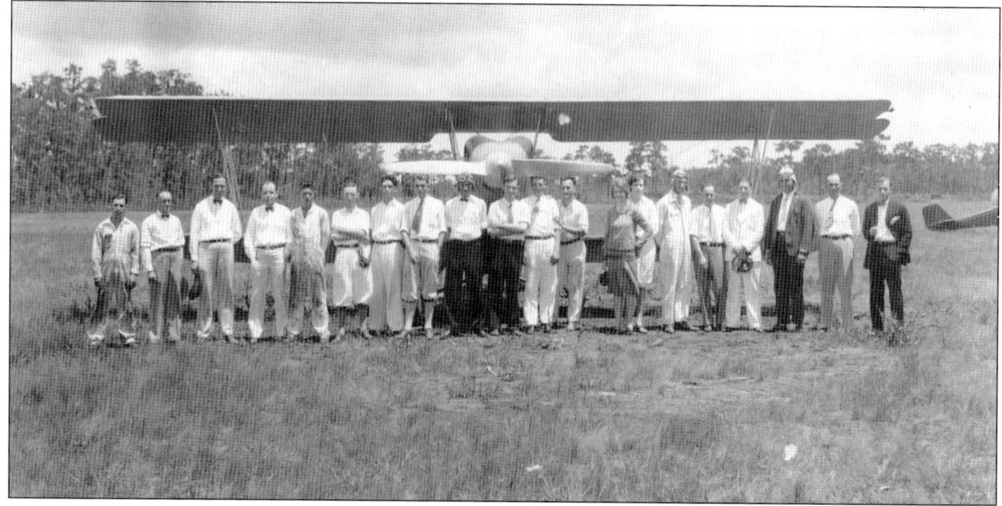

A group from the A.B. McMullen School of Aviation lines up for a photograph at Drew Field on July 16, 1928. Drew Field was establishing itself as a top airport during its first decade of operation, which was fitting given the importance of commercial aviation to the Tampa Bay area. The world's first scheduled commercial passenger air flight occurred when pilot Antony Habersack Jannus flew former St. Petersburg mayor Abram C. Pheil from his city to Tampa in a Benoist XIV plane on January 1, 1914. (Courtesy of the Tampa–Hillsborough County Public Library System.)

Drew Field took on a significant role during World War II, when the US Army Air Corps moved onto the airfield in 1940. The Army converted Drew Field into a military base with barracks, administration buildings, and a prisoner of war camp for Germans. Over the course of the war, some 100,000 combat aircrews were trained at Drew Army Air Field, which served as a subpost to MacDill Army Air Field in South Tampa. This photograph captures Drew Army Air Field as it appeared during its peak of activity in World War II. (Courtesy of Tampa International Airport.)

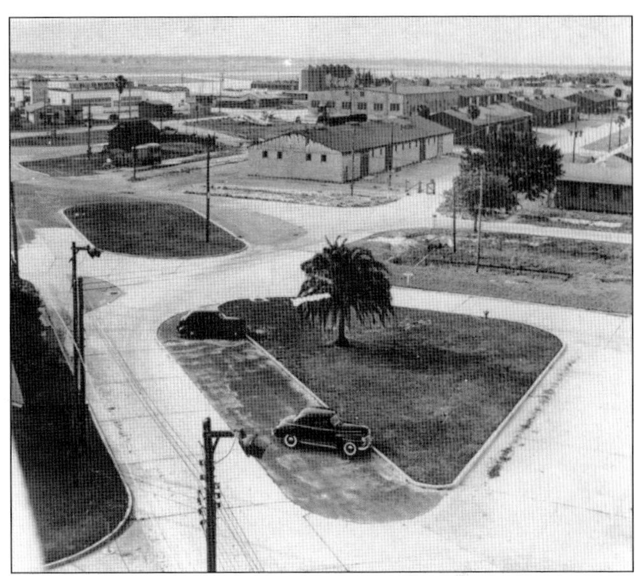

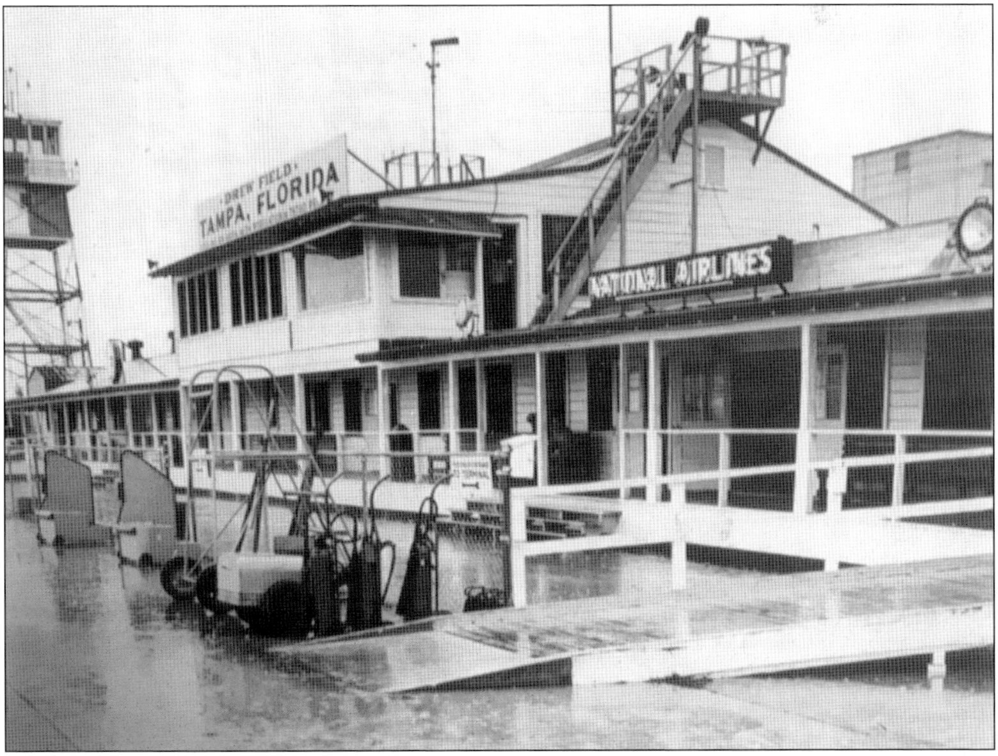

Following the end of World War II, the US government returned Drew Field to the City of Tampa in 1946 as a facility that had received significant upgrades to ensure its viability as a top-flight base for the US Army Third Air Force. Among the many improvements that Drew Field saw was the construction of several permanent buildings, which were well utilized during the airport's return to commercial service. Seen here is the former Drew Army Air Field base operations facility, which was being repurposed in the late 1940s as the main passenger terminal for the municipal airport. (Courtesy of Tampa International Airport.)

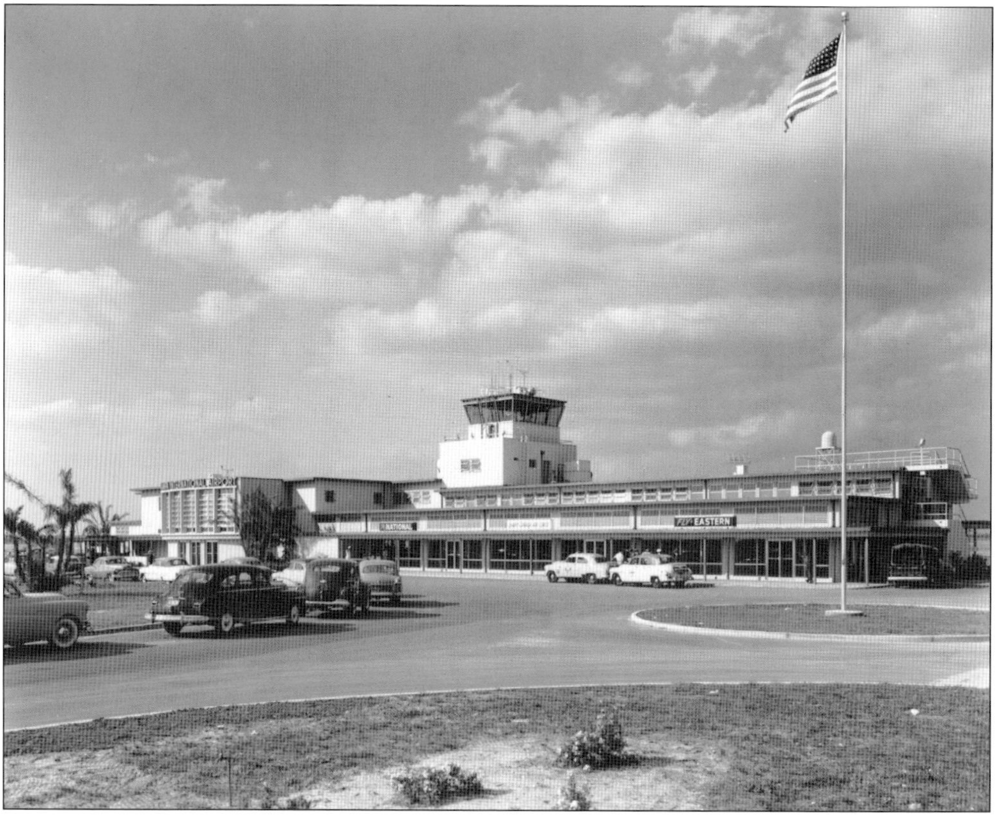

By 1950, Drew Field was fielding flights beyond US borders from Trans-Canada Air Lines, thus prompting the air transit hub to become known as Tampa International Airport. The Hillsborough County Aviation Authority was formed and began preparing the construction of a new passenger terminal that could lure more airlines and handle larger crowds. The new Tampa International Airport, seen above and below, opened on August 17, 1952, at the three-way intersection of what was then West Columbus Drive and North West Shore Boulevard. (Both, courtesy of the Tampa–Hillsborough County Public Library System.)

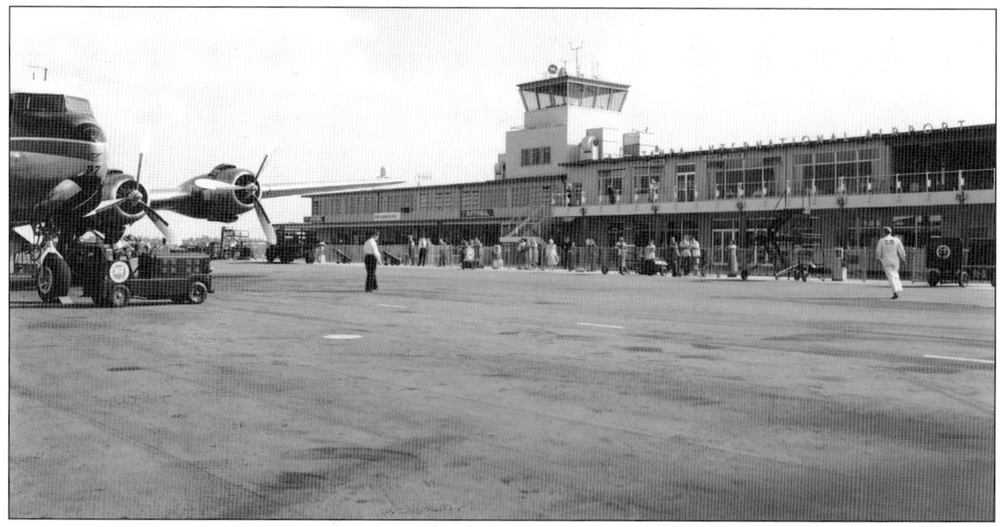

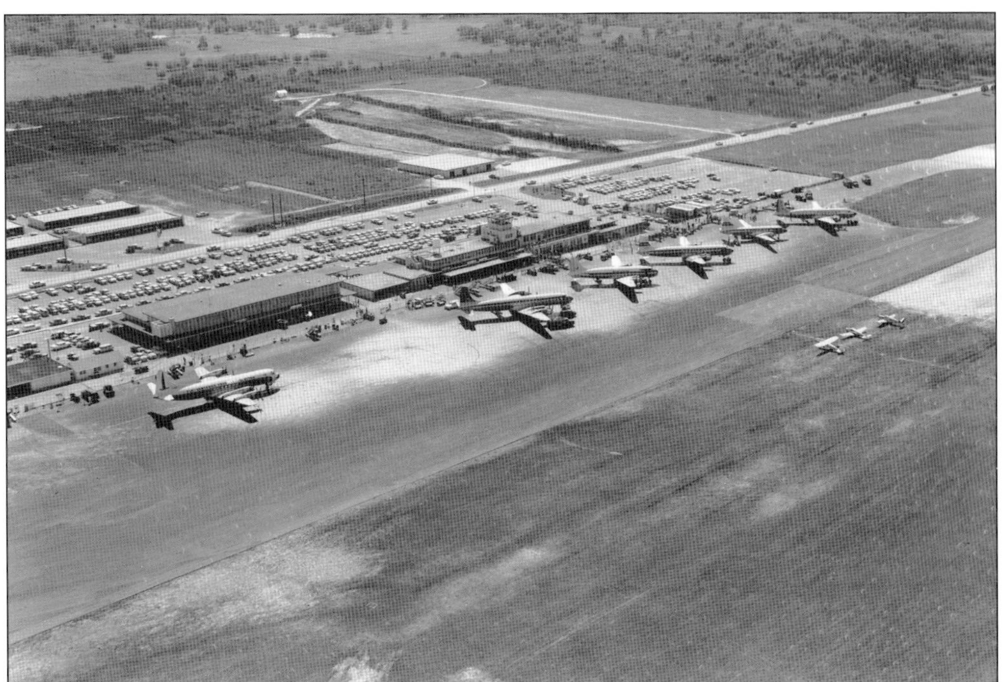

Trans World Airlines brought passenger jet flights to Tampa by the early 1960s, ushering in a wave of more travelers taking bigger, faster airlines. Tampa International Airport quickly proved to be too small for the needs of the booming postwar tourism economy. Above, a parking lot brims with cars while planes line up on the tarmac. Below, an expansion is underway on November 9, 1959, to increase the airport's capacity. As can also be seen, the corridor for Columbus Drive west of North West Shore Boulevard was cut off by the project, permanently diverting the arterial flow of motor traffic farther south of the airport. (Both, courtesy of the Tampa–Hillsborough County Public Library System.)

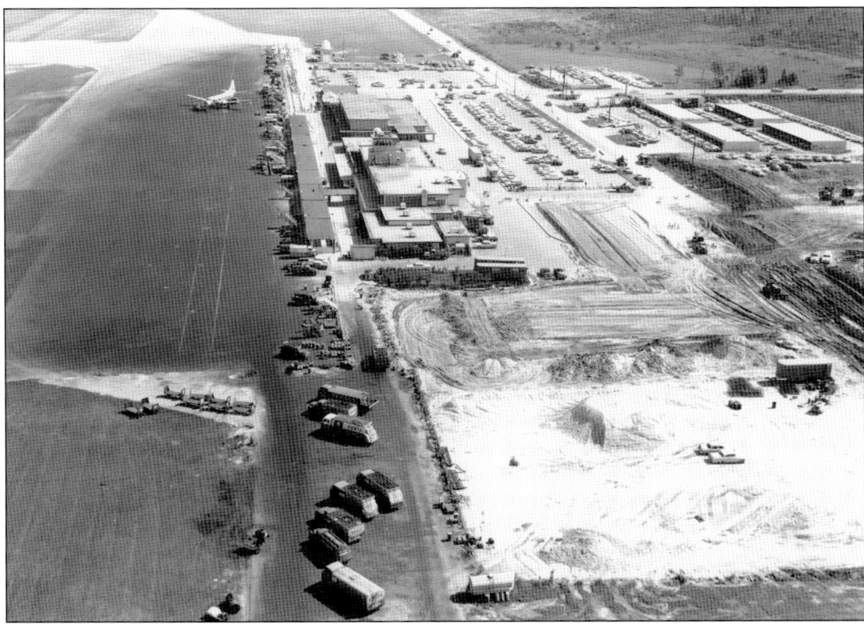

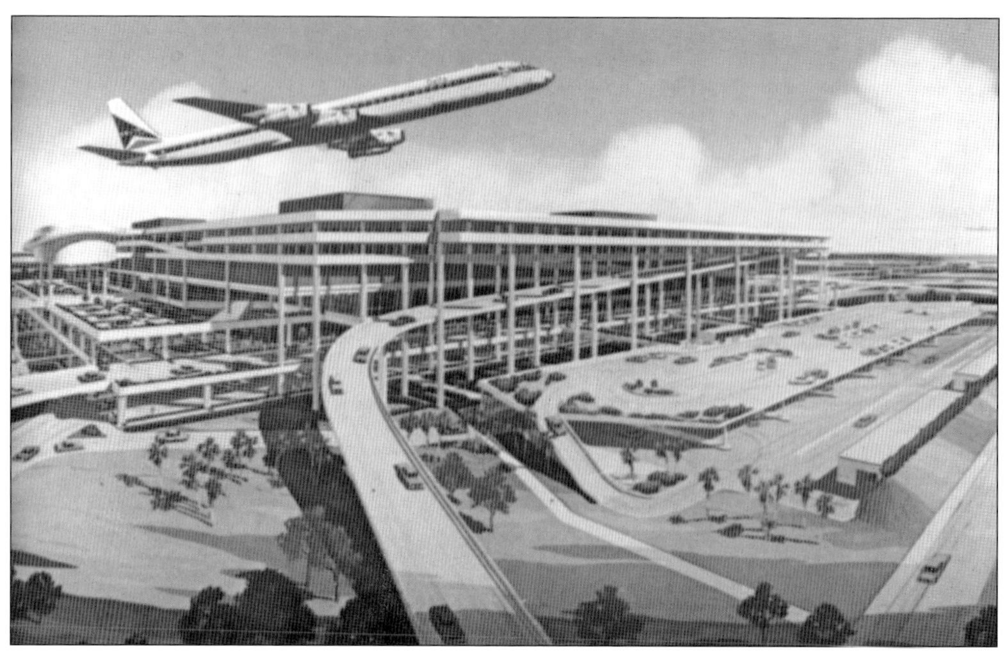

Make-do expansions on the vintage-1952 Tampa International Airport facility never seemed sufficient for increasing traffic at the airport. By the early 1960s, the Hillsborough County Aviation Authority began planning a futuristic Tampa International Airport (above) capable of handling more passengers and ever-larger jet planes. Construction began on the new airport in 1968. Below in the background, construction crews build the current Tampa International Airport facility in 1970 while business snugly carries on at the 1952 terminal in the foreground. (Both, courtesy of Tampa International Airport.)

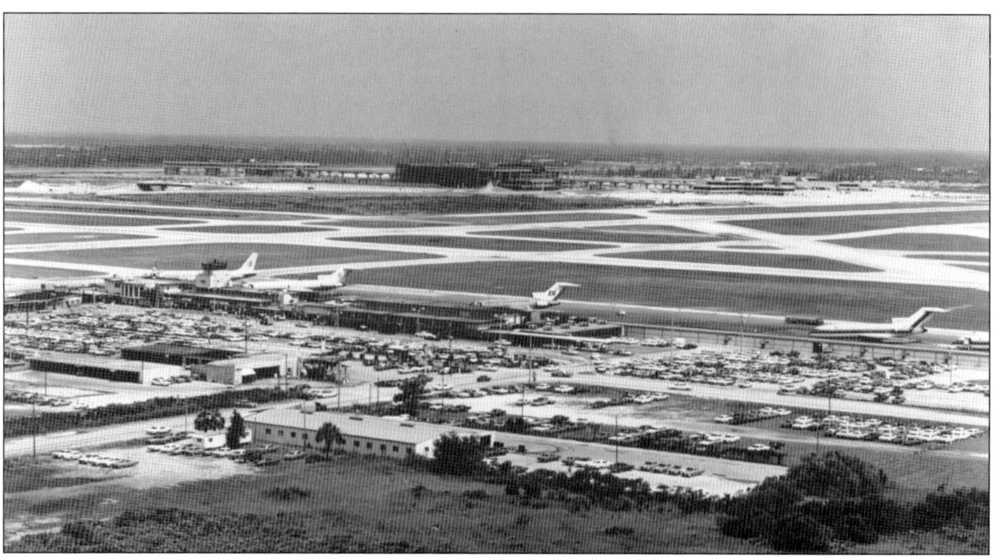

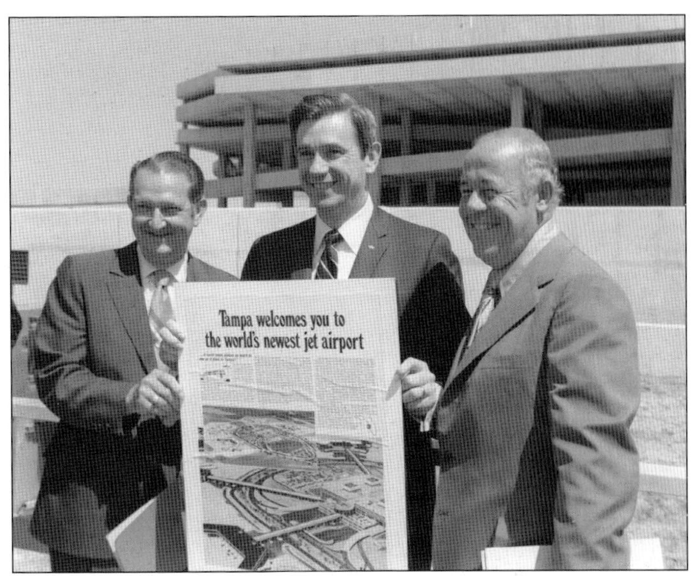

After years of anticipation, planning, and construction, the new Tampa International Airport was dedicated on April 15, 1971. Among the festivities were appearances by many dignitaries, including Florida governor Reuben Askew (center), joined here by Tampa International Airport manager Stewart D. Mast (left) and Hillsborough County Aviation Authority director George J. Bean (right). (Courtesy of Tampa International Airport.)

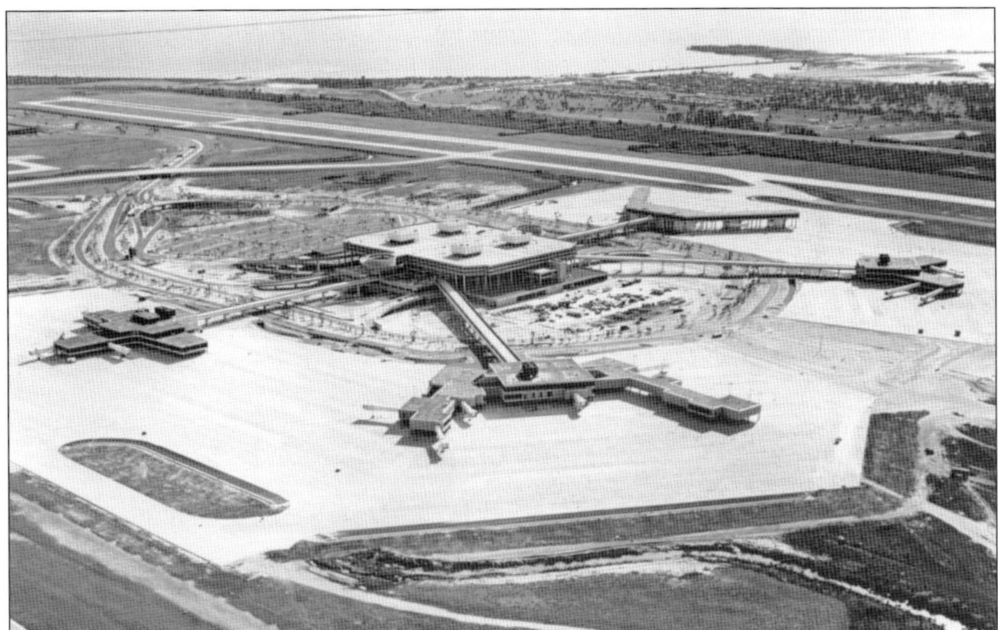

The $80-million Tampa International Airport broke new ground with its hub-and-spoke design, with satellite airside terminals each connected to the central landside terminal by way of electric train, which was a first for any airport in the world. With the addition of parking decks atop the central terminal and convenient curbside pickup locations, typical travelers would never need to walk more than a few hundred feet between a car and their plane. The landside terminal and its four original airside terminals are seen in this 1971 photograph, which also captures Rocky Point and Dana Shores in the upper right corner. (Courtesy of Tampa International Airport.)

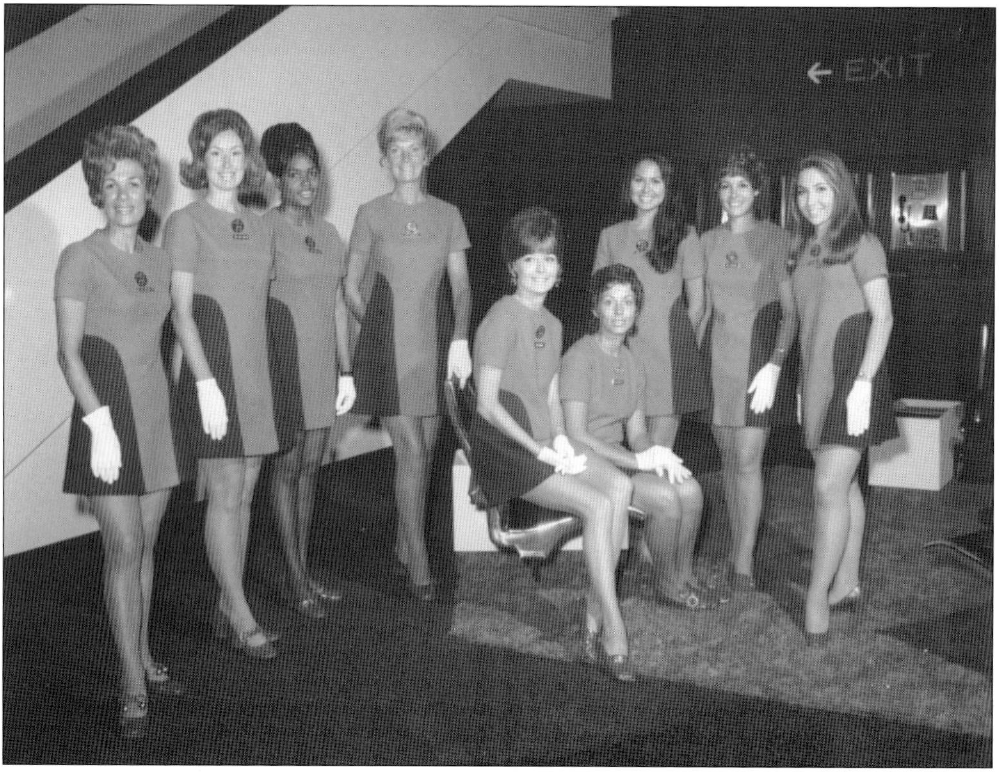

The new Tampa International Airport became a world unto itself, with more spaces and places than travelers of the time were accustomed to seeing. Tour guides (above) and information desks (below) helped tourists—and locals picking up and dropping off friends and loved ones—navigate their way around the airport. The revolutionary airport drew praise from many, including *Esquire* magazine, which in 1976 named it the "best in America." (Both, courtesy of Tampa International Airport.)

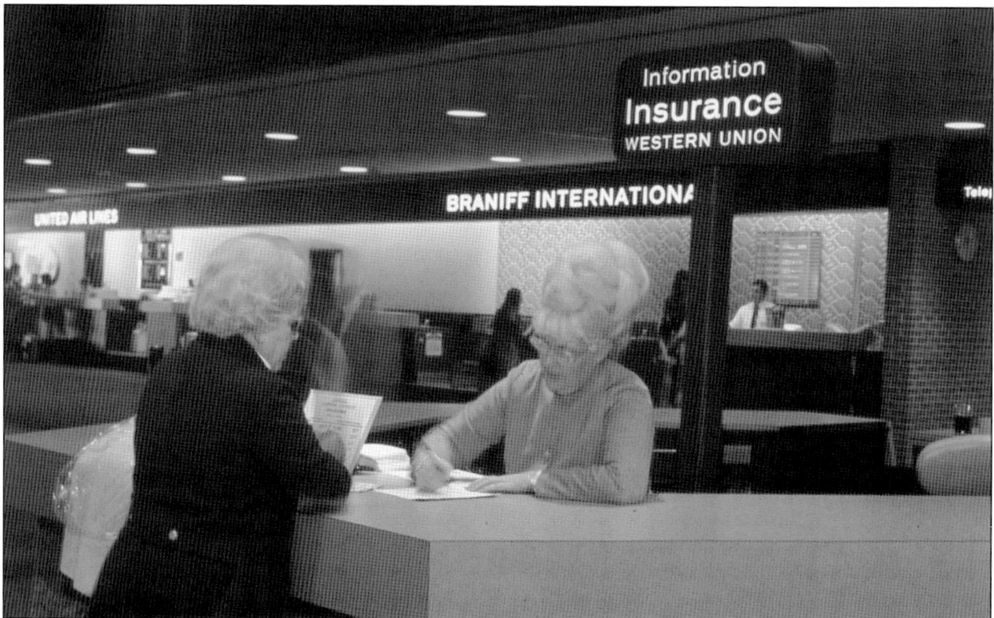

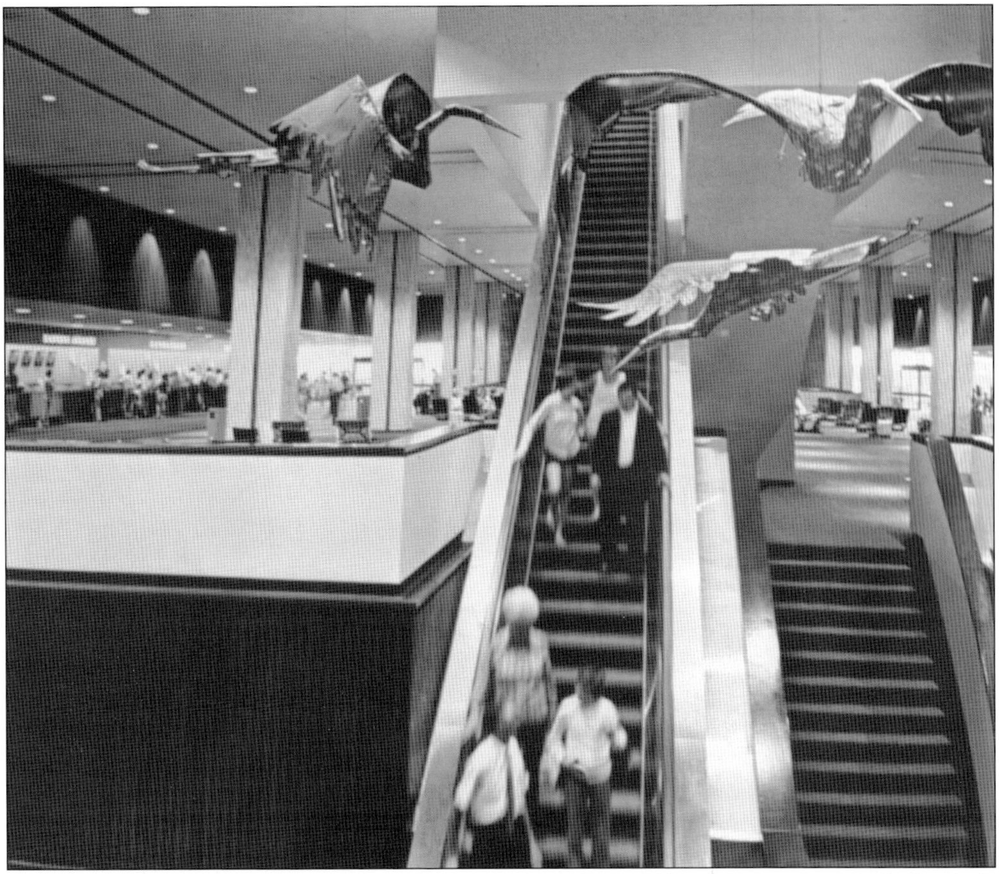

One of the missions at Tampa International Airport is to keep walking to a minimum. The landside terminal and any airside terminals with multiple levels are served with banks of escalators (above) and elevators (below) to help ensure everybody can get where they need to go without breaking a sweat. (Both, courtesy of Tampa International Airport.)

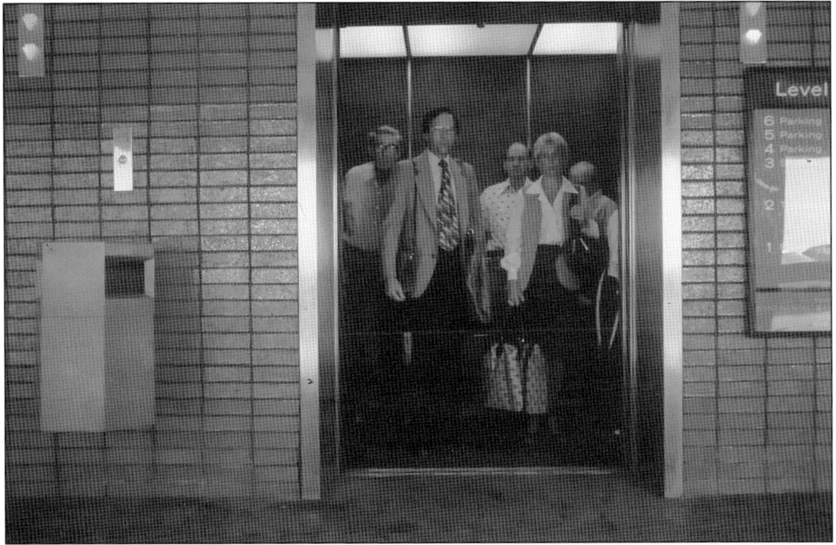

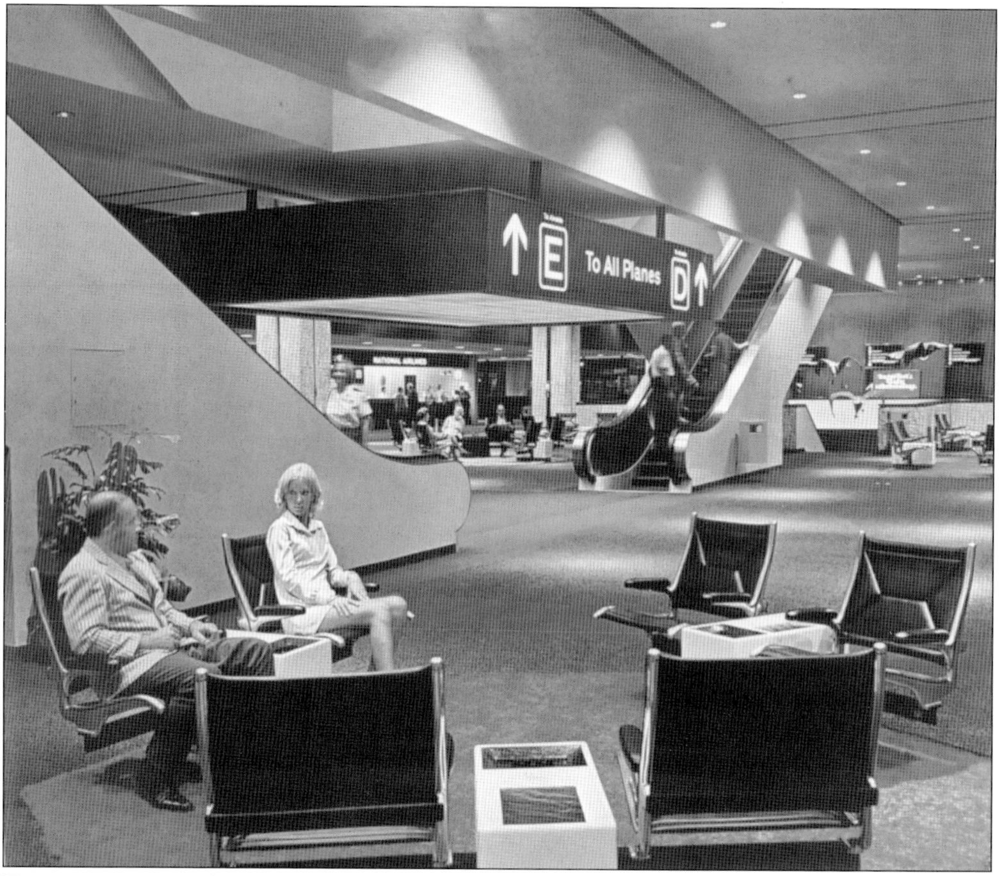

Tampa International Airport's mission is not just about hustling travelers from landside to airside (or vice versa). There are many important reasons Tampa International Airport has long ranked among the most popular airports in the United States. Among these factors is a plethora of amenities aimed at making Tampa International Airport a destination itself. Travelers can rest in comfort when they need a moment to catch a breath (above), ticketing and luggage counters are spacious (below), and there are plenty of things to do while waiting for flights. (Both, courtesy of Tampa International Airport.)

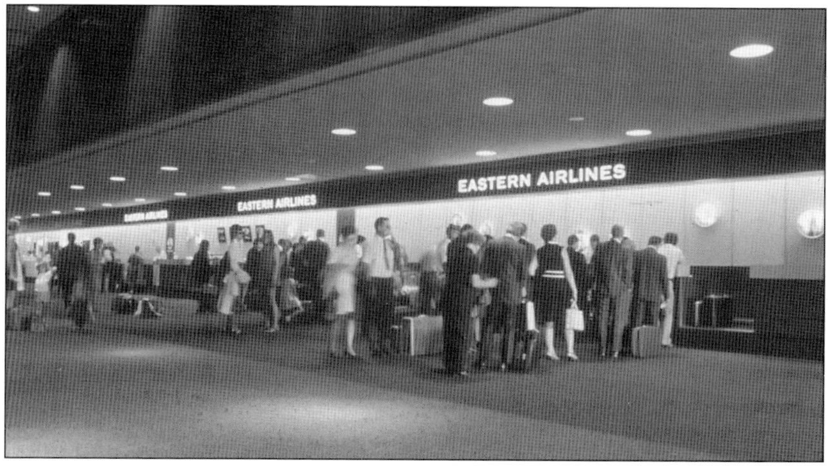

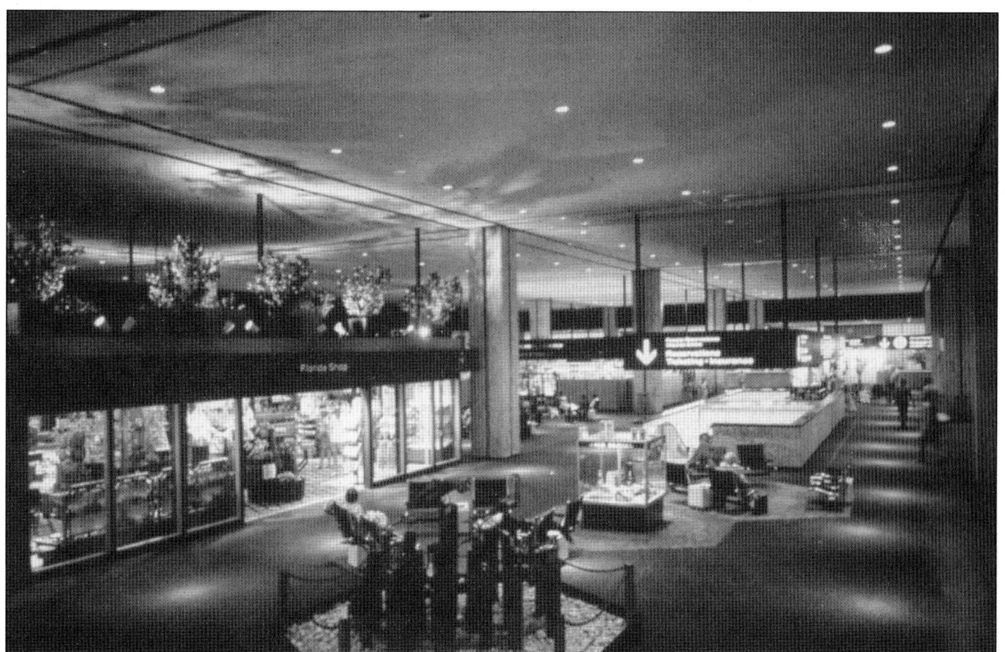

The landside terminal has always boasted an abundance of cafés and shops, as seen in this 1971 photograph. The Florida Shop was a traveler favorite for many years, offering everything from camera film and postcards to snacks and sundries. Duty-free stores, cafeterias, and lounges were also fixtures in the landside terminal. (Courtesy of Tampa International Airport.)

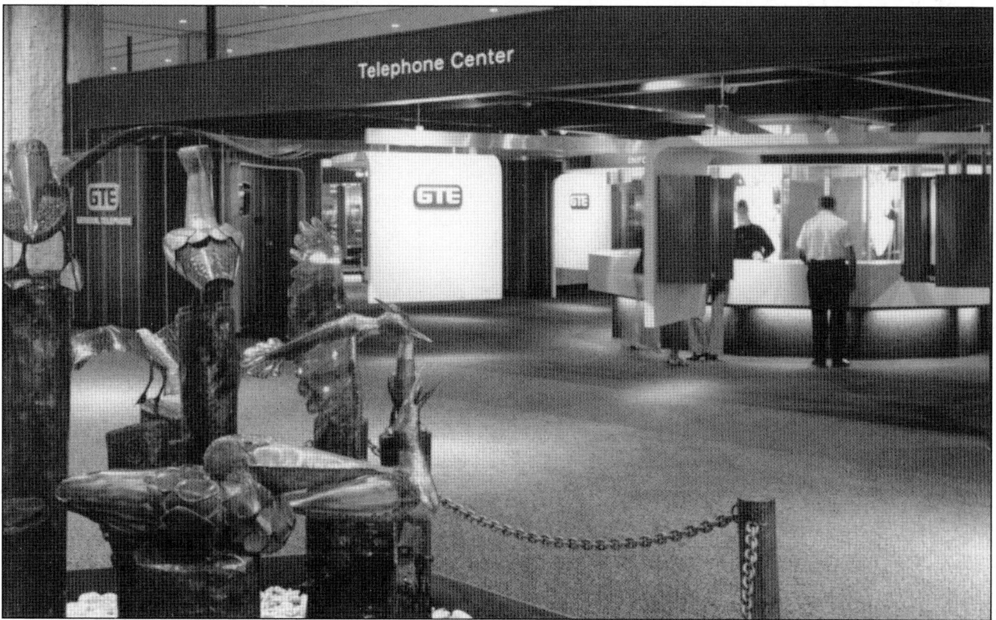

Before cellular phones emerged in the mid-1980s, using pay phones was about the only way a typical traveler could place a call on the go. Tampa International Airport made reaching out and touching someone as convenient as possible for the time with its expansive pay phone center, offering plenty of telephones operated by General Telephone and Electronics Corporation (GTE). (Courtesy of Tampa International Airport.)

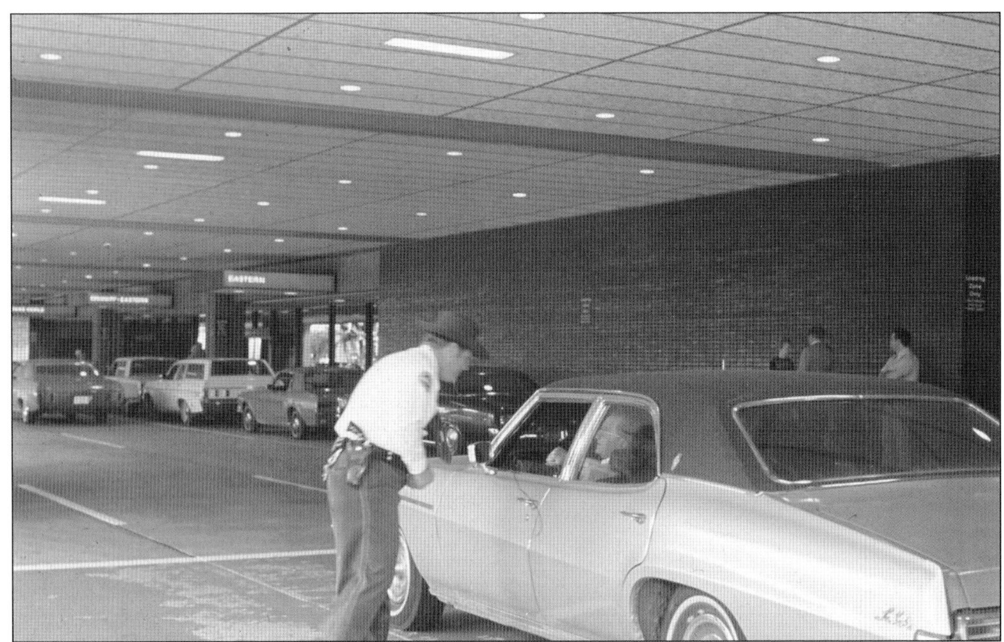

Operating an airport involves so much more than selling tickets and flying planes. It takes a team to make a place like Tampa International Airport function efficiently. The airport has a crew of thousands who work together to make sure everyone stays happy and safe. Above, a Tampa International Airport Police officer assists a driver, while the Tampa International Airport Fire Department (below) is poised to help in an emergency. (Both, courtesy of Tampa International Airport.)

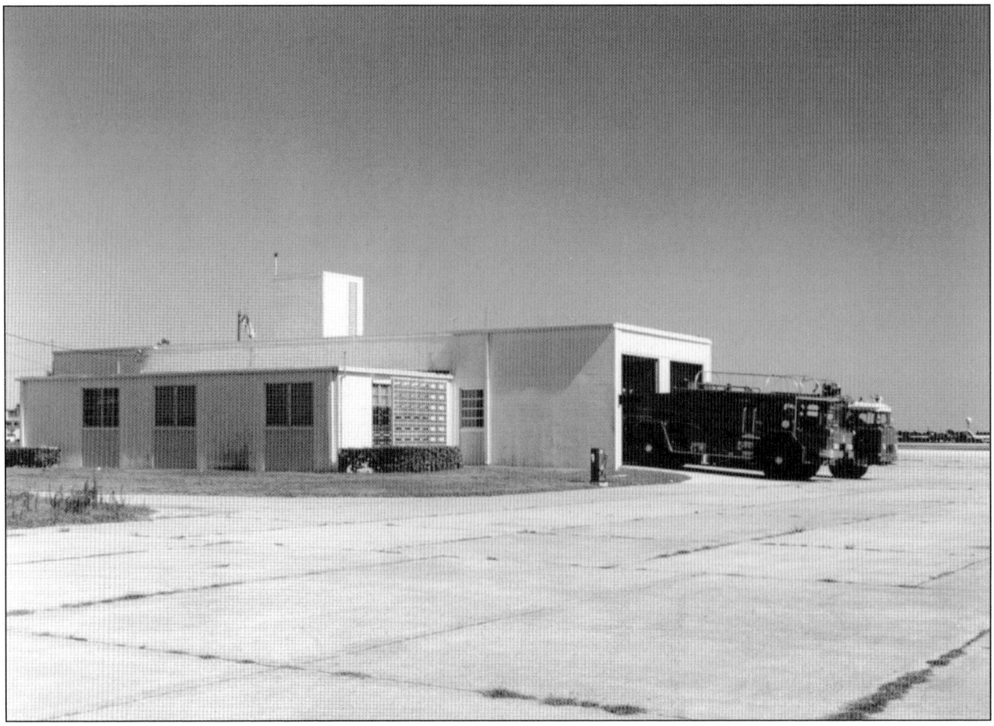

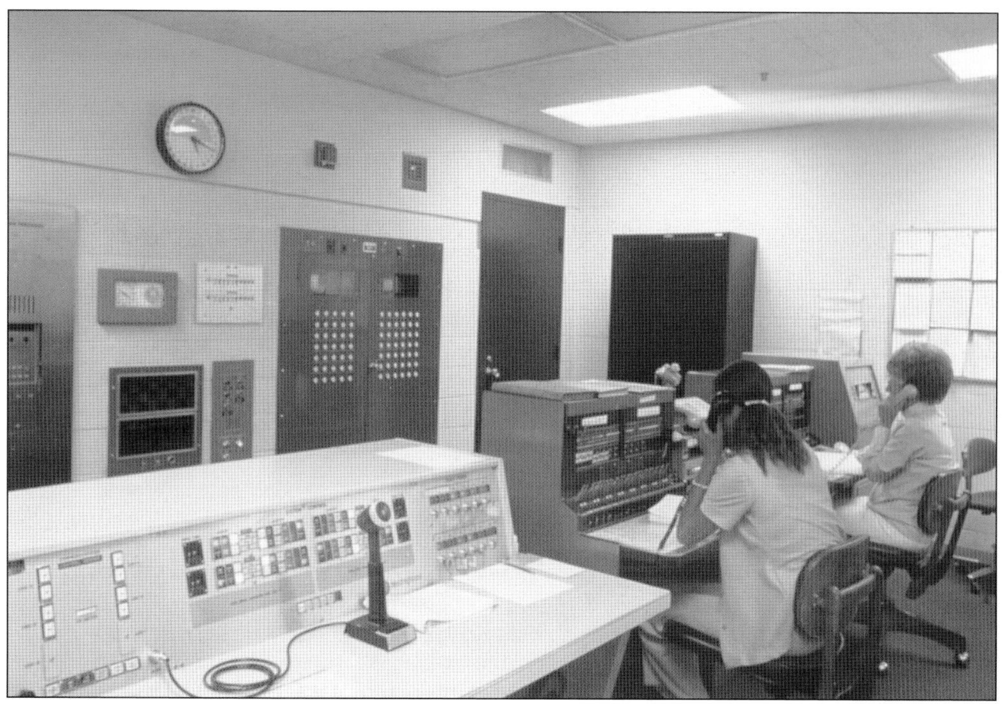

The Tampa International Airport communications team (above) handles everything from telephone calls to public announcements. Meanwhile, the luggage crew works around the clock to make sure bags, suitcases, and freight are securely moved between the landside and airside terminals. (Both, courtesy of Tampa International Airport.)

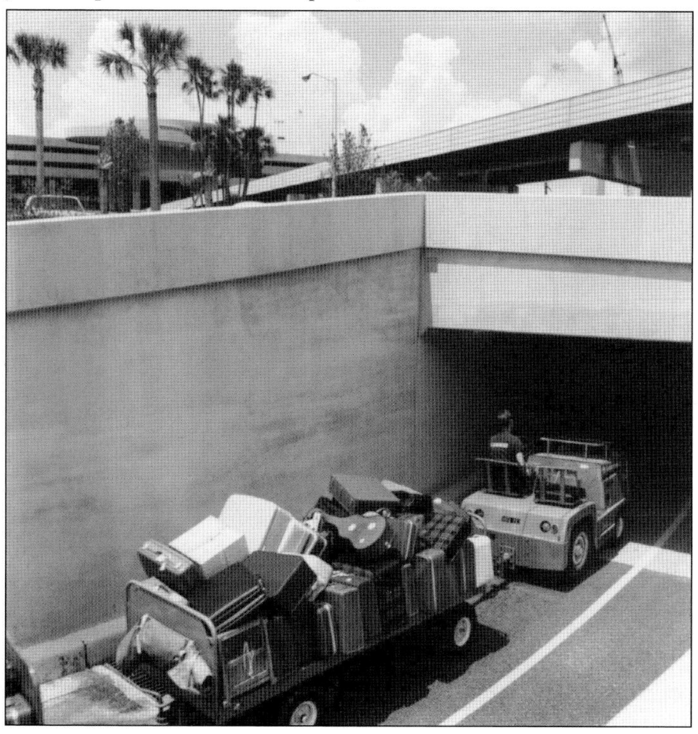

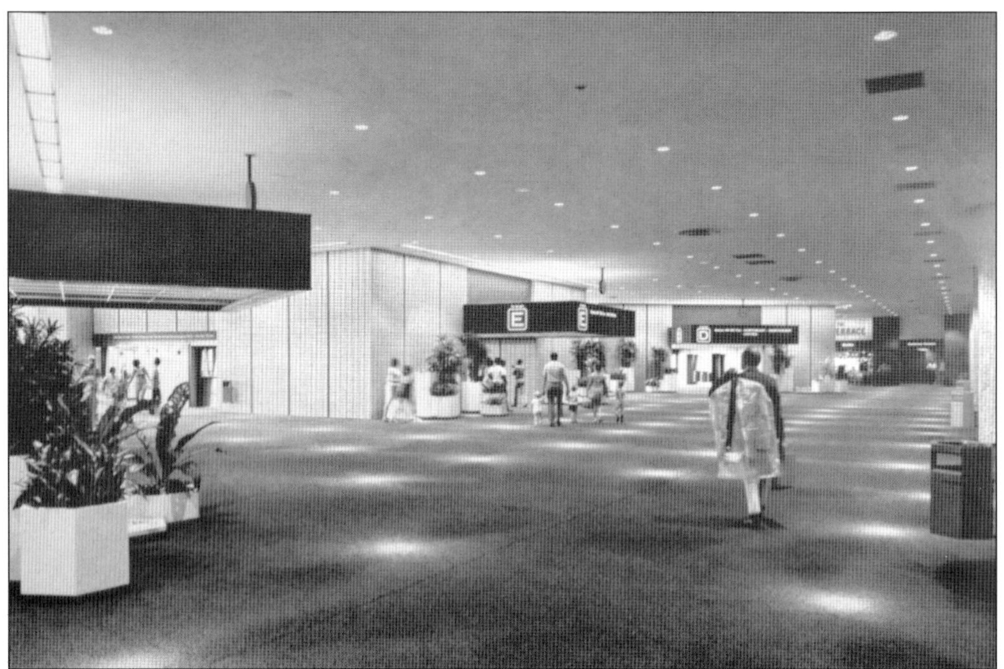

Tickets are in hand and baggage has been checked, so now it is time to hop aboard the people mover to take a ride from the landside terminal to an airside terminal. This 1971 photograph shows people getting ready to board a people mover bound for Airside E. (Courtesy of Tampa International Airport.)

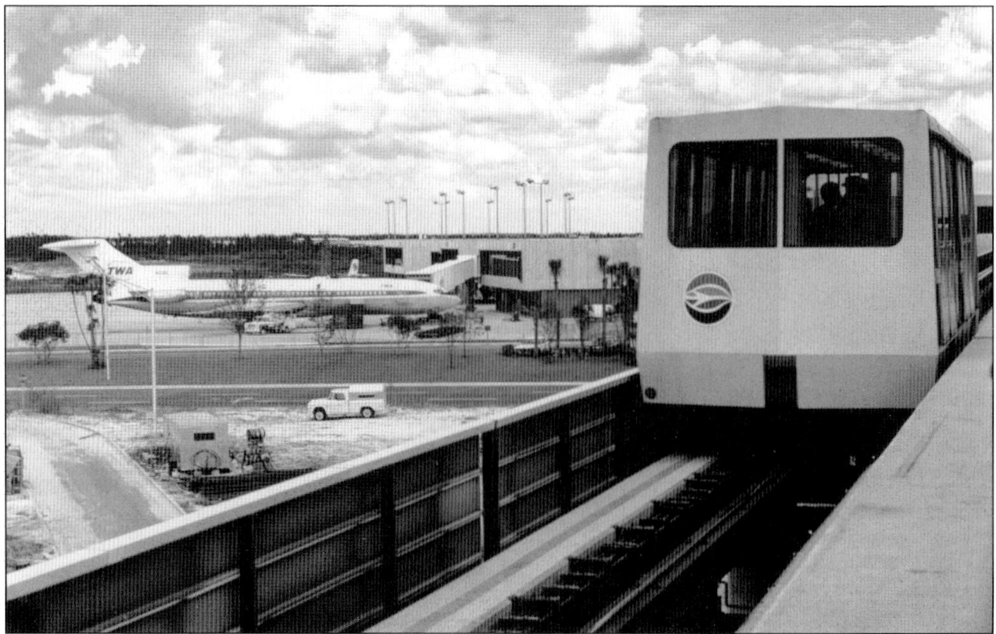

An airline trip to or from Tampa International Airport means a ride on the people mover, which is a vital part of what makes traveling through this Tampa transportation hub so easy. Rain or shine, the people mover will help get travelers to the plane on time. (Courtesy of Tampa International Airport.)

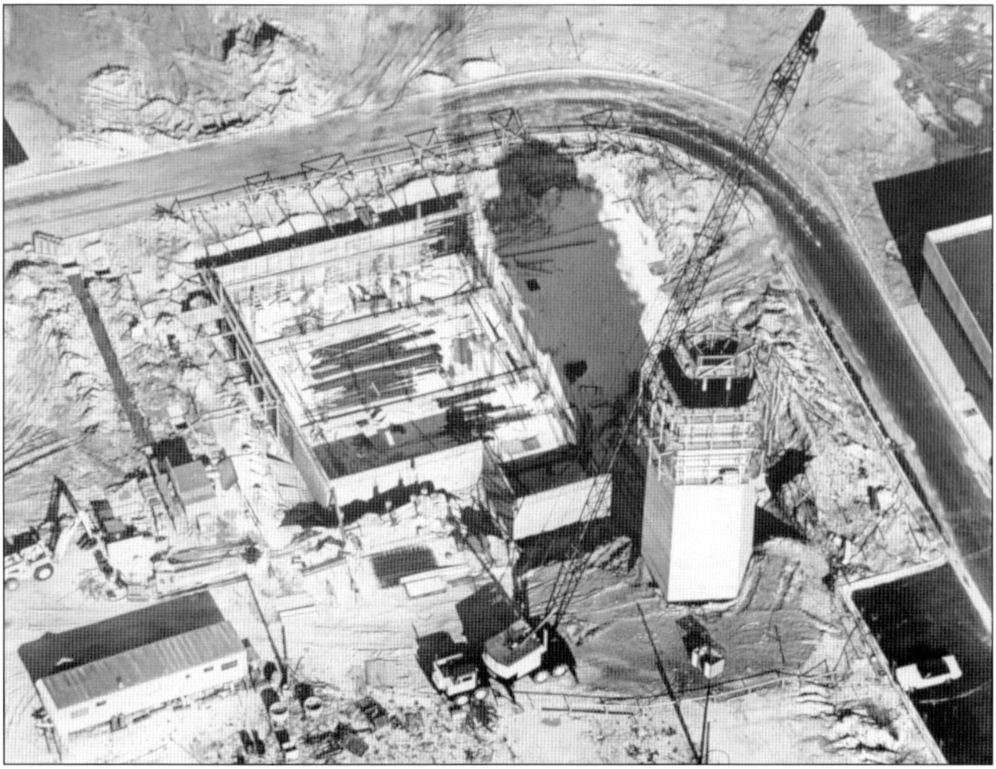

Construction crews have never been bored at Tampa International Airport, dating back to at least the days of the 1952 terminal. In this 1972 photograph, workers construct the air traffic control tower, which would stand more than 200 feet high beside a hotel and its revolving rooftop restaurant, also under construction here. (Courtesy of Tampa International Airport.)

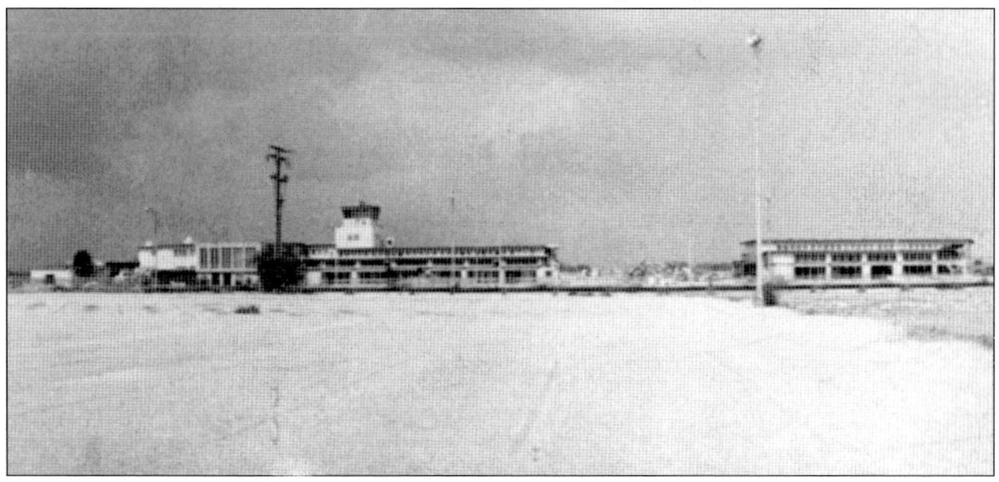

The 1952 terminal was vacated by planes and passengers with the opening of the current airport in 1971. But the decades-old building seen here did not stand empty for long. It served a function as the temporary home for Hillsborough Community College. After the school left for its permanent campus about a mile to the northeast, the terminal was razed, as seen in this November 1975 photograph. In 1981, the site of the old airport was redeveloped as a private airport. (© Fraser Hale/*Tampa Bay Times* via ZUMA Wire.)

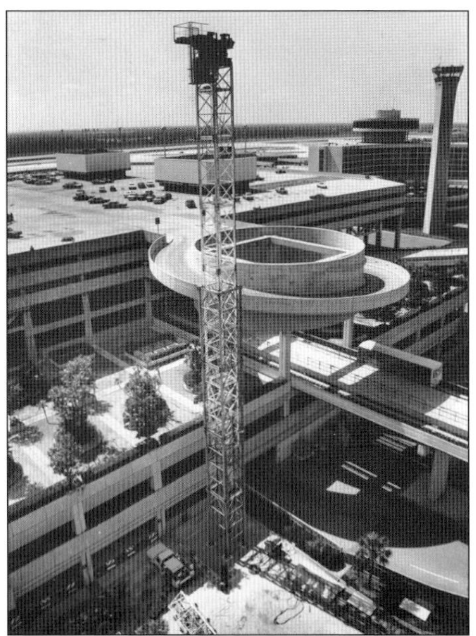

The new Tampa International Airport closed out its first decade of service on a note of expansion. In this May 15, 1981, photograph, crews erect a crane that will help construct more parking decks atop the landside terminal to add thousands of new parking spaces for the airport. (© *Tampa Bay Times* via ZUMA Press.)

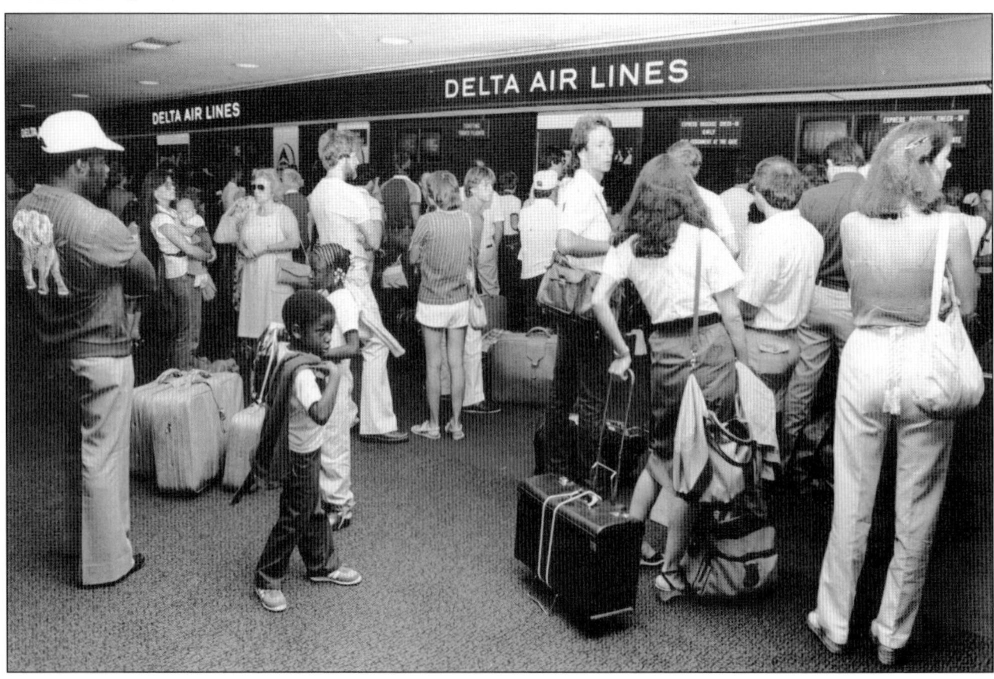

Antsy passengers wait in long lines at the ticketing counter in this June 21, 1981, photograph as tensions rise between air traffic controllers and the US government. When negotiations between the Professional Air Traffic Controllers Organization (PATCO) and the Federal Aviation Administration failed to materialize, the vast majority of the union employees declared a strike with hopes of improved working conditions and better pay. The government ordered the striking PATCO employees to return to their duties, but they maintained their position. Following a 48-hour standoff, Pres. Ronald Reagan fired the more than 11,000 PATCO strikers who refused to return to their jobs, severely hindering the flow of air travel in the United States for some time. (© *Tampa Bay Times* via ZUMA Press.)

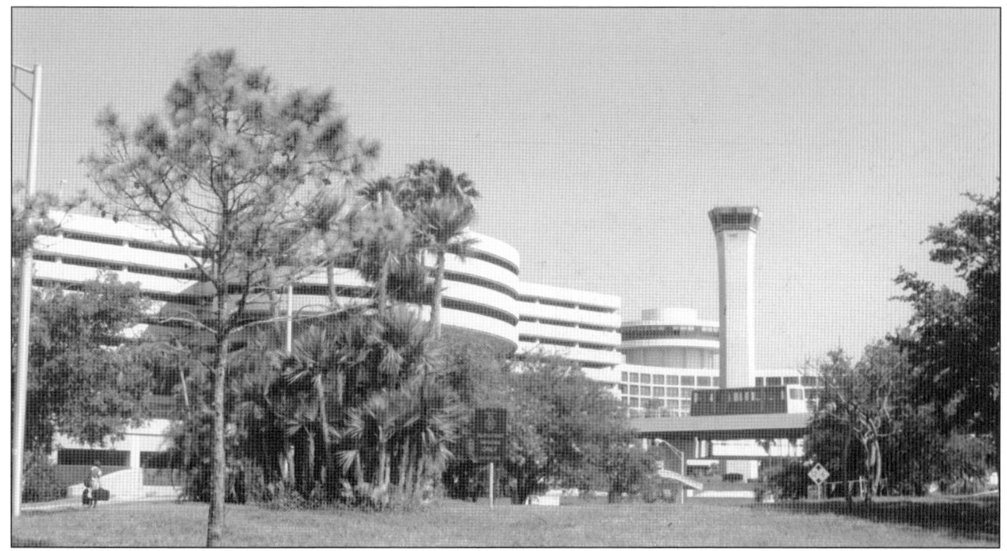

As the 1980s rolled on, Tampa International Airport firmly positioned itself as one of the nation's leading airports. By the closing decades of the 20th century, air travel was no longer restricted to only the wealthy. It had become a normal mode of transportation for everyone from young Tampa Bay area families going on a trip to see grandparents in New England to Central Florida executives needing to give a business presentation in Europe. (Courtesy of the University of South Florida Special Collections Department.)

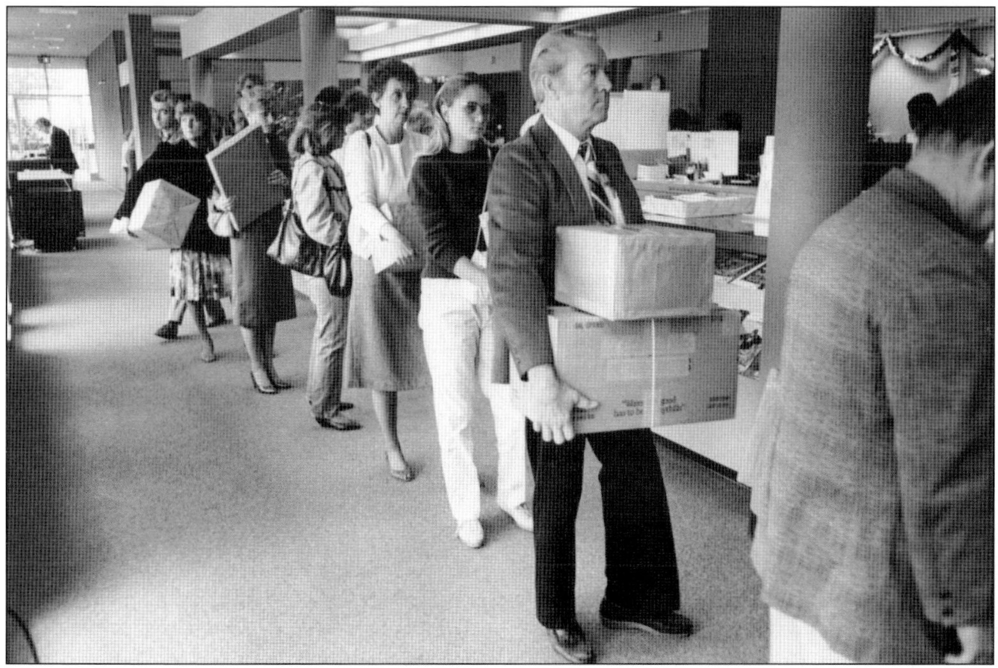

Customers wait in line on December 17, 1985, to drop off holiday packages and greeting cards at the US Postal Service (USPS) station at Tampa International Airport. Serving as the main USPS office in Tampa, the airport's post office has bustled with activity since opening its doors in 1975. (© *Tampa Bay Times* via ZUMA Press.)

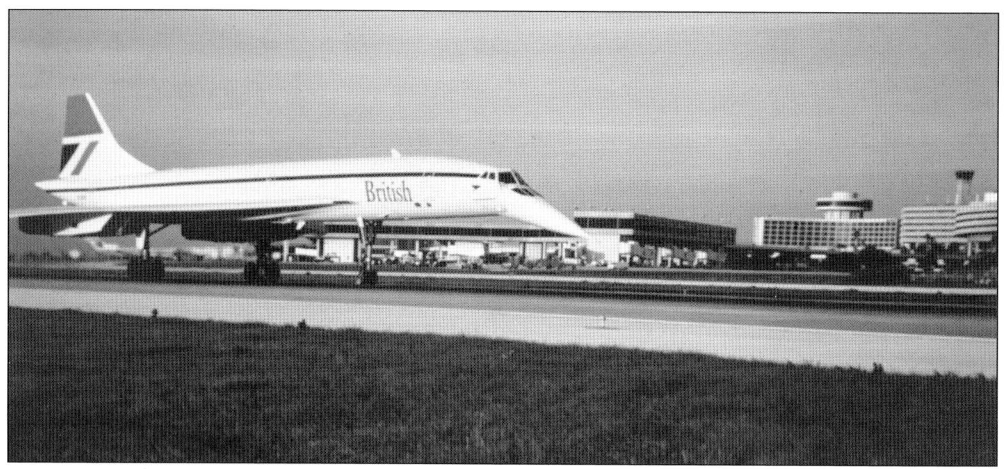

Tampa International Airport moved to the supersonic age on March 30, 1985, upon its first visit by the Concorde, a jet airliner capable of whisking passengers from New York City to London in fewer than three hours. The British Airways Concorde jet seen here flew at speeds averaging 1,250 miles per hour, otherwise measured as nearly Mach 2, or about twice the speed of sound. (Courtesy of Tampa International Airport.)

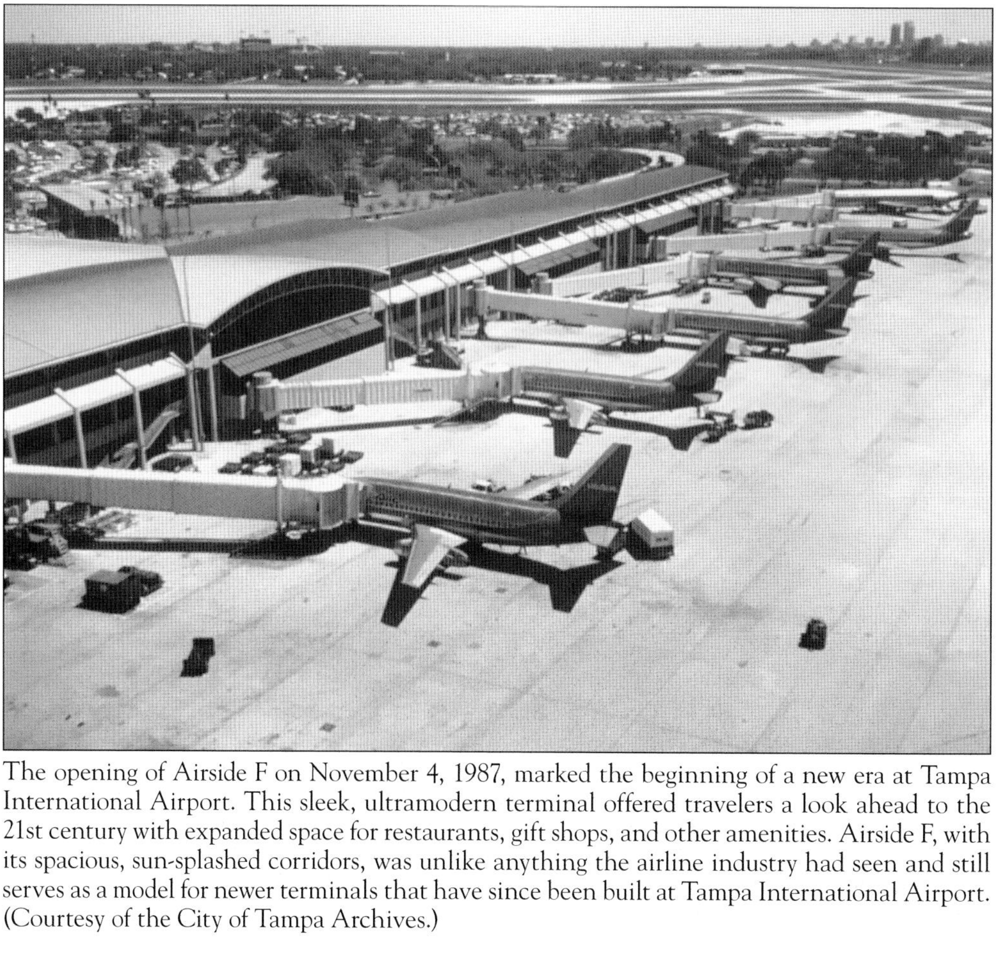

The opening of Airside F on November 4, 1987, marked the beginning of a new era at Tampa International Airport. This sleek, ultramodern terminal offered travelers a look ahead to the 21st century with expanded space for restaurants, gift shops, and other amenities. Airside F, with its spacious, sun-splashed corridors, was unlike anything the airline industry had seen and still serves as a model for newer terminals that have since been built at Tampa International Airport. (Courtesy of the City of Tampa Archives.)

Seven

In the Community

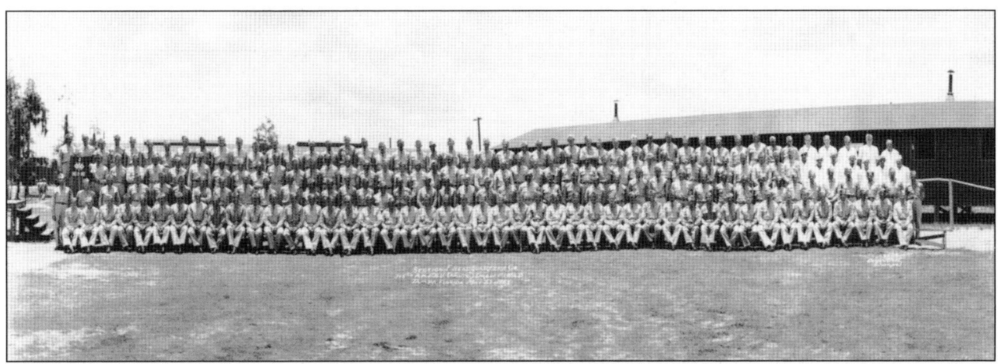

Seen here are troops from the 315th Army Air Force Base Unit at Drew Army Air Field on May 27, 1944. They were among the tens of thousands who came through the Westshore military installation to prepare for battle in various theaters of World War II, which would come to an end the following year. (Courtesy of the Tampa–Hillsborough County Public Library System.)

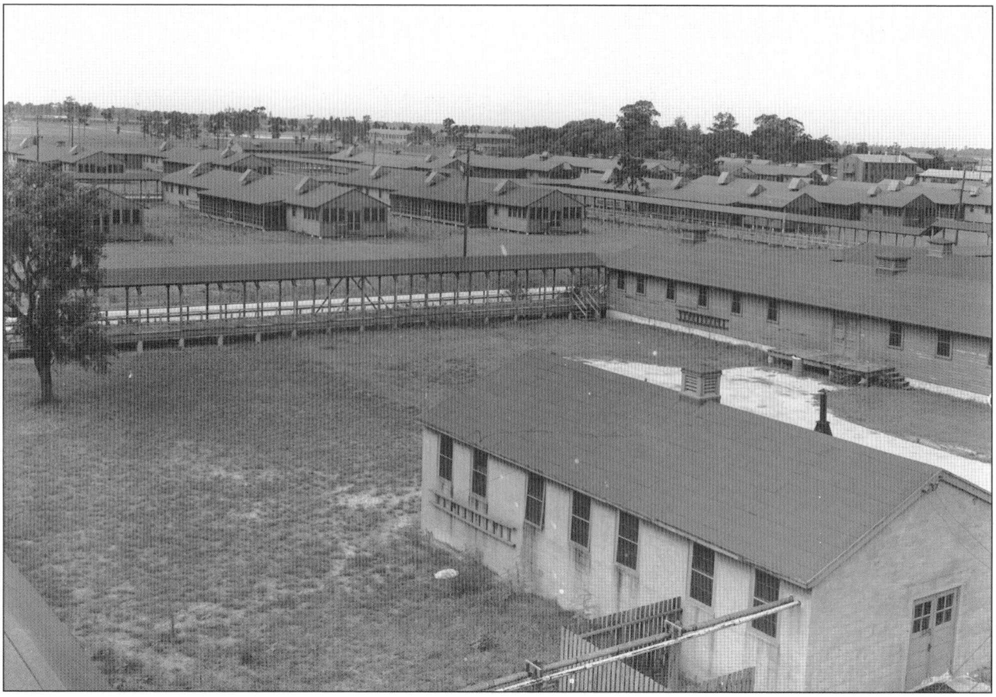

Thousands of individuals lived at Drew Field during their military tours there. Above is a sweeping view of the many barracks that were built to house the troops while they were in Tampa. Below is the Tampa Army Reserve Training Center at the southwest corner of Lois Avenue and South Avenue in Drew Park, as seen on November 14, 1956. (Both, courtesy of the Tampa–Hillsborough County Public Library System.)

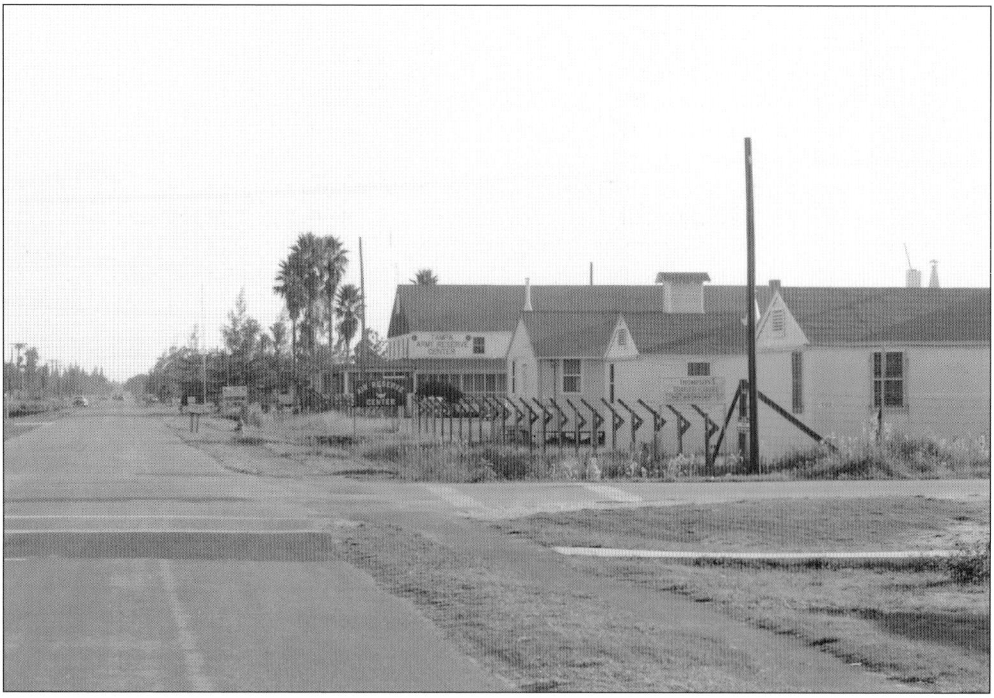

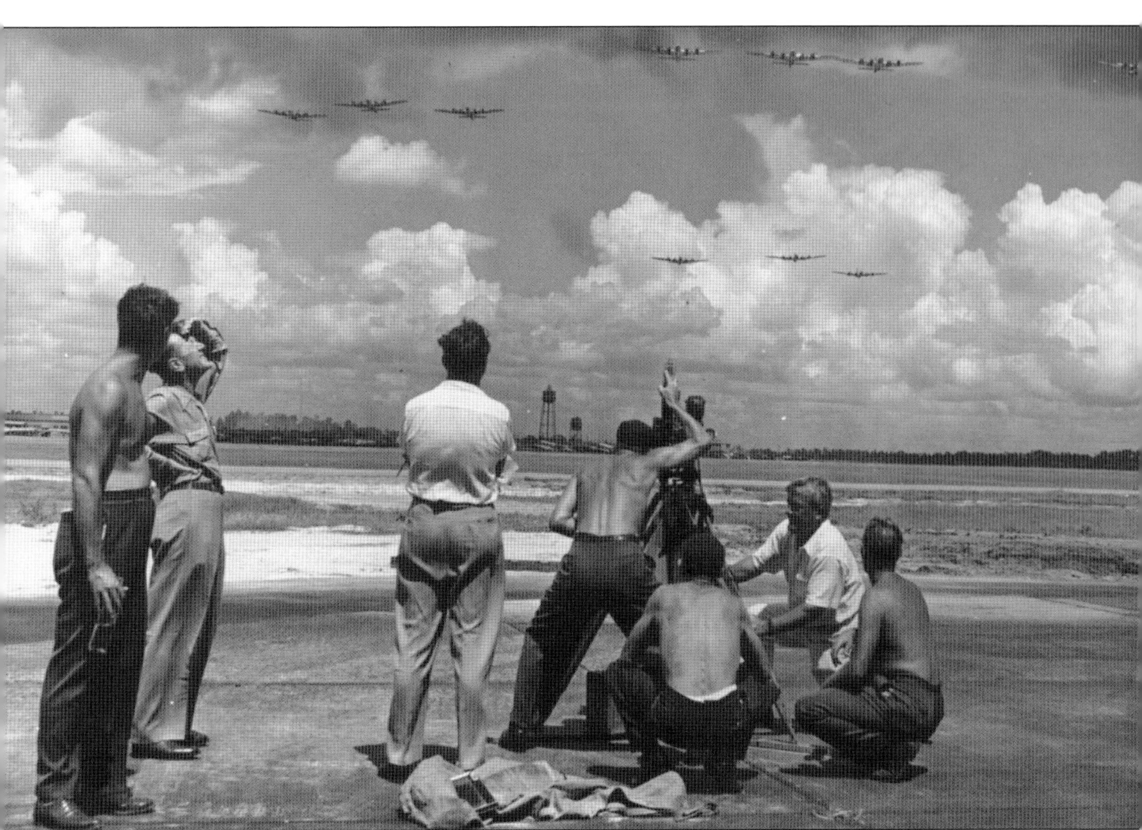

The critically acclaimed 1943 World War II film *Air Force* was partly filmed in Tampa at Drew Army Air Field, as seen here. The movie, starring John Ridgely, George Tobias, John Garfield, and Faye Emerson, tells the high-flying story of a US Army Air Corps B-17 Flying Fortress bomber crew that takes to the skies for thrilling action in the turbulent Pacific theater of World War II. Production of the movie occurred in 1942, with Drew Army Air Field setting the stage for the filming of many aerial scenes during the summer of that year, as seen in this photograph. The 124-minute Warner Bros. feature film was released on February 3, 1943, during the height of World War II, and drew sensational reviews, with *New York Times* film critic Bosley Crowther naming it among the "Ten Best Films of 1943." The movie, one of the top-grossing films of the year, earned multiple Oscar nominations and scored the Academy Award for Best Film Editing. (Courtesy of the University of South Florida Special Collections Department and licensed by Warner Bros. Entertainment, Inc. All Rights Reserved.)

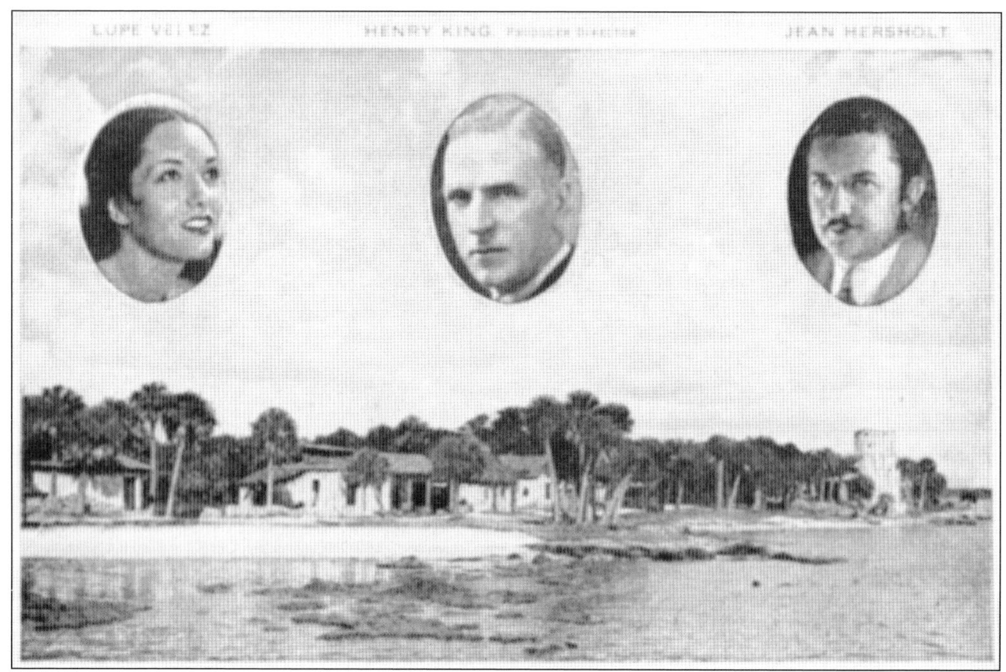

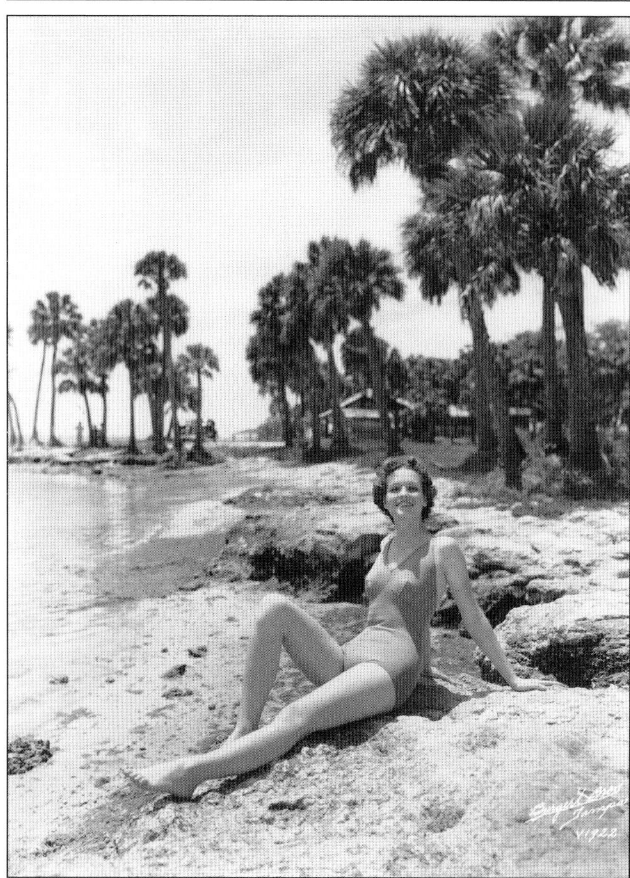

Hell Harbor is a 1930 film about a young woman living in the Caribbean who falls in love with a visiting American and dreams of moving to Havana with him. The movie was shot on Rocky Point, where elaborate sets were constructed to create the film's tropical locale. The film was produced and directed by Henry King and starred some of the leading actors of the day, as depicted on this commemorative card, including Lupe Velez and Jean Hersholt. (Courtesy of the Bell family.)

The picturesque landscape of Rocky Point was more than just a popular place for shooting feature films. It was also an ideal location for taking glamor shots. Alice Robles, a descendant of the local pioneer family, is seen in this 1938 image posing by the palms on Rocky Point. (Courtesy of the Tampa–Hillsborough County Public Library System.)

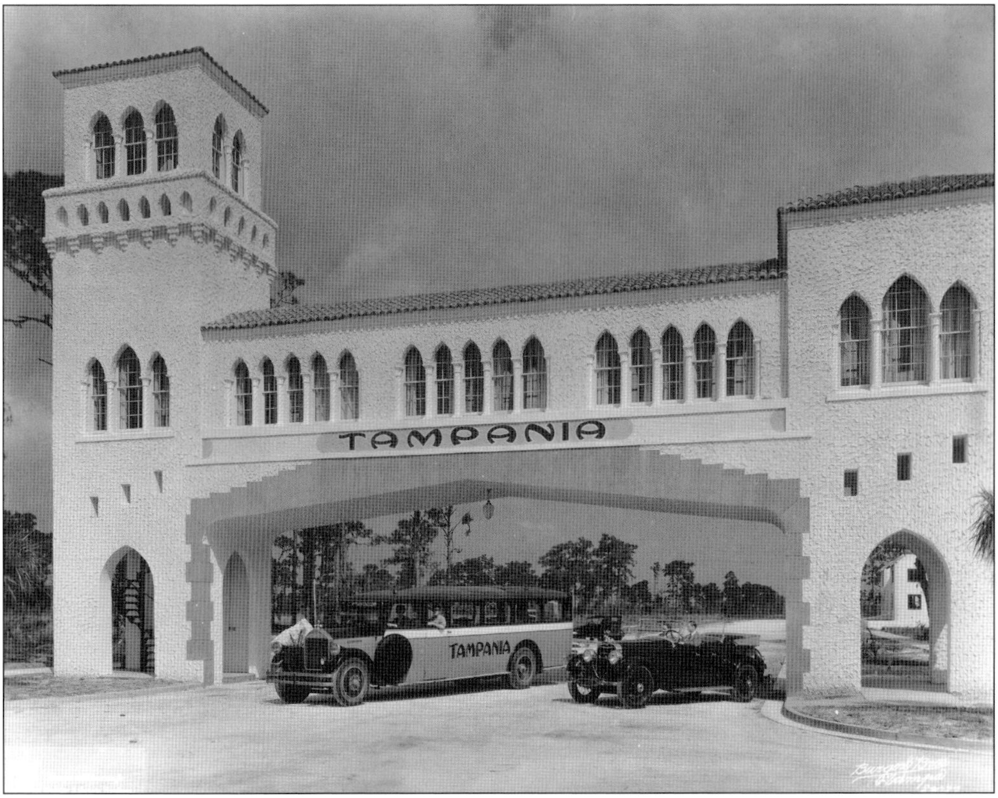

The Tampania neighborhood was one of the first major subdivisions in the Westshore community. The upper image shows the ornate, Mediterranean-style entrance gate that spanned over modern-day North West Shore Boulevard at the location of West North A Street. Below is a panoramic view of some of the many beautiful homes in the community, which was first developed in the mid-1920s. Many of these homes still stand today. (Both, courtesy of the Tampa–Hillsborough County Public Library System.)

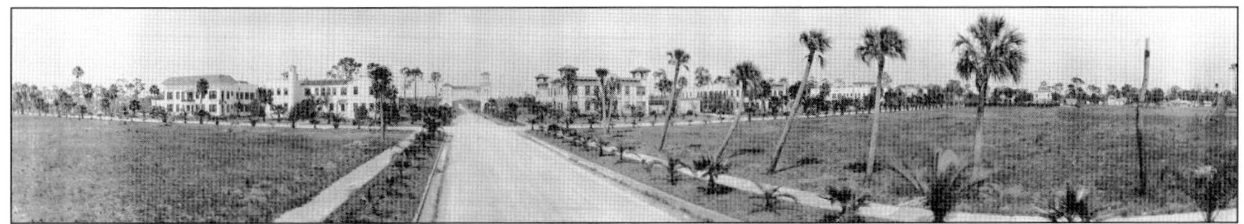

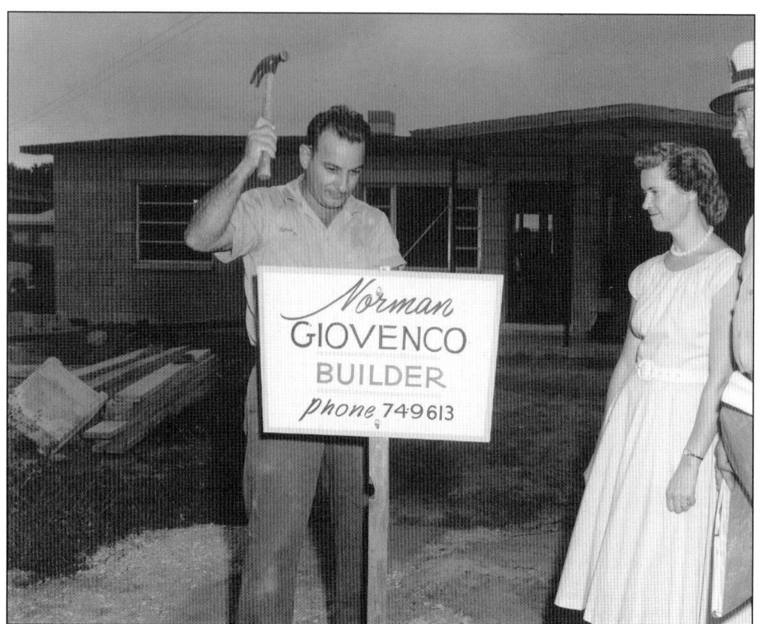

The couple on the right just bought a home at 4609 West Osborne Avenue. This home, seen under construction on October 14, 1957, is one of many single-family homes that were built in Drew Park in the years following World War II. (Courtesy of the Tampa–Hillsborough County Public Library System.)

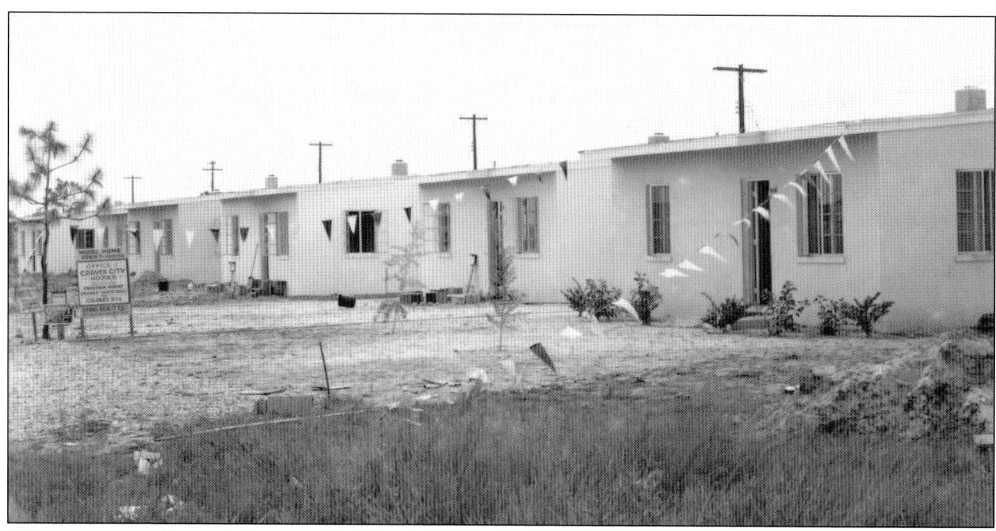

The area now known as Carver City and Lincoln Gardens saw the arrival of its first African American residents in the late 1920s. After World War II, the Veterans Administration coordinated the development of Lincoln Gardens in 1948 as a planned subdivision designed for African American troops returning home from service. Seen above in 1950 are homes under construction in adjacent Carver City. The Lincoln Gardens and Carver City subdivisions formally merged in 1983 to establish a single civic association to help oversee the welfare of the neighborhood, which has become one of the most diverse in the Westshore area. (Courtesy of the Tampa–Hillsborough County Public Library System.)

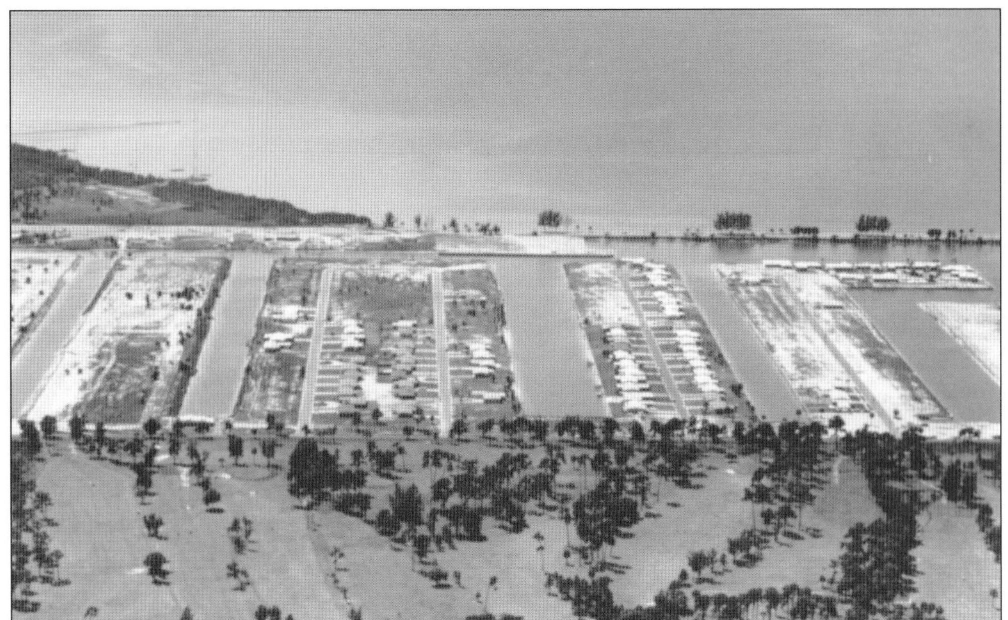

Dana Shores is a waterfront community developed in the early 1960s between the Tampa side of the Courtney Campbell Causeway and Rocky Point Golf Course. Dana Shores remains a coveted community today and is prized for its stunning nature views and close proximity to many of the area's best shopping destinations and recreational amenities. (Courtesy of the Tampa–Hillsborough County Public Library System.)

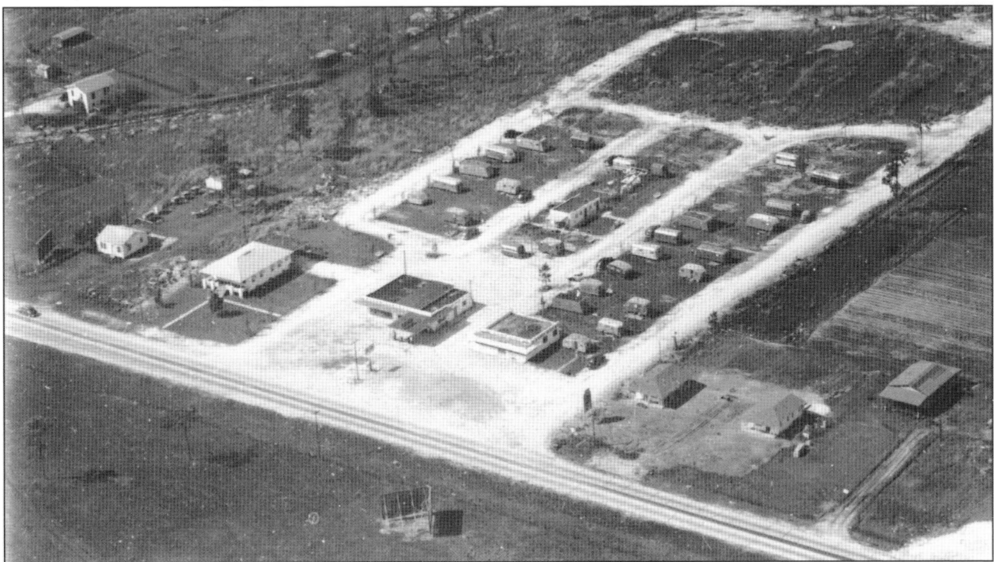

Richard's Trailer Park was located on the north side of West Hillsborough Avenue between what became North Dale Mabry Highway and North Himes Avenue. Offering a gas station and tavern, Richard's Trailer Park opened in the 1940s with 100 trailer lots. Vestiges of the trailer park remained through the years leading up to construction of a T.G.I. Friday's restaurant in 1983 and Greenhouse Shoppes in 1985. Much of the original shopping plaza remains, but the T.G.I. Friday's and other western portions of the property were replaced by a Walmart Neighborhood grocery store in 2014. (Courtesy of the University of South Florida Special Collections Department.)

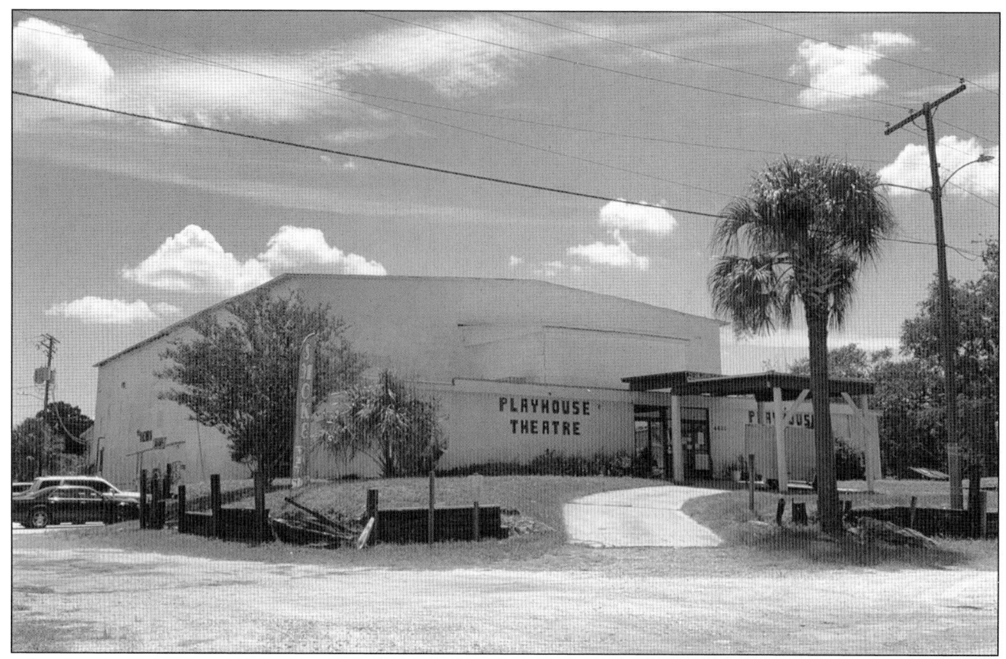

This building at 4421 North Hubert Avenue once served as a theater to entertain the troops at Drew Army Air Field during World War II. After the war, the 1942-vintage structure was repurposed as a civilian entertainment venue known as Drew Park Playhouse, capable of seating 800 and serving as the performance stage for productions by Tampa Little Theater, later known as Tampa Community Theater and the banner under which the Drew Park theater operated from the late 1960s through the 1970s. By the mid-1980s, the Drew Park landmark was operating as Playhouse Theatre.

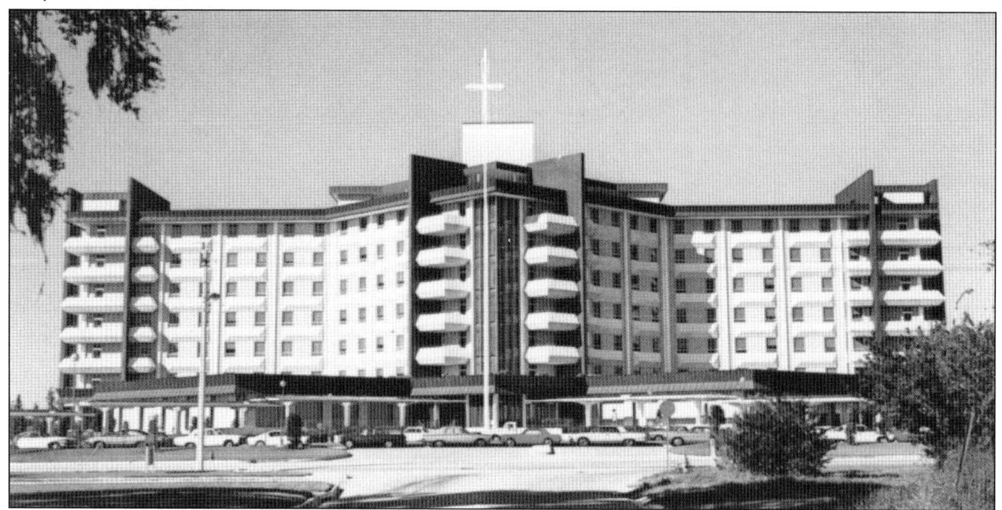

St. Joseph's Hospital, at 3001 West Buffalo Avenue (now Dr. Martin Luther King Jr. Boulevard), opened in 1965 as the much larger replacement of the former St. Joseph's Hospital, started in 1934 as a 40-bed facility near downtown Tampa operated by the Franciscan Sisters of Allegany. Straddling the communities of Westshore and West Tampa, St. Joseph's Hospital is now part of the BayCare Health System and has built several expansions on its campus, including wings designated for neonatal, pediatric, trauma, and cancer care.

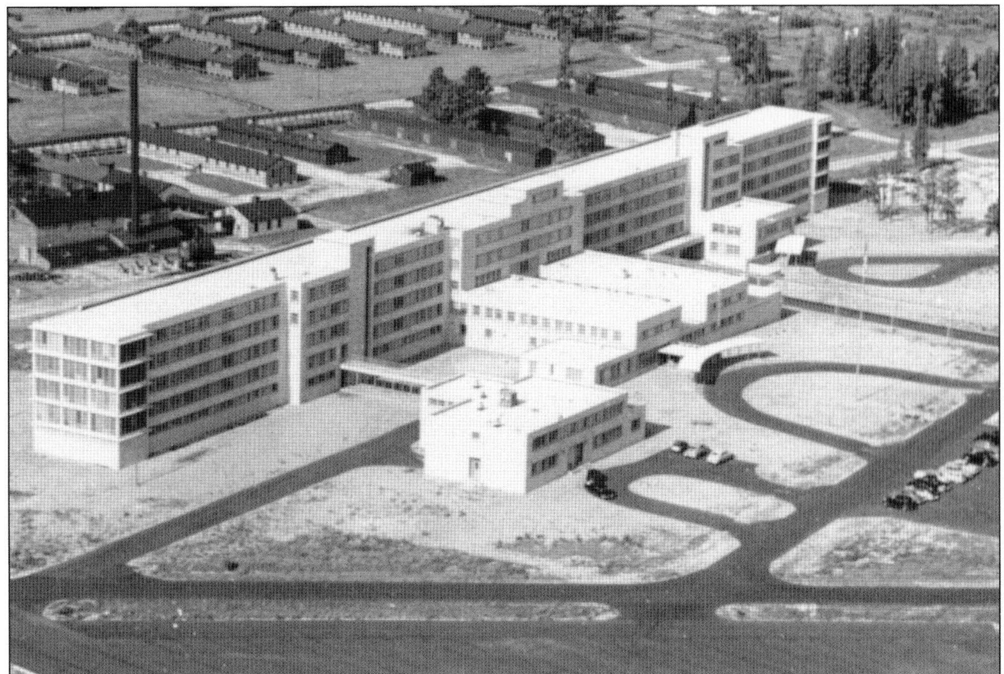

W.T. Edwards Tuberculosis Hospital opened in 1952 as a state-of-the-art treatment facility offering both advanced medical treatment and isolation areas. However, with the rise of medicines effective in treating tuberculosis, the hospital saw a subsequent decline of tuberculosis admissions, and the facility at 4000 West Buffalo Avenue (now Dr. Martin Luther King Jr. Boulevard) closed in 1974 and was demolished years later. The property eventually became part of the adjacent Hillsborough Community College Dale Mabry campus. (Courtesy of the Tampa–Hillsborough County Public Library System.)

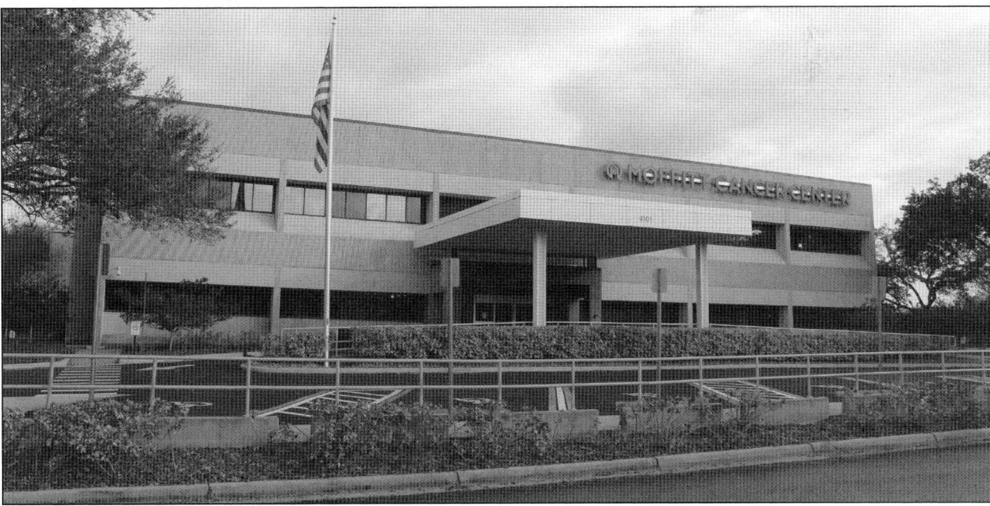

This building at 4101 Jim Walter Boulevard near International Plaza was built in 1980 and was the reservation office for Eastern Airlines, which shuttered in 1991. In more recent years, the property has become the home of H. Lee Moffitt Cancer Center's Westshore branch, serving patients in Tampa's western communities and convenient to those driving from across Tampa Bay in Pinellas County.

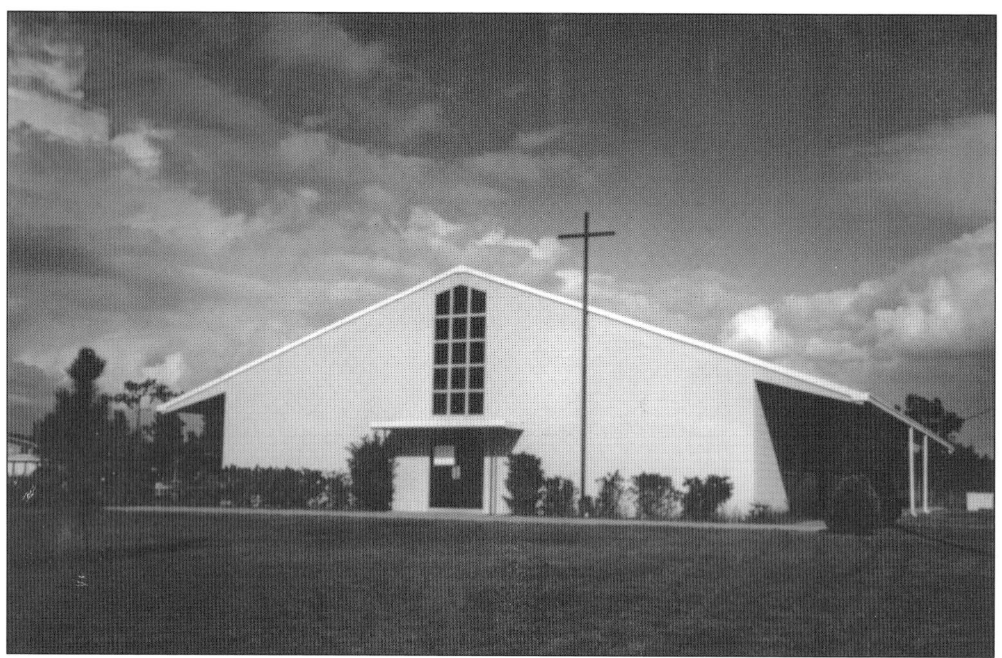

Seen above in 1967 is the provisional sanctuary for St. Lawrence Catholic Church at 5225 North Himes Avenue. The parish started in 1958 as a mission assigned to Fr. Laurence Higgins (pictured below around 1976), a young priest from Ireland. The mission held Masses at various places, including Hillsborough High School, until funds were raised to build a temporary church on 20 acres of pastureland at the southeast corner of North Himes Avenue and West Hillsborough Avenue. "I never asked people for money," Higgins told the author in a 2015 interview. "The church was built from pennies." (Above, courtesy of the Diocese of St. Petersburg; below, courtesy of St. Lawrence Catholic Church.)

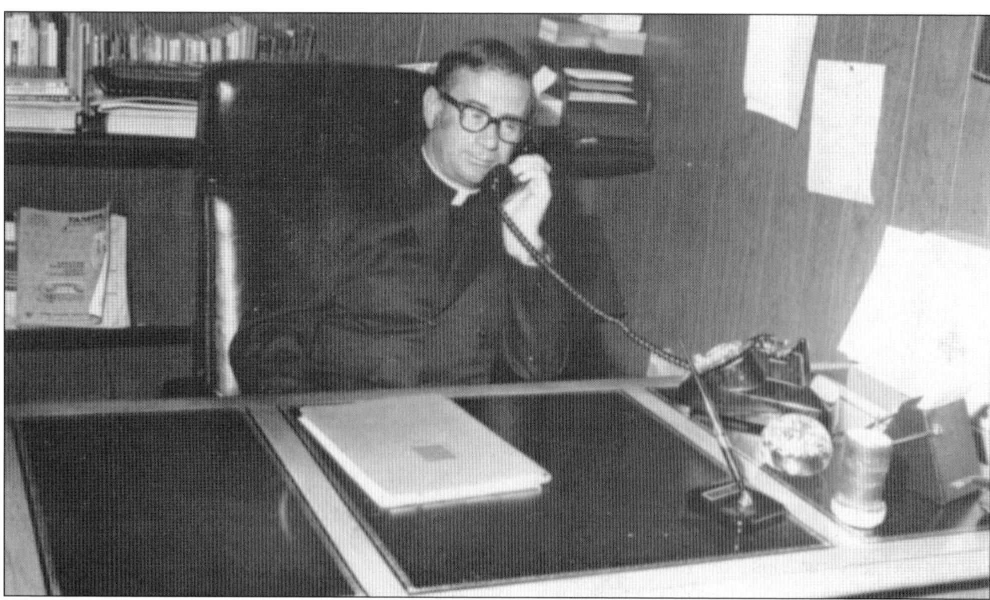

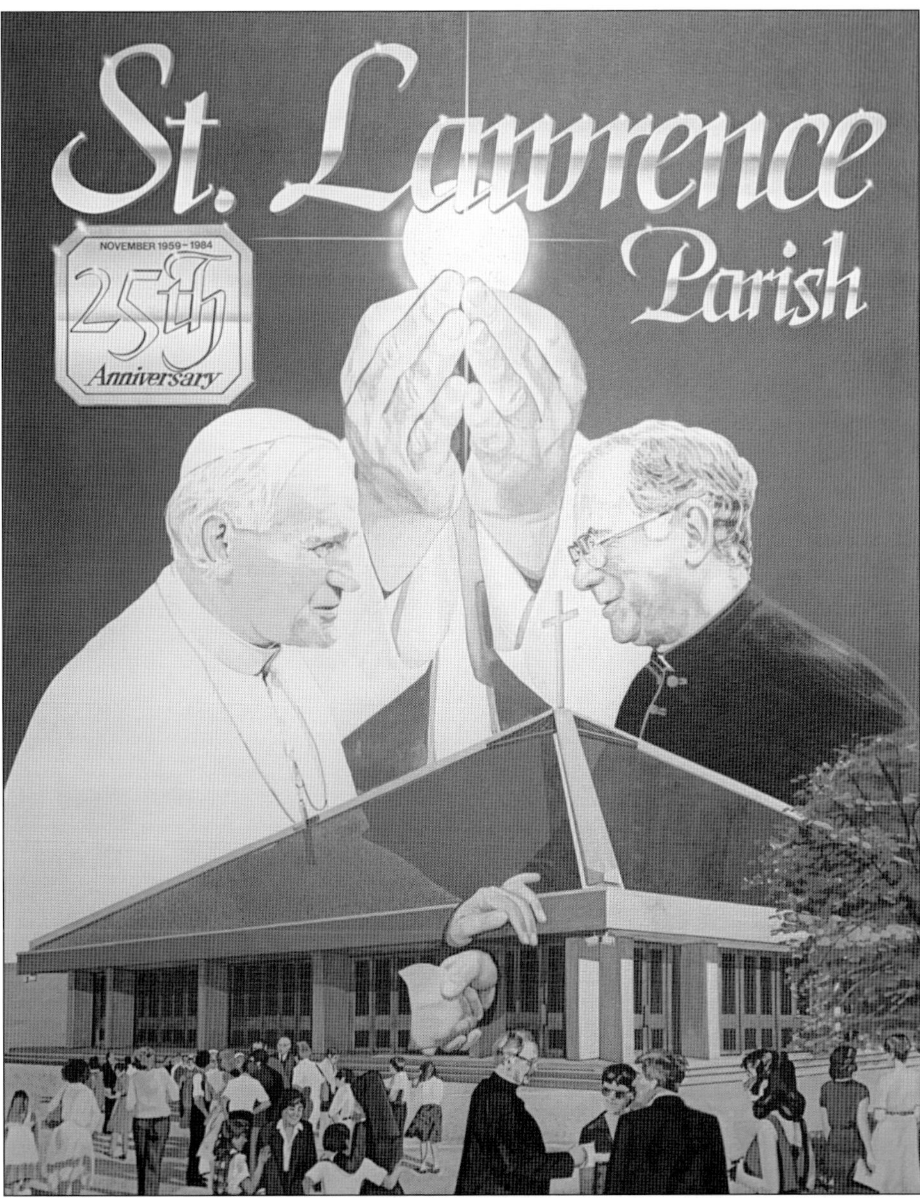

Fr. Laurence Higgins may have hailed from Ireland, but he embraced Tampa as his permanent home. Serving as the pastor of St. Lawrence Catholic Church parish since its beginning as a mission in 1958, he became a prominent community leader and trusted spiritual advisor to many as well as chaplain for the Tampa Bay Buccaneers. He served on the boards of many local organizations and reached beyond Tampa's large Catholic community to serve as an ambassador of goodwill and faith to people of all religions. The Tampa priest was bestowed the title of monsignor by Pope John Paul II during a visit to the Vatican in Rome, an event depicted in this poster, which also showcases St. Lawrence's permanent church, dedicated in 1981. Over the decades, Monsignor Higgins saw his Tampa parish grow to include more than 2,000 families and become one of the biggest in the Diocese of St. Petersburg. Even after his retirement in 2007, Monsignor Higgins continued serving Mass at St. Lawrence until passing at the age of 87 in 2016. He is buried in Tampa. (Courtesy of St. Lawrence Catholic Church.)

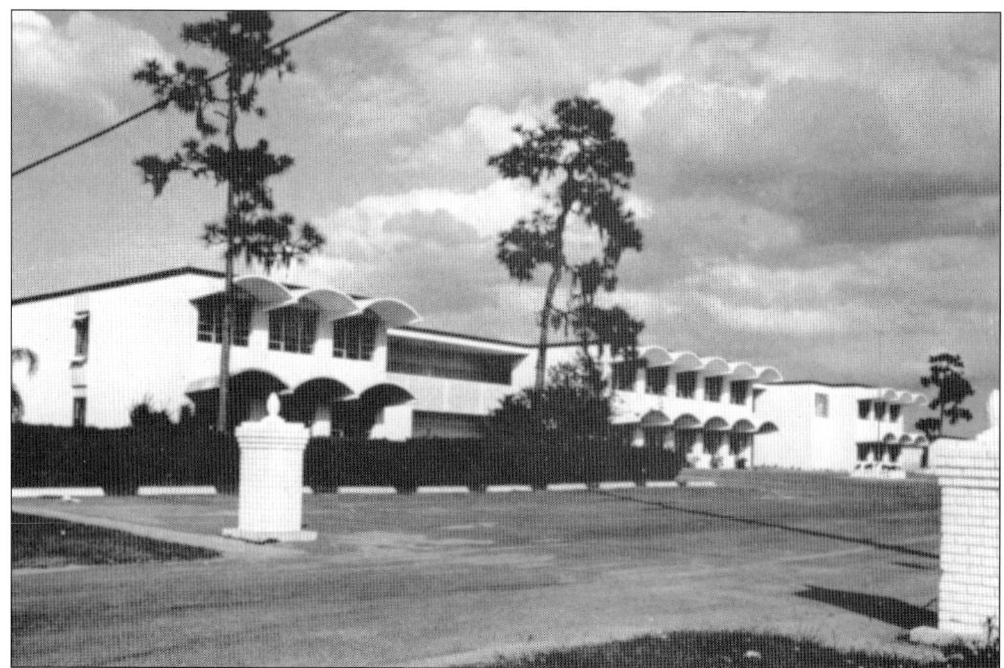

Above is St. Lawrence Catholic School, which was founded in 1961 with four classrooms serving 91 students. It has grown to include more than 500 children ranging from pre-kindergarten through the eighth grade. Below is Jesuit High School, which was founded in downtown Tampa by Jesuit priests as Sacred Heart College in 1899. Renamed Jesuit High School in 1940, the educational institution moved to its permanent campus at 4701 North Himes Avenue in 1956. (Above, courtesy of St. Lawrence Catholic Church; below, courtesy of the Diocese of St. Petersburg.)

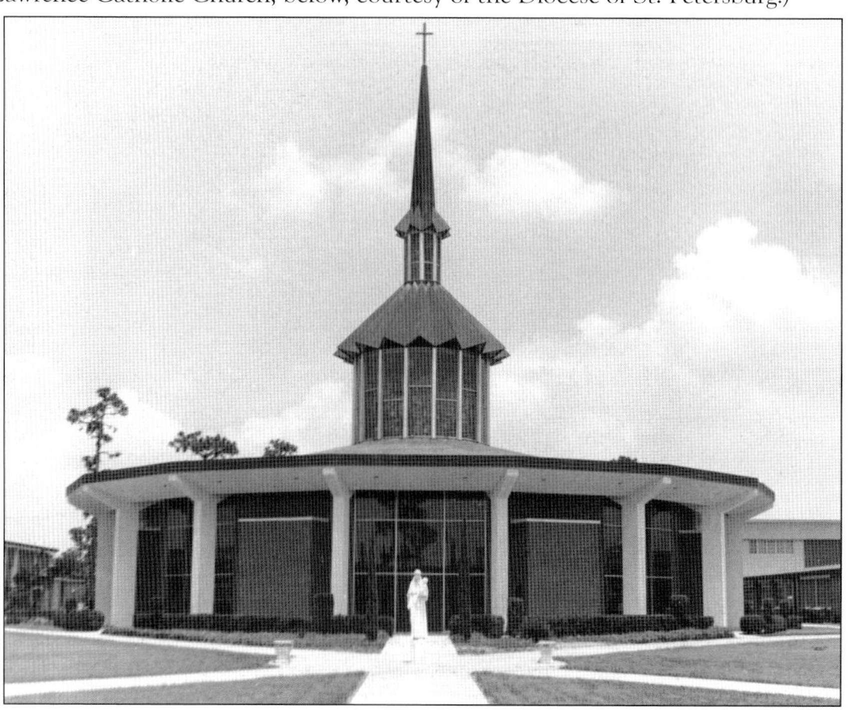

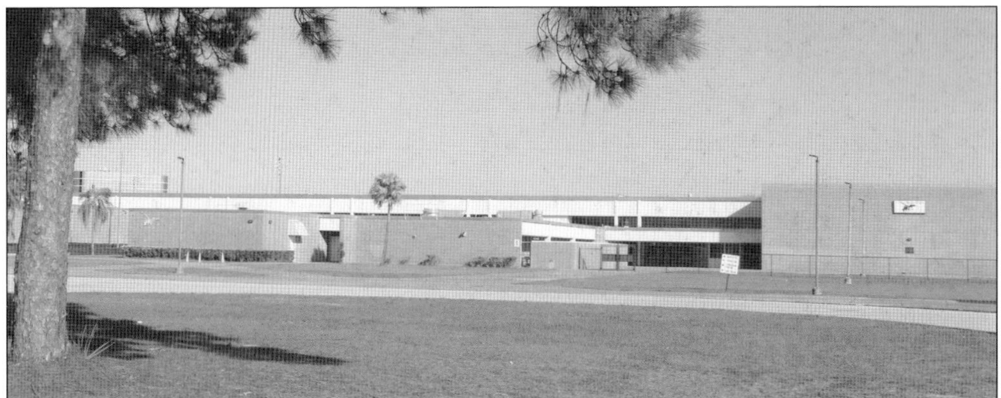

Thomas Jefferson High School was founded in 1939 and originally served students at 2704 North Highland Avenue in Tampa Heights. However, the school's small quarters there proved inadequate for a rapidly growing Tampa, and the Hillsborough County School Board decided to close that location in 1967. Thomas Jefferson High School students were distributed to various local high schools until the completion of the current incarnation of the school at 4401 West Cypress Street in 1973. Students revel in school spirit by donning the blue and gold colors and cheering on Thomas Jefferson High School Dragons athletic teams.

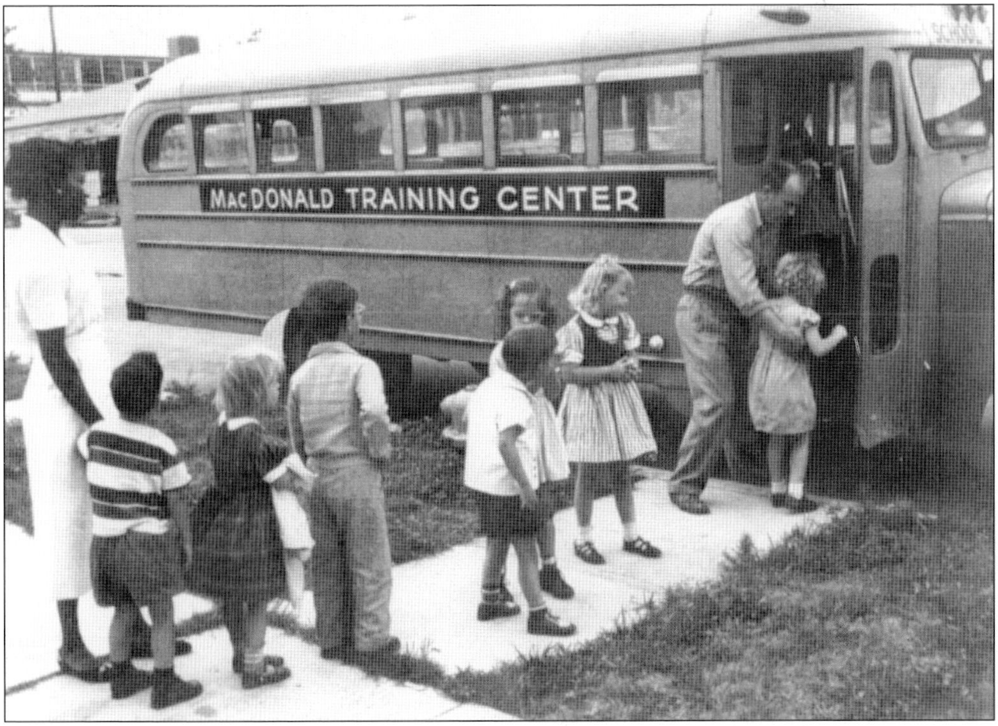

MacDonald Training Center opened in 1953 in Drew Park and was one of the first schools in the nation for children with special needs. The school, founded by J. Clifford MacDonald and parents of individuals with disabilities, moved to a location on Boy Scout Boulevard in the 1960s and grew to include therapies and educational programs for children, teenagers, and young adults. Workforce training programs were started in the 1970s and became one of several life-enrichment and support initiatives offered by MacDonald Training Center, now located at 5420 West Cypress Street and serving more than 500 people with all disabilities. (Courtesy of MacDonald Training Center.)

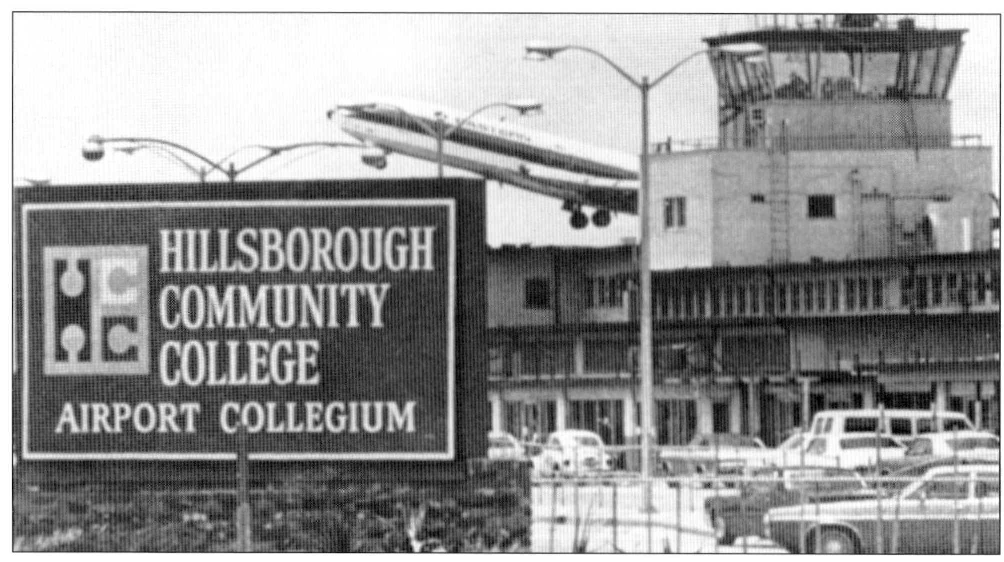

Originally founded as Hillsborough Junior College, Hillsborough Community College started serving students in 1968 with humble beginnings. The two-year public college began with 1,625 students enrolled in classes held at Hillsborough High School. After Tampa International Airport left its terminal at the corner of West Columbus Drive and North West Shore Boulevard in 1971, Hillsborough Community College took up temporary residence there, as seen above and below. (Both, courtesy of Hillsborough Community College.)

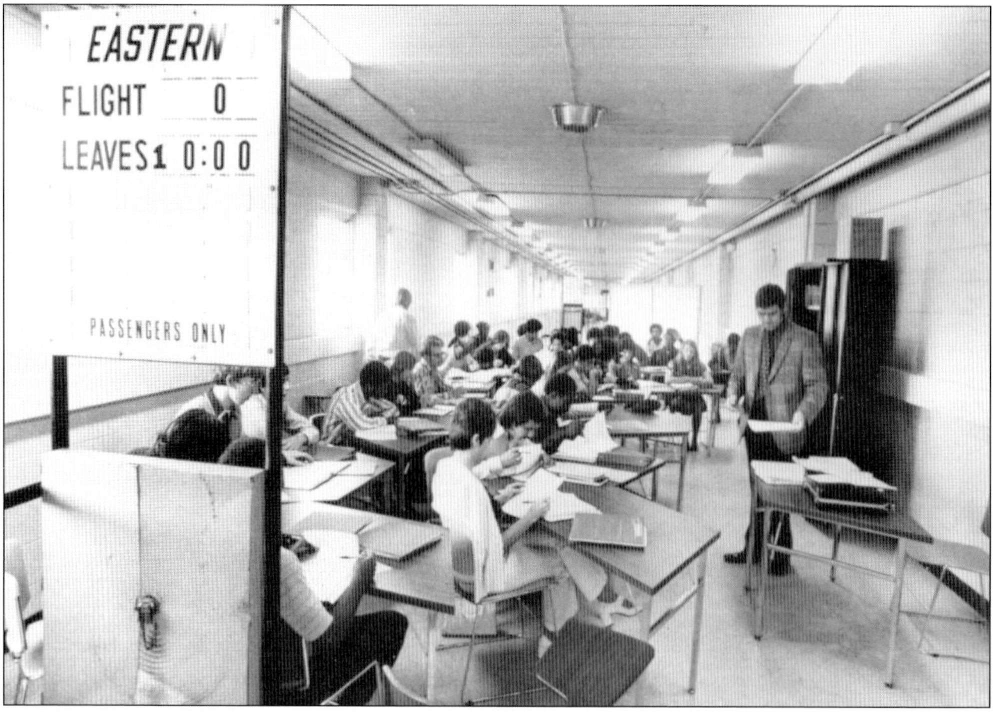

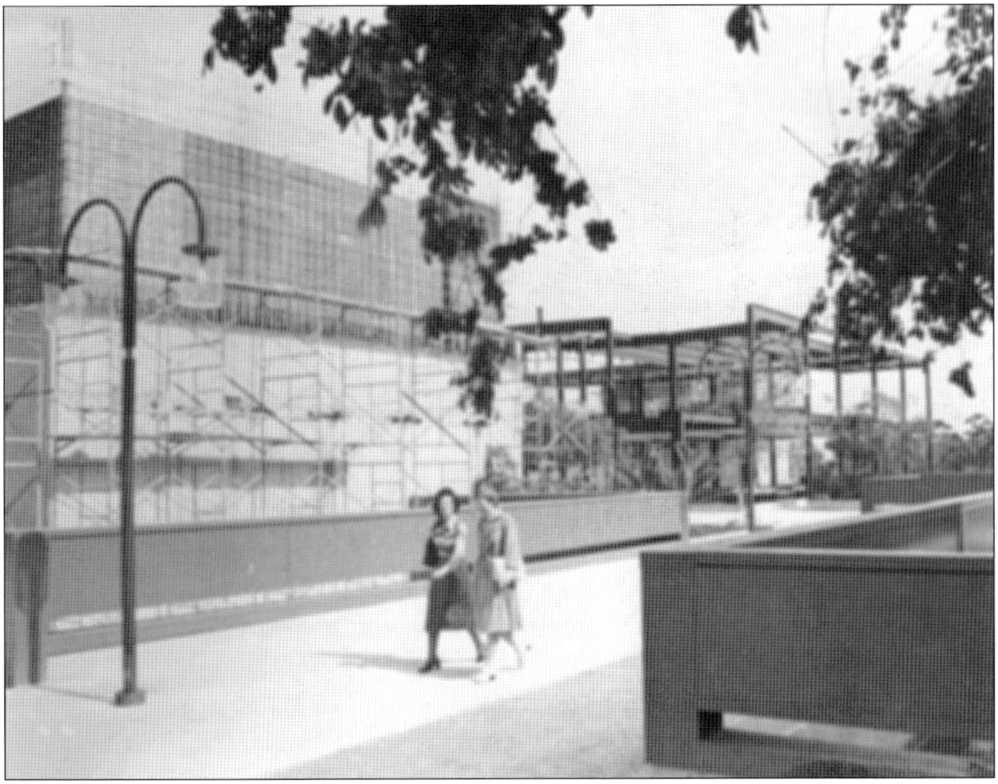

Collegium 1 (now the school's social sciences building) became the first permanent structure at the Hillsborough Community College Dale Mabry campus in 1972. Construction of a second classroom building (above) followed in short order to help handle the influx of students enrolling at the school (below). Over the course of the 1970s, other Hillsborough Community College campuses opened in Ybor City and Plant City and saw student enrollments skyrocket as more career programs were offered. Today, Hillsborough Community College has five primary campuses and several satellite locations that cumulatively educate more than 40,000 students. (Both, courtesy of Hillsborough Community College.)

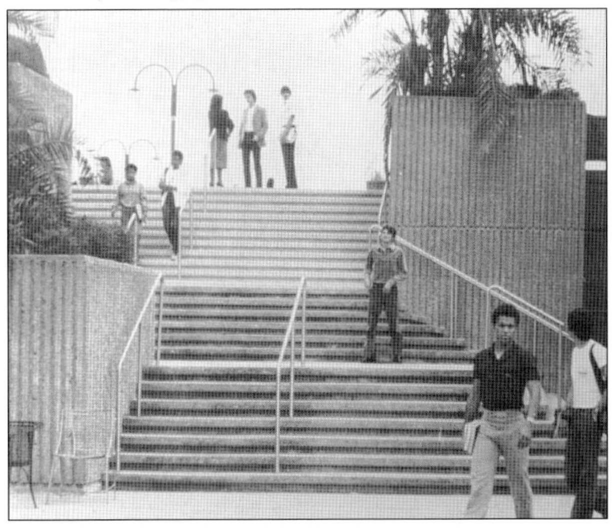

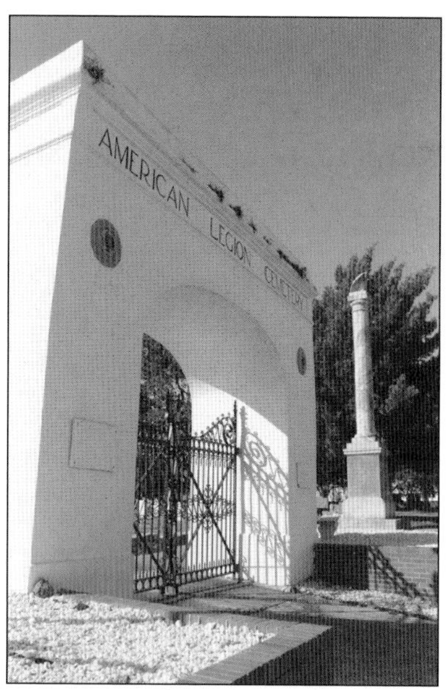

The American Legion Cemetery, at 3810 West Kennedy Boulevard, features an ornate entry gate adorned with a World War I veterans memorial that was originally located at the intersection of Howard Avenue and West Grand Central Avenue in 1921, the latter road having been dedicated as Memorial Highway for a long stretch running from Howard Avenue west out to Oldsmar. The monument at West Grand Central Avenue and Howard Avenue was moved to the American Legion Cemetery after several cars crashed into it, while an identical monument farther west is situated near the intersection of what is now West Kennedy Boulevard and Memorial Highway.

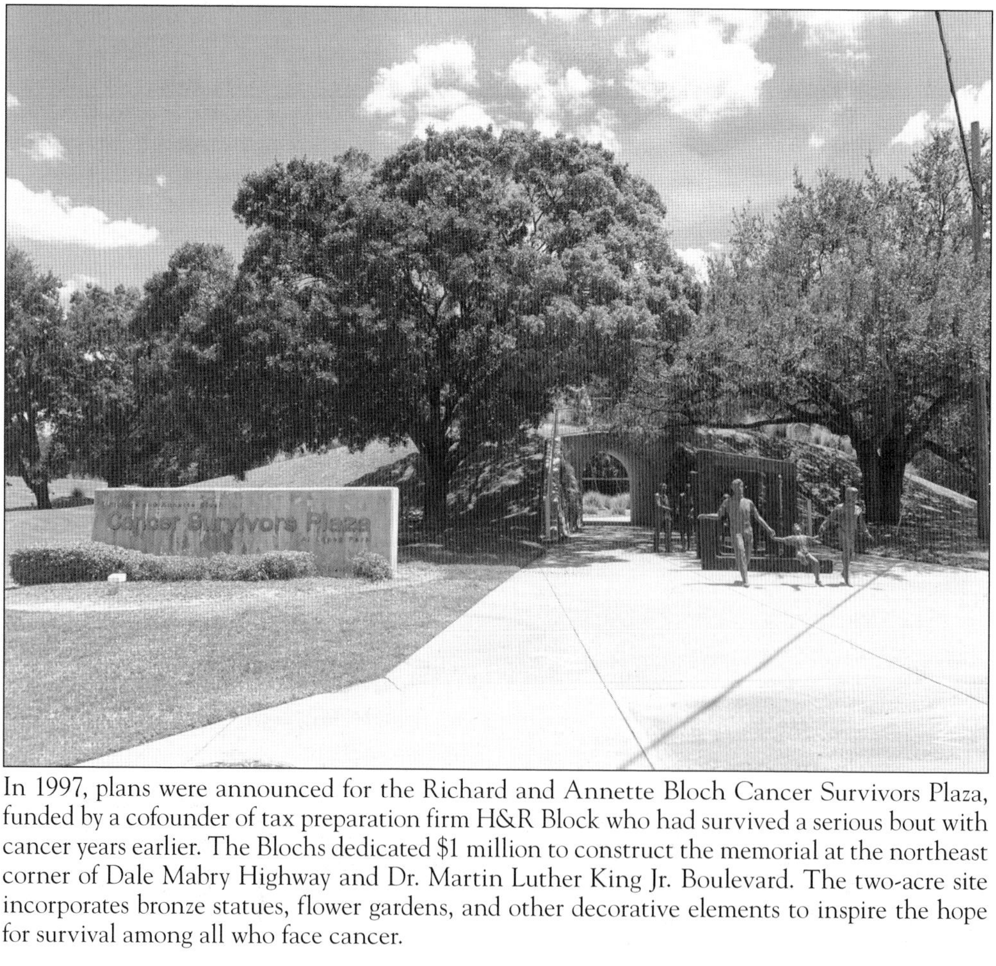

In 1997, plans were announced for the Richard and Annette Bloch Cancer Survivors Plaza, funded by a cofounder of tax preparation firm H&R Block who had survived a serious bout with cancer years earlier. The Blochs dedicated $1 million to construct the memorial at the northeast corner of Dale Mabry Highway and Dr. Martin Luther King Jr. Boulevard. The two-acre site incorporates bronze statues, flower gardens, and other decorative elements to inspire the hope for survival among all who face cancer.

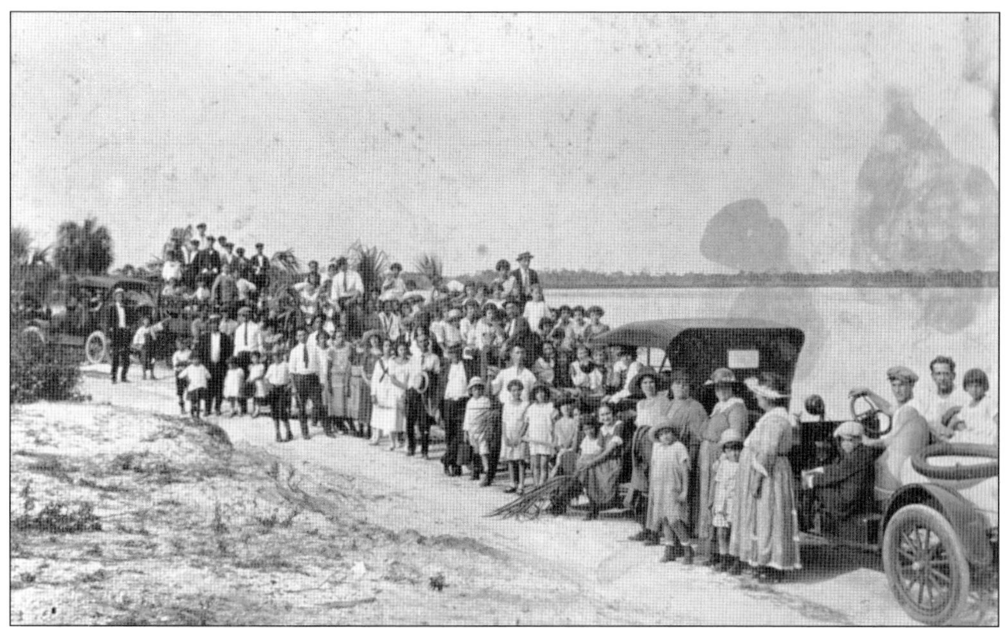

Rocky Point has long been a draw for civic clubs wanting to bring their members together for good times and memorable moments. Above, members of Tampa's Cuban Club gather for a photograph in the 1920s. Below, a business and professional women's club holds a banquet at Bartke's Rocky Point Restaurant on October 1, 1955. (Above, courtesy of the University of South Florida Special Collections Department; below, courtesy of the Tampa–Hillsborough County Public Library System.)

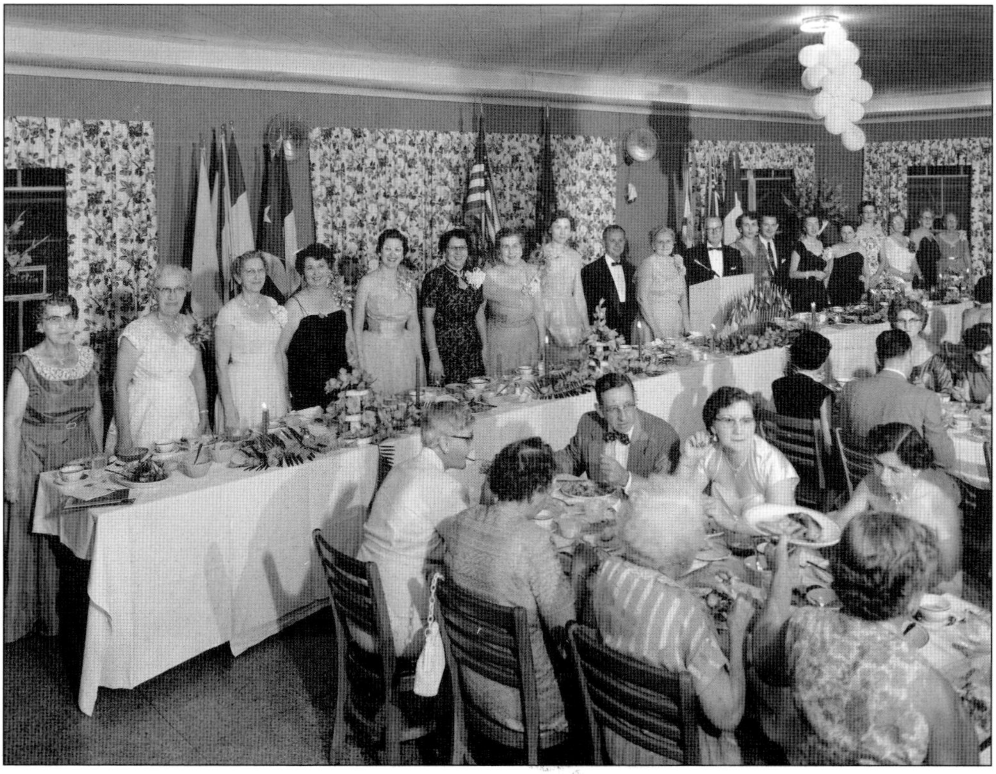

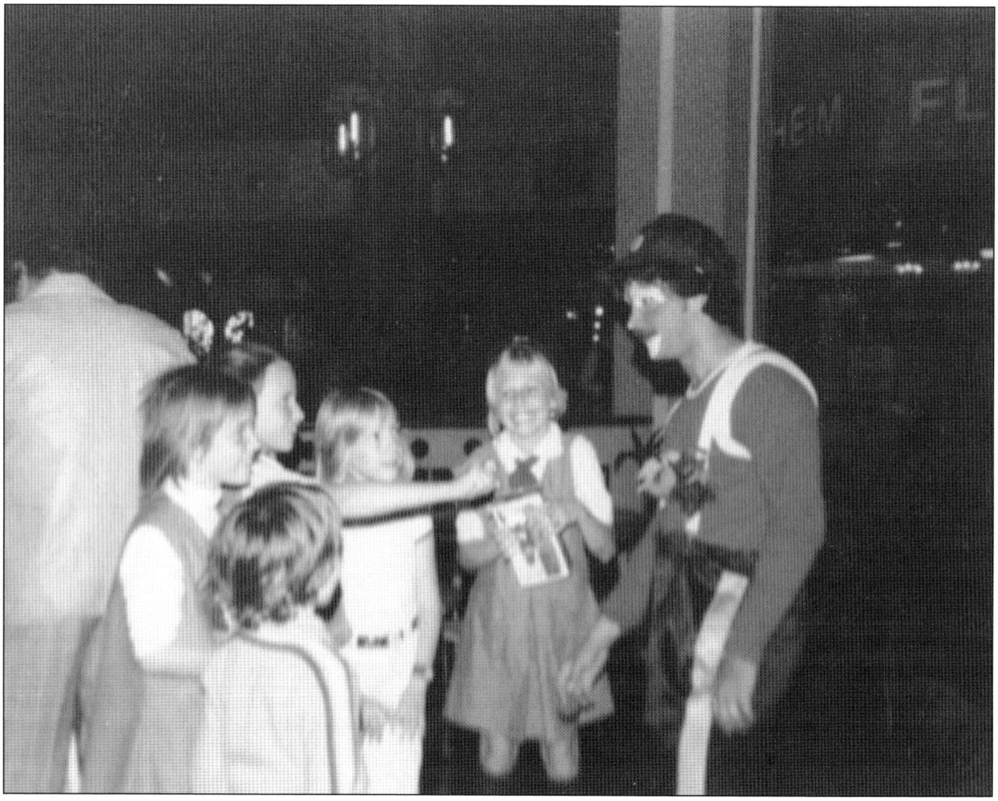

Westshore has long served as a hub of community joy and entertainment. Above, Tampa magician Frank Rudy Hernandez entertains young children at Tampa Bay Center around 1980, while below, Tampa Bay area FM radio station Q-105 raises a larger-than-life stereo boom box high over Interstate 275 by the former Embassy Suites at 4400 West Cypress Street around 1990. (Below, courtesy of Mason Dixon.)

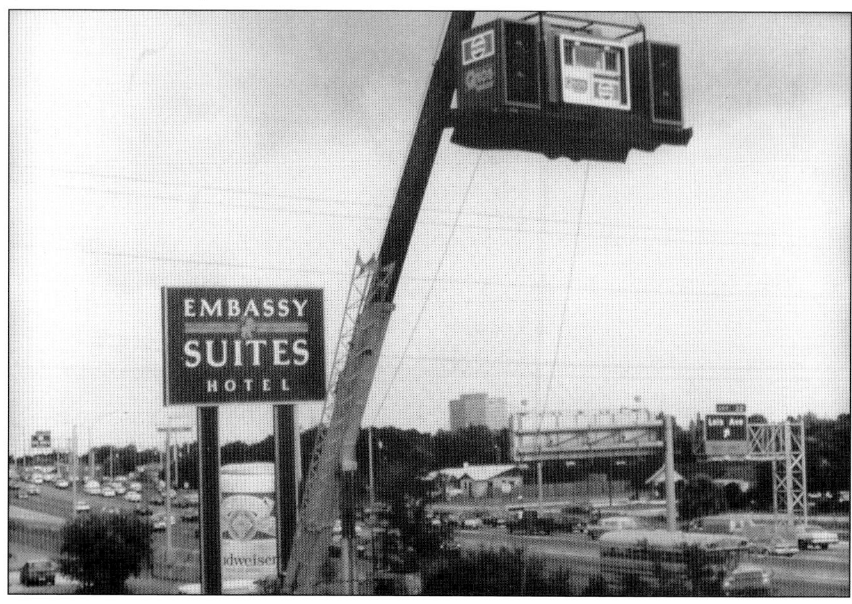

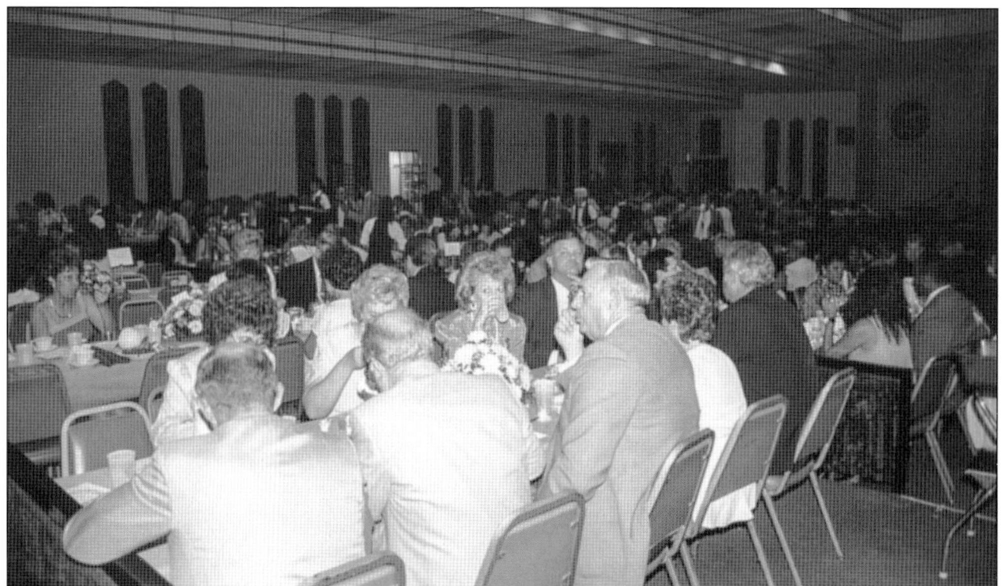

The Egypt Temple Shrine at 4050 Dana Shores Drive was built in 1966 and originally served as a meeting place for the Egypt Shriners philanthropic fraternity. Over the years, the 56,000-square-foot hall grew to host many events ranging from wedding receptions to civic association banquets, as seen here in the mid-1980s. In the early 2000s, the hall was leased out to a company that renamed the convention center A La Carte Pavilion. The 13-acre property was sold in 2017 and converted into a residential development. (Courtesy of the City of Tampa Archives.)

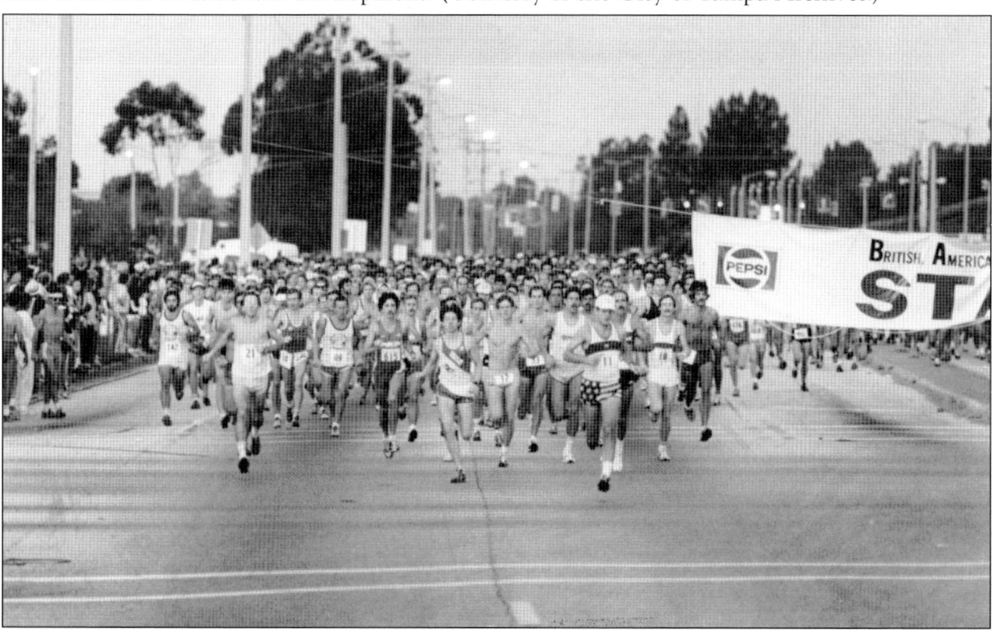

The British American Marathon lured 1,400 runners in its inaugural November 1982 event, with runners seen here making their way down then–Buffalo Avenue between Himes Avenue and Dale Mabry Highway. The 26.2-mile race started at Tampa Stadium and ended at Al Lang Stadium in St. Petersburg. It was renamed the Tampa–St. Petersburg Marathon in 1984 but was discontinued by 1986 due to financial reasons. (© Kathleen Cabble/*Tampa Bay Times* via ZUMA Press.)

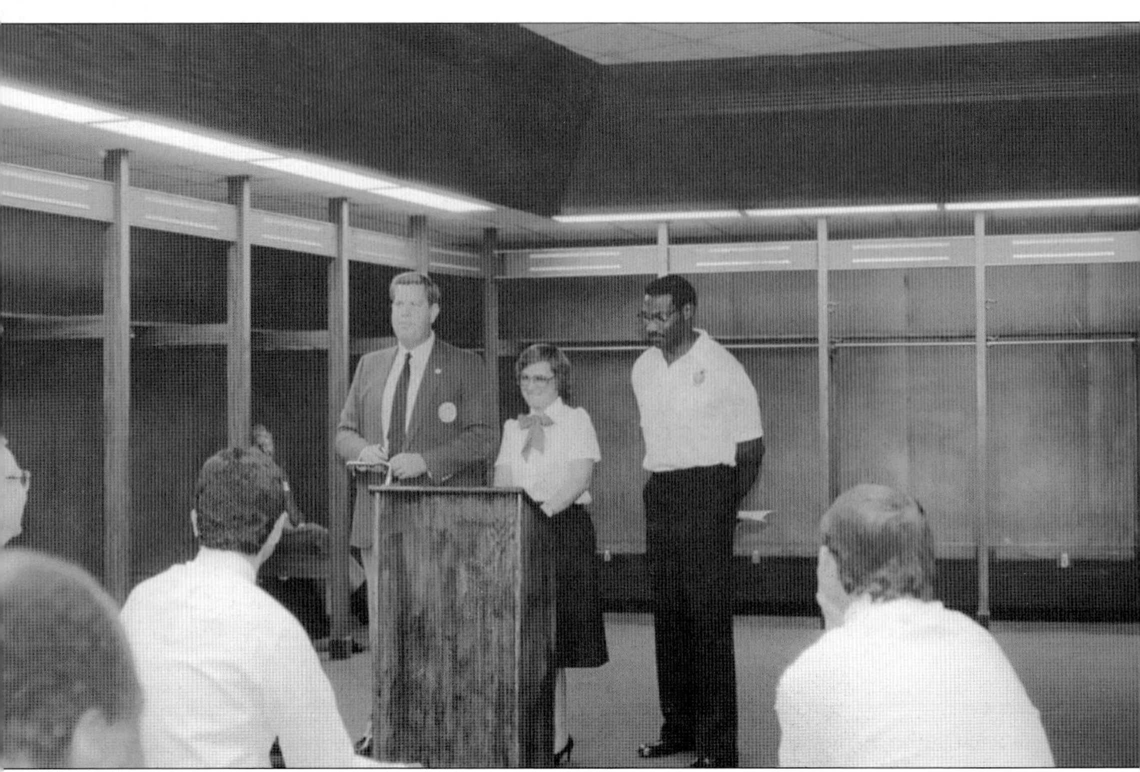

Lee Roy Selmon, seen here at center right, was the first overall pick in the National Football League draft in 1976, marking the first year of regular-season action for the Tampa Bay Buccaneers franchise. Selmon joined the Tampa Bay Buccaneers playing for the team's defensive squad and wearing jersey number 63. He quickly rose as a standout star, playing in six Pro Bowls and being named as the 1979 NFL Defensive Player of the Year. He continued playing for Tampa until a back injury forced him to retire in 1984. He was named to the Florida Sports Hall of Fame, and his jersey number was retired by the Tampa Bay Buccaneers in 1986. He later served as the head of the University of South Florida Athletic Department and was the first player named to the Tampa Bay Buccaneers Ring of Honor in 2009. The namesake of the Lee Roy Selmon Expressway, which traverses east and west through Tampa, passed away at the age of 56 in 2011. (Courtesy of the City of the Tampa Archives.)

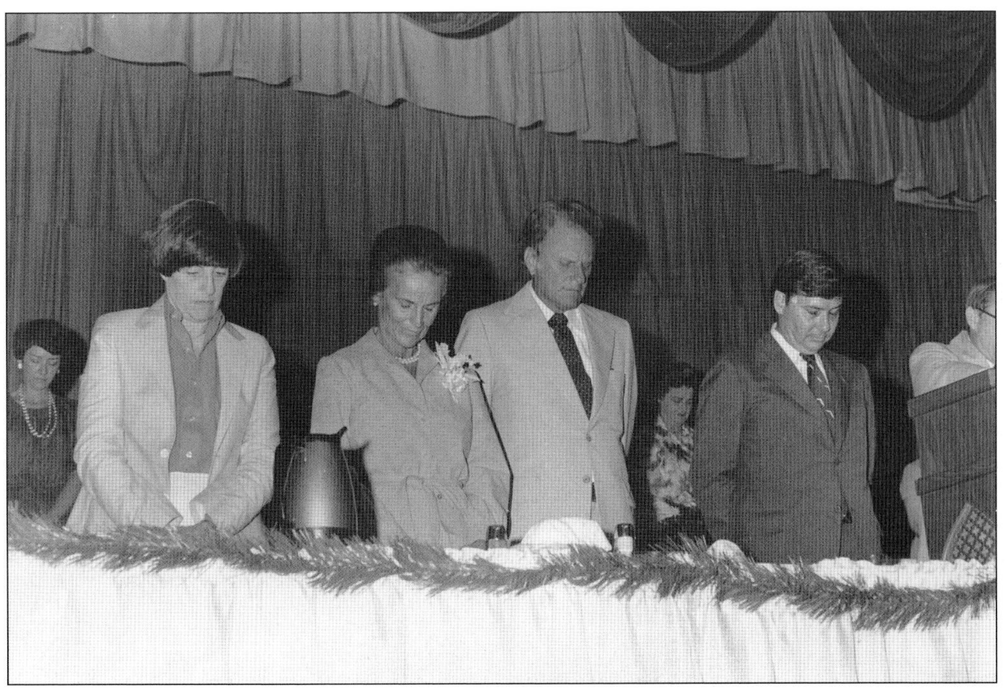

Legendary evangelist Billy Graham is seen here (center, with his wife, Ruth Graham) at the Egypt Temple Shrine with St. Petersburg mayor Corinne Freeman (left) and Florida governor Bob Graham (right) during the religious leader's multiday Tampa crusade in March 1979, when 175,000 people attended his services at Tampa Stadium. (© *Tampa Bay Times* via ZUMA Press.)

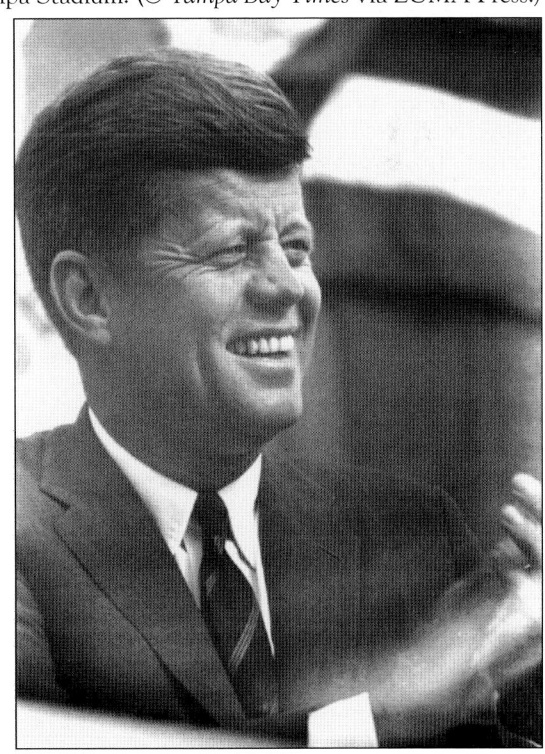

Pres. John F. Kennedy visited Tampa on November 18, 1963, to make a variety of appearances in the city, including a motorcade procession throughout West Tampa and Westshore and a speech at the International Inn at West Grand Central Avenue and West Shore Boulevard. Here, he is seen addressing the crowds who came to see him at Al Lopez Field. Sadly, he was assassinated during his motorcade procession in Dallas, Texas, just a few days later, on November 22, 1963. In the fallen president's memory, most of Grand Central Avenue was renamed Kennedy Boulevard in 1964. (Courtesy of Tony Zappone.)

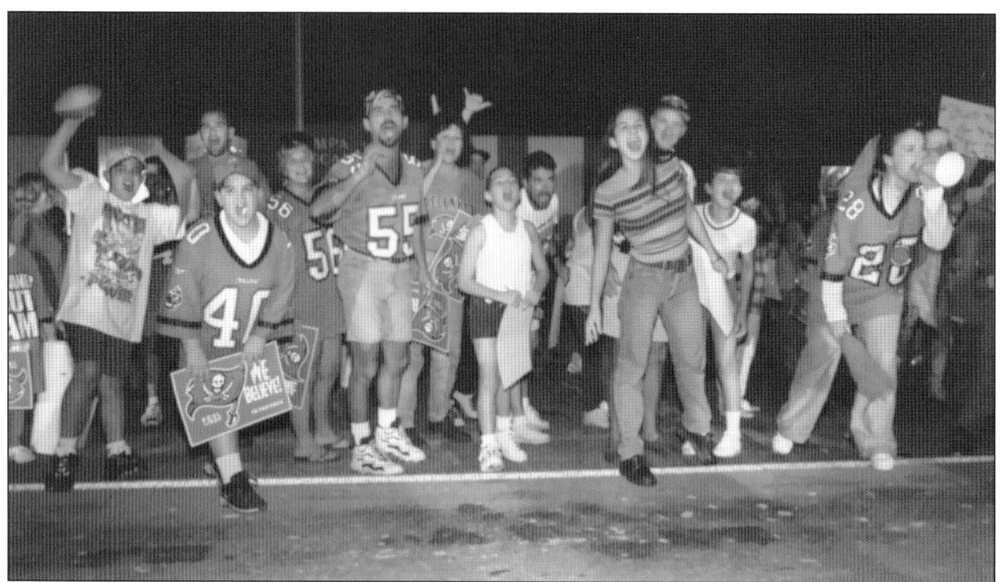

The Tampa Bay Buccaneers started off on a winless streak during their first year. But their fortunes changed within a few years under the leadership of their first head coach, John McKay, and an improving squadron. They made playoff runs during their 1979 and 1981 seasons but fell into a long patch of losing seasons until the arrival of head coach Tony Dungy in 1996. The team saw its first playoff run under Dungy at the end of the 1997 season, compelling the community to cheer for the team before its then-training facility, known as "One Buc Place" (background), on North West Shore Boulevard. The Tampa Bay Buccaneers went on to win their first Super Bowl Championship on January 26, 2003. (© *Tampa Bay Times* via ZUMA Press.)

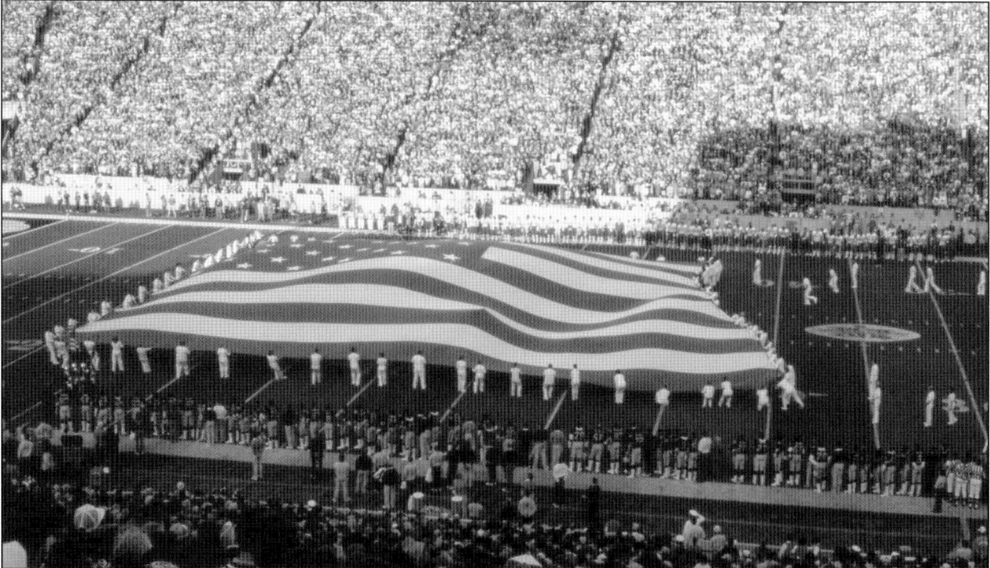

Tampa's first Super Bowl, seen above, was played at Tampa Stadium on January 22, 1984, before some 75,000 people in the stands and tens of millions watching on televisions worldwide. Tampa hosted three more Super Bowls in 1991, 2001, and 2009. Tampa's fifth Super Bowl, held on February 7, 2021, saw the Tampa Bay Buccaneers become the first team ever to play the game on their home turf. The Bucs won that championship against the Kansas City Chiefs 31-9. (© TNS/ZUMA Press.)

Bibliography

Brower, Ralph. *Remembering Tampa.* Nashville, TN: Trade Paper Press, 2010.
Cinchett, John V. *Vintage Tampa Signs and Scenes.* Charleston, SC: Arcadia Publishing, 2009.
Crawford, Denis M. *Hugh Culverhouse and the Tampa Bay Buccaneers: How a Skinflint Genius with a Losing Team Made the Modern NFL.* Jefferson, NC: McFarland & Company, 2011.
Dunn, Hampton. *Yesterday's Tampa.* Miami, FL: E.A. Seemann Publishing Inc., 1972.
Florida Division of Historical Resources. *Florida Historic Golf Trail.* Tallahassee, FL: A Florida Heritage Publication, 2015.
Grismer, Karl Hiram. *Tampa: A History of the City of Tampa and the Tampa Bay Region of Florida.* St. Petersburg, FL: St. Petersburg Printing Company, 1950.
Lisicky, Michael J. *Remembering Maas Brothers.* Charleston, SC: Arcadia Publishing, 2015.
Mormino, Gary R., and Anthony Pizzo. *Tampa: The Treasure City.* Tulsa, OK: Continental Heritage Press Inc., 1983.
Rajtar, Steve. *Historic Photos of Tampa in the 50s, 60s, and 70s.* Nashville, TN: Turner Publishing, 2012.
Tash, Paul. *125 Years: Tampa Bay through the Times.* Vancouver, WA: Pediment Publishing, 2008.